# TAKE BACK THE LIGHT

The Circle Women's Centre
Brescia University College
1285 Western Road  London ON  N6G 1H2

# New Feminist Perspectives Series

*General Editor: Rosemarie Tong, Davidson College*

# TAKE BACK THE LIGHT

## A Feminist Reclamation of Spirituality and Religion

**Sheila Ruth**

Littlefield Adams Quality Paperbacks

LITTLEFIELD ADAMS QUALITY PAPERBACKS

Published in the United States of America
by Rowman & Littlefield Publishers, Inc.
4720 Boston Way, Lanham, Maryland 20706

British Cataloging in Publication Information Available


The Library of Congress has cataloged the
    Rowman & Littlefield edition as follows:

Ruth, Sheila.
Take back the light : a feminist reclamation of spirituality and
religion / Sheila Ruth.
p.    cm. — (New feminist perspectives series)
Includes bibliographical references and index.
1. Women and religion.  2. Feminist theory.  I. Title.
II. Series.
BL458.R87    1993    200'.82—dc20    93-6061    CIP

ISBN 0-8226-3031-1  (paper : alk. paper)


Printed in the United States of America

The paper used in this publication meets the minimum requirements of
American National Standard for Information Sciences—Permanence of
Paper for Printed Library Materials, ANSI Z39.48–1984.

for
Amity

*that her life may be spirit led*

*Know that you are one—only one, yet indeed one—of the beauties of the Earth.*

*Remember that you are in the heart of God, and She is in you.*

*With Her, each of us is our own mother. Love your child fiercely, without reservation. Because you are precious, keep yourself with infinite care.*

She told me this one night to tell to you.

# Contents

# Preface

To win, *we must know exactly what it is we want, why
we want it, and why we think it is best.* To win for all
time for all people we must see beyond our own transient time and place. From what source shall we obtain
such clarity?

Feminists have spoken clearly for positive social change to reverse
the world's history of exploitations, war, cruelty, and arrogance. In
1970 Shulamith Firestone said, "If there were another word more
all-embracing than *revolution* we would use it."[1]

Feminism begins with an analysis of gender, but its range goes
far beyond that, to all culture, all nature, all life. It is about striving for quality, for an elemental shift toward goodness. If we are
to obtain the change we desire, we are going to have to provide
and make clear, for ourselves and for others, the broad framework,
the wider philosophical and spiritual context into which feminism
fits, in other words, a metaphysic and an ethic. Such a framework
already exists. It needs only to be articulated and refined. What that
framework is and how it may be articulated will be the subject
before us here.

To be transforming, not merely cosmetic, change must be radical—situated at the root. It cannot be formulated only out of what
is familiar and easily apprehended; nor should it be mystified with
the exotic or obscure. Rather it must come out of the profoundest
comprehension of the nature of life, of creatures, and of the processes that bind us.

Change presupposes a framework of values. Additionally, it must have a plan, however hazily defined, some idea of where it wants to go. In other words, positive social action requires both an ethical base and a sense of direction.

Ethics, ideas about how we should behave toward one another and toward life itself, is impossible without a metaphysical foundation, an articulation of what life is ultimately about. Without either one—a sense of the meaning and purpose of life and a set of behavioral values drawn from that meaning—social action becomes mere tinkering, random experimentation with superficial modifications that can produce good only by the greatest luck. People who care deeply about life and are committed to its improvement, then, must tend their metaphysical gardens. At least as much as ever before, what is required of us is the widest thinking, the deepest sensitivity to the creatures and events around us, and finally diligent and persistent action.

We live in difficult, demanding times. As often happens when things go arduously, a disproportionate share of the suffering has fallen upon women. These are cold times for social justice, times that are hostile to the feminist program—to our drive for liberty and well-being and to our global agenda: peace and environmental responsibility. The predicted backlash to feminism appears to be upon us, opposing our goals and values with claims that we are guilty of moral decay. Once again, feminists are charged with destroying the social order, the economy, and the family, and with disobeying God's will and the laws of nature. Women are on the brink of losing many, if not most, of our gains of the past two decades, perhaps of the past two centuries.

Feminists agree that to survive in such a climate, let alone to continue to take what ground we may, we must be strong, active, and endlessly energetic. We cannot be timid. What is more, we cannot just react to every strike against us, allowing the spoilers to set the terms of battle, the rhetoric, and the field. Our opponents have claimed the moral right and are winning the popular mind, while feminists have been forced into a defensive posture. This cannot continue. To win, we must lead. On every level—political, social, philosophical, religious—we must take the initiative and act with incredible persistence and purpose. *We* must demonstrate that we provide the ethical choice. *We* must set the terms of the argument, claim the moral good, and show that our goals represent the best interests of women and the best interests of society. *We* must show that our agenda, not theirs, reflects the long, historical unfolding of liberty, that our agenda, not theirs, is motivated by spiritual goods.

We must, for example, demonstrate that insisting upon women's right to share equally in the determination of society is a moral and spiritual activity, not only because it seeks to avert the material and emotional suffering of women (which is reason enough), but because opposing such suffering serves the harmony and fullness of all life. We must show that the decision *not* to have a child can serve life as deeply as its converse, and therefore the fight to preserve the right to abortion is not only pragmatic but moral. We must show that our goals are grounded in the commitment to the human spirit and to the good in life—to the sacred. To show that, we must understand and believe in that commitment.

Leaders lead by drawing people to them, by translating people's needs into understandable terms and then by providing strategies to meet those needs. The entire process rests upon trust. People follow those they trust. It is obvious, then, that if we want society to adopt our program, we must comprehend society's profoundest needs and show how our plan best satisfies them. Perhaps it is less obvious that leaders must also rely upon those that follow, must always be receptive and listen to people as they express their needs. It is not at all obvious, but just as true, that to be a leader and to elicit trust in others, one must trust oneself, one's understanding, and one's abilities. The deepest trust emerges from the deepest conviction.

To regain the lead, we feminists must reestablish trust in ourselves—in our goals, our motives, and our actions. Such confidence is engendered by shared, self-consciously sought, thoughtful judgments. From such judgments we can speak and act assertively without apology or undue hesitation.

It is not enough for activists to articulate the flaws we see in our world; we must also be able to present alternatives, not just abstractions, but real solutions to real problems. To win the support of an ever-widening portion of women, we need to articulate essential feminist values and the visions they are built upon. We must not just explain what exists today, but also point our societies in a better direction. Because women's circumstances are so diverse and the needs so complex, because focus and unity are so elusive and yet so crucial, our understanding must be supremely creative, and, as much as possible, uncontaminated by destructive, parochial thinking.

Somehow, we must find directions that serve the whole planet, that make sense enough to engender wide agreement. We must discover perspectives beyond the transient insularity that has never worked and that leaves us coldly unconvinced, despairing of a way ahead. We must find a source to validate our beliefs, which rises above our superficial selves, which rises above our troubled cultures. And we can do it.

But how do we uncover insights that transcend the limitations of our social experience? We are, after all, largely creatures of our past and of our societies. Some argue that it is impossible to break free from inherited perspectives, that we are at the mercy of our personal and social histories, and that "knowledge" is at best a fiction created by power, and truth is no more than a majority opinion.

Such ideas are partially correct. Certainly, for most people, social discourses represent the whole of what is considered knowledge, and even among thoughtful and reflective persons, social beliefs contribute a major portion of their understanding. But in each of us is a counterforce to what we learn from the external world— it is what we come to understand through the inner world, the deepest level of experience, what some have called the "center," the "private self," the "deep mind." We tap this awareness when we think very deeply, meditate, or reflect. This part of ourselves can be difficult to access, because it lies far from ordinary surface awareness. But because it is farther from the surface, it is less accessible to culture, less subject to it, in some sense insulated from it, and therefore less contaminated. Not a separate entity, but a part of the way we process life experience, this inner self, our deep mind, is the agent that interacts with the external world, but which preceded it and is not wholly a creature of it. Our deep mind functions in a different context from ordinary thinking, uses different modes of validation, and so it produces different fruit. (A great deal more will be said about the inner life in the following chapters.)

In this profoundest center of experience we find conviction. Very likely, for most of us our belief in social justice was born here, and it is here that our feminist values have their roots. Ultimately, this is the center we must tap to find the knowledge and the validation that we require to empower ourselves and motivate others.

For feminist values not only to survive but to prevail, they must come out of such profound thinking. *To know clearly what we want, why we want it, and why it is best*—such knowing flows from an understanding deeper than superficial social consensus, a level which we tap through the deep mind. Thus, that level of understanding, what it is, what it yields, and how it may be used, is a legitimate, even a necessary consideration for feminists.

As productive as such a sensibility and mode of thinking can be to feminism, there have been impediments to its use. It has been the primary subject of what is called the humanities, "the study of the human spirit." It has also been a focus of religion. And therein begins a problem.

Many, if not most, contemporary social activists and feminists have a long tradition of hostility, or at least suspicion, toward "spirituality" and toward religion, both as an institution and as an individual practice. After all, most of the "world's great religions" have unfalteringly opposed women's rights (despite avowals otherwise). They often have been the most active opponents of many crucial feminist programs, among them, full participation in the cultural and political life of society, reproductive and sexual autonomy, access to divorce, the right to economic parity, even personal freedom. Worse, often "piety," obedience to religious dogma or churches, has in one form or another kept many women from acting in their own best interests.

At the hands of the father-god religious institutions, women have been brutalized, exploited, and manipulated. What is worse, from time before remembering, the patriarchs have assailed women's sense of self and sought to destroy confidence and pride. It has been their aim not just to control us, but to make us willingly obedient. We have been required to believe that we are intellectually and spiritually inferior, and therefore we should be happy, grateful to be "guided." To gain this end, a contemptible picture of women was created and propounded as real. Our authentic history was erased, our experience negated, and a series of lies set in their place. People can be hurt physically, robbed of labor, time, wealth, or comfort, and yet still somehow survive with pride and affirmation. The loss from which a person rarely emerges intact is the theft of self, of one's sense of worth apart from any instrumental utility, of one's belief in one's own intrinsic goodness, the right to be, to live as seems fit, to make decisions for oneself.

Feminists are sharply aware that for all their talk about higher values and the goodness of God, the powerful establishments of patriarchal religion have failed to meet their moral responsibilities. They have often perverted the human scene with hatred and violence and maligned the Earth and life upon it, bringing the planet to the edge of the end. For the most part, the religions of the patriarchs have gone wrong. They have deflected the communities of the world from developing healthy values and instead have focused people's minds upon the darkest elements of existence. They have fostered the worst kind of irrationality and illogic. Inherent in their very nature is overwhelming hostility to over half of the human population—women. Feminists know it is impossible that all this error should be accidental, but rather that such consistent wrongdoing must emanate from an inherent warp. In fact, we are increasingly discovering what the warps are and how they work, and we have learned that patriarchal religion's contempt for women and its destructiveness towards life in general are intimately related.

The feminist struggle to articulate the mistakes of the patriarchal religions and to free women from their consequences has been monumental. Such freedom is hard won. The influence of the "world's great religions" is pervasive and complex. Their belief systems are integrated so completely into the fabric of our societies and are so much a part of our own psychic interiors, that we are only just beginning to understand what damage we have suffered, and we can but barely hope to convince those who have not yet begun to see. Feminists know that in taking on patriarchal religion, our age-old foe, we stand on dangerous ground, because we face the prospect of war with all the priests of patriarchy—the ones inside our heads as well as those at the altars.

Small wonder that one of the earliest themes of the current women's movement was the disclaiming of religion. The majority of feminist activists said "no" to religion—actually, what they rejected was the usurpation of moral prerogative, oppressive, antilife orientations, the kind of manipulative games that are played with one's mind. They argued, and continue to insist, that feminism is a social-political-economic movement: Its business is concrete change in the circumstances of women's lives and ultimately in the institutions and culture that affect all people. They correctly point out that effecting such change requires enormous amounts of labor, commitment, time, and energy: energy that must not be siphoned away into unproductive or counterproductive channels. Recognizing that historically religion has often functioned as a tranquilizer for the powerless and oppressed, these feminists fear a religious or spiritual orientation in women; we cannot, they point out, afford to be tranquilized. And of course, we cannot.

Unquestionably "religion" or "spirituality" defined by and in the service of patriarchy is a force against freedom, vitality, and survival. But patriarchy's definition of religion is not the only one possible. *Religion* and *patriarchal religion* are not synonymous. Often the distinctions between religion as such and religion as a particular institution in a particular time and place have been blurred. The predisposition to misperceive this fact is understandable, but it is also regrettable, because it causes so many to rebuff a resource that contains incredible value to women as individuals and to the women's movement.

Liberation for women entails more than parity, more even than economic or political power. It presupposes self-definition and the opportunity to radically redefine the meaning of life and how it should be lived, for ourselves personally, and for our societies. To do this is a matter of the spirit. It requires a far more profound sense of what life is about, a more profound perspective than we usually carry in everyday life; again, it requires that we look inside the essential inner core of us, individually and collectively.

Uncontaminated by the perversions that have beset the greater part of patriarchal religions, looking "deep" can be an extraordinary catalyst for more exuberant, more powerful living. It provides a trail to meaningfulness, which is, after all, the essential source of direction, empowerment, and commitment. Because looking into the self leads one inevitably to consider other selves and other kinds of selves, it generates empathy and ultimately concern for the whole planet and beyond. It provides a wider and deeper viewpoint and a different context in which to confront events. It leads to powerfully felt insight, which is why it so often leads to action.

Consciously or not, the inner life directs the outer life; we cannot afford to neglect it. What is more, attention to the inner life is entirely consistent with the mainstream of feminist thought. Feminists are not cynics, and the women's movement has always had a strong spiritual element, although in this century it has not usually been articulated or acknowledged as such. Feminism and its programs are based on discernable values and a particular vision of life, which is, after all, the stuff of spirit. Why not articulate those values and visions? Why not use all the means that have been used and may be used to deepen and refine them? Why not harvest the best in all kinds of human understanding? And why not share what we find, use it to improve our lives, and celebrate it together? Certainly we could call doing this spirited (spiritual) endeavor.

Should we call it religion?

What might religion be like free of the patriarchs' control? How might we experience spirit from a truly life-embracing stance? Why can't we, shouldn't we create an alternative to the spiritual devastation so many of us have come to associate with the familiar traditions?

If our trek inward and then outward is to be different from what we knew before and rejected, we must identify the elements in the traditional approaches that have rendered them toxic. As we shall see, the trapfall in the patriarchal religions is the warrior mentality: the principles of conflict, power, and aggression as a paradigm for reality; the wholehearted embrace of pain, suffering, and death; the substitution of a one-sex metaphor for a two-sex reality. We must be careful to avoid this mentality and its paraphernalia. But we must do more. We must construct something healthy and life-serving to replace the martial paradigm. What that something might be, how we might discover it, and how we might best use it is the subject of this book.

The search for a life-embracing spirituality is presented here through a variety of means: analysis of existing religions, especially the strains that led to their distortion; examination of certain current religious terms—*grace, faith, sublimity, spirit, religion*—and their radical reinterpretation; conceptualizations or approaches to religion not weighted with the familiar destructive currents—irrationality, contra-naturalism, perverse asceticism; and finally the sharing of stories, myths, prayers, and rituals grounded in another religious orientation—pagan and woman-centered.

I am a feminist, unregenerate, no less emphatic than I was in the 1960s when I first became involved in women's liberation. I am a social activist, committed to practical change, somewhat experienced in the rigors of life on the line. I am a professional philosopher, a women's studies scholar, a political theorist, a "trained academician." I am also a mystic, a pagan, and a Quaker; I stand positively toward the life of the spirit and toward religion when it is an expression of Spirit.

I am the child of a first-generation orthodox Jewish American family. I fled the religion of my birth in my early twenties. I experienced it as implacable, and through the people closest to me, I was presented with a belief system that I found irrational, repressive, and sexist. I did not know until many years later that there was any other way to find it. By that time, the associations with Judaism that I had forged out of those early experiences were ineradicable. I could not go back. In this I am typical of many feminist activists. Years later, my intellectual life, my encounters with people and life events, and my feminism reconfirmed my original rejection of religion as I knew it. However, perhaps despite my resistance to religion, perhaps because of it, those same factors that separated me from my original beliefs have pressed upon me a new and reconstructed spiritual world-view, the conviction that health, wisdom, and freedom, personal and social, are grounded in an ongoing, serious attention to the inner life, to *Spirit*, mine and the world's. Furthermore, I believe that for feminists to prevail in our most far-reaching goals, we require the balance and the potency that comes from personal *centeredness* and from possessing a viable metaphysic. In this I am probably not typical of most feminist activists; in some cases, I risk their disapprobation. It is my intention in this work to persuade some portions of the feminist community to reconsider the meaning and potential significance of attending to their spiritual lives and in so doing contribute to our ultimate success.

## A Story (Quite True)

"It doesn't need to be hard," she said, riveting me with her eyes. She held my hands tightly in her own, forcing me to face her squarely, as one might a rattled, unruly child. Seeing in my expression that I didn't quite understand her, but that I wanted to, she said it again, slowly, softly (considering how much power she transmitted), "Your book, it doesn't need to be hard. That's ego; let it go."

I was conducting a workshop in feminist spirituality at a small university in Illinois. Perhaps fifty or sixty people were present, including students, some townspeople, and faculty, but she had drawn my attention from the start. A little older than the rest, she seemed especially vital; although she spoke little, she watched intently, and I would catch myself looking for her, trying to read her reactions from her expressions. During the session I had mentioned that I was struggling to write a book about feminist spirituality. It was, I said, the hardest thing I had ever tried to do. Later, toward the end of coffee-and-cookies-and-meet-the-speaker time, the woman approached me, said she had enjoyed the workshop, took my hands, and spoke her message.

Following that workshop, it was days before I returned to my home, my desk, and my book. In between, there were more presentations, motel rooms, airplane rides at night, noise and static, but her words kept echoing inside my head: "It doesn't need to be hard. That's ego; let it go."

By the time I reached home, the message had become no longer a puzzle, but a mantra. Over and over I repeated it to myself (it repeated itself to my self?), and it was still reverberating inside me as I sat down to write, this time with greater calm than usual. As I put pen to paper, what printed itself on the page before me were the words

Let me be a conduit for Spirit.

Early in the writing of *Take Back The Light*, I was slowed almost to a halt by a host of fairly typical author worries: Who would be reading this book—academicians? feminist scholars? women in general? philosophers? To whom should I address myself, at what "level," and in what voice? What did I hope to accomplish with this writing? How should the book be organized—around what theme, in what tone? More troubling: Who was I, a social philosopher and not a (credentialed? official? traditional?) theologian, to be writing a book about spirituality and religion?

Round and round I had gone in my head, unsettled and undecided, until that striking woman caught hold of me and delivered her message. "That's ego," she had said, and she was right, for outside of a wholesome desire to be understood, such stumbling self-doubt is obviously a form of self-protection: Who will be reading *my* work? How can I be assured of *my* acceptance? How can I persuade readers to agree with *me*? Once all that (ego) is discarded, what remains is: What do I have to say, and how can I make myself understood?

What I have to say is already a part of me. I need only to access it. Making myself understood, on the other hand, is difficult; there is such a chasm between the soul and the lips. In a conversation with Elizabeth Janeway in 1987, she told me, "It is not a writer's responsibility to be simple, only to be clear." The subject of this book resists clarity, but, although I am certain I have sometimes missed the mark, I have endeavored to be clear—albeit in unusual ways. Communication is always a joint venture; I urge the reader to strive with me for understanding in the following pages.

The elusive character of the subject of this work presents one challenge, but another factor here may give the reader even more pause. I have mixed two modes of understanding which usually are kept separate.

Two general spheres of "knowing" have been postulated within Western thought, each with its own mode of verification, its own subject matter, even its own language. On the one hand is the cognitive, the *ef*fective, what is termed analytical, rational, linear, documentable, the kind of information that is deemed publicly verifiable. Even though the meanings of these terms are controversial and open to widely divergent interpretations, they circumscribe the major portion of what is considered respectable scholarship.

On the other hand stands experiential thinking, the *af*fective, the personal, the holistic, the epistemologically private. This realm of discourse is tolerated in poetry, some aspects of theology, aesthetics, and so on, but for the majority of Western thinkers it is considered inferior to the other—everyone knows thinking is better (more dependable, more productive) than feeling—and is either relegated to a very particular kind of project or is viewed as beyond the ken. The status of *knowledge* is generally reserved for analytic cognition.

As a rule careful thinkers are expected to confine themselves to one sphere or the other (mixing the two in the same work amounts to a kind of unseemly miscegenation), and it is believed that the best thinkers (such as scientists, mathematicians, and certain philosophers) are those who avoid the affective altogether. (Scholars who stray are often talked about as if they had "lapsed.")

Nonetheless, a mixing of the cognitive and the affective is precisely what I am attempting here. It is very difficult to use both, but also very enriching. At least for certain kinds of issues, such as the subject of this book, splitting the two into exclusive spheres may be both incorrect and counterproductive. Clearly a thin line exists between what is sensible and what is subjective, and since Descartes, all researchers have been sensitive to the problems of "public" knowledge. The line between the rational and the nonrational is equally thin. To further complicate matters, there are times when ideas themselves cross the various boundaries of thought. Territorializing the two modes of thought may have caused more confusion than it has repaired. Precisely because they reflect two very different dimensions of understanding or even reality, their integration might yield richer, more accurate knowledge than what can be gleaned by either one used alone. Being prudent, being alert to the differences between modes of thinking is not necessarily the same as isolating them. Difficult though it may be to build bridges, it may help us to comprehend and communicate some very slippery ideas.

Early readers of this manuscript had very different reactions to aspects of *Take Back The Light*. Some who applauded the analysis advised me to drop the "other stuff." Just as many, however, enjoyed the meditations and poetry and thought the analysis superfluous. I was advised on not a few occasions to separate the mystical and the didactic and publish two books. That would be one way to handle this material, but it had always been my express intention to show that the two elements not only could be, but should be, joined. For the integrity of my project, I decided to preserve the current design.

Some wondered about my tone, judging it in turn to be "angry," or "tranquilized (not angry enough)," didactic or sentimental, and in some cases "embarrassingly autobiographical." Apparently, tone, like understanding, can be jointly created. This work was meant to be subjective, experiential, and uncompromisingly authentic, as well as thoughtful and analytic. Certainly it is personal. If it is embarrassing, perhaps that is because we live in a world in which the self is supposed to hide, and we become uncomfortable when it does not. It is at times angry. So am I—although not exclusively. It is also at times joyful. So am I.

The question was posed whether the work might be reactionary. That means it would tend to reverse important gains women and I myself had made in understanding, attitude, and resolve; it would be detrimental to the women's movement. Quite the opposite. *Take Back The Light* stands squarely for each woman's and all women's right to our own articulation of the meaning and purpose of life. It suggests ways to decide for ourselves, consistent with those articulations, what we desire in our relationships with others, with the world, and with our own emerging selves. It calls for better stewardship of ourselves, the earth, and beyond, based on conviction, not on external, alien constructions. If this work "appears" or "feels" reactionary, because of its language or its realm of discourse, then perhaps a choice must be made between honesty and ideology.

This book was written in a spirit of regeneration and empowerment. It is an invitation to share in insights that can lead *away* from the spiritual deprivation and damage many of us have suffered, *to the possibilities and pleasures of connecting the self with the cosmic.*

This book is also an entreaty: to take back unequivocally our right to create our own spiritual core; to resolve that, out of that core, as feminists we can and do pursue those goods that may keep ourselves and our world safer.

## Notes

1. Shulamith Firestone, *The Dialectic of Sex: The Case for Feminist Revolution* (New York: Bantam, 1970), p. 1.

# Acknowledgments

*Take Back The Light* has been in process for several years. During that time, there have been very special people who have helped and supported me in my intellectual and spiritual development.

In the writing and organizing of this manuscript, it is impossible to exaggerate the help I received from Professors Thomas Paxson and Clyde Nabe of the Department of Philosophical Studies and Professor John Taylor of the Department of History at Southern Illinois University at Edwardsville. They read each chapter again and again, shared with me their ideas and their own spiritual harvest, and prompted me to tackle the most difficult questions. Their advice and suggestions are interwoven throughout this book, and I am extremely grateful for the time and energy they gave so generously.

This work could not have been completed without the support of the Department of Philosophical Studies. For granting me the time and the flexibility to work on this project, my thanks go to Professor Carol A. Keene, chair of the department.

In a more personal vein, heartfelt appreciation goes to Mary Helen Osborne, who has shared her insights with me and has nourished me in mind, heart, and spirit; to Judith Ferren, whose unfailing warmth, kindness, and strength have made me feel grounded and secure; and to John Taylor, who has graced me with ceaseless stimulation of mind and friendship that sustains.

Very special thanks go to the people at the St. Louis Religious Society of Friends (Quakers). They have helped me learn to listen, to reach for Vision, and to love the stillness. They have made me a friend, for which I am grateful.

For the renewal that comes of camaraderie, laughter, and a gladsome sharing of the Mother's gifts, I am indebted to Bill Budke and the rest of my friends at the Media Club in St. Louis.

For the personal joy and vitality that undergirds *Take Back The Light*, for the ongoing connectedness, for the love that restores, my deepest gratitude goes to Amity Ruth and Michael Allaband.

Permission to reproduce previously published material is gratefully acknowledged.

Mahnaz Afkhami, "Iran: A Future in the Past," from *Sisterhood Is Global: The International Women's Movement Anthology*, edited by Robin Morgan. Copyright © by Robin Morgan. By permission of Edite Kroll Literary Agency.

Zsuzsanna Budapest, "Self-Blessing Ritual," *The Feminist Book of Lights and Shadows*, edited by Helen Beardwoman (Luna Press, 1976). Copyright © 1976 by Zsuzsanna Budapest. The material is also now in *The Holy Book of Women's Mysteries*, published by Wingbow Press, 1989.

Joseph Campbell, Excerpts from *Masks of God: Occidental Mythology*. Copyright © 1964 by Joseph Campbell. Used by permission of Viking Penguin, a division of Penguin Books USA Inc.

Mary Daly, *Gyn/Ecology*. Copyright © 1978, 1992 by Mary Daly. Reprinted by permission of Beacon Press.

John A. Hardon, Excerpts from *Modern Catholic Dictionary*. Copyright © 1980 by John A. Hardon. Used by permission of Doubleday, a division of Bantam Doubleday Dell Publishing Group, Inc.

Carol Ochs, "Categories of Opposition in Matriarchy and Patriarchy," from *Behind the Sex of God*. Copyright © 1977 by Carol Ochs. Reprinted by permission of Beacon Press.

Sheila Ruth, "A Feminist Analysis of the New Right," in *Women's Studies International Forum*, volume 6, number 4, pp. 345–351, 1983. Copyright © 1983. Reprinted with kind permission from Pergamon Press Ltd., Headington Hill Hall, Oxford OX3 OBW, UK.

Sheila Ruth, "Bodies and Souls/Sex, Sin and the Senses in Patriarchy: A Study in Applied Dualism." Reprinted from *Hypatia: A Journal of Feminist Philosophy*, volume 2, number 1 (Winter 1987), pp. 149–163.

Starhawk, Excerpts from *The Spiral Dance*. Copyright © 1979 by Miriam Simos. Reprinted by permission of HarperCollins Publishers, Inc.

Diane Wolkstein and Samuel N. Kramer, Excerpts from *Inanna, Queen of Heaven and Earth*. Copyright © 1983 by Diane Wolkstein. Published by HarperCollins Publishers, Inc.

# Part One

# CHAPTER ONE

# Feminist Vision

## *Beginnings*

A young woman told once of her earliest memories of religion and of how she had left it behind, she believed, forever. When she was very small, she and two younger sisters had attended church every Sunday with their parents. From those earliest times, she could remember only the colors and sounds and smells of the place, the darkened room, the polished wooden pews, the choir, sitting and standing and sitting and standing again, hushed voices or toneless singing in between. Some time later her parents stopped attending with their daughters, but her father continued to take the three girls to church every week, leaving them at the door and returning for them at the end of the service. Church had always been depressing and tedious to this energetic girl, but she had been obedient until her parents' defection. Then she conceived a plan of escape. Each Sunday morning, directly after her father drove off, she and her sisters would slip out through the side door of the church to the woods behind. They would remove their Sunday dresses, uncovering the play clothes they had secretly worn beneath, and sprint into hiding among the trees, where they would laugh, climb, run, play hide-and-seek, chase butterflies, and share secrets. Later they would tell their father, yes, church had been all right, and it had been a pleasant enough morning.

In truth, it had been pleasant. The sisters felt so free, she recalled. The very fact that no one knew where they were to call them back or call them down added to the delectation of the moment.

3

The colors of the woods were especially vivid, the smell of mud and leaves particularly sweet. She recounted that as she ran, her body fairly sailed over stones and logs. She loved the feel of the sun and the breeze. And no, she said with only small consternation, she had not felt guilty about her deception. Perhaps, she had mused, her morning had made infinitely more sense to her than the one planned for her by her parents, and because they had been content in their ignorance, and she had been happy, this independent young woman believed her actions had been right. It was a simple act in her own behalf. She had concluded early in her life that religion was shackling, dark, and senseless. By its own nature, it dictated escape.

Indeed, the girl had acted well in her own behalf. In some profoundly knowing, small-child way, she had chosen Life. What she did not realize or could not have articulated was that she had fled the church to tend to her spirit.

The girl had chosen liberty, joy, expansiveness, affectionate interchange with her sisters, relationship with nature, which she loved and which heartened her. The church and the people in it might have provided her avenues to those things, but they did not. In fact, there she was blocked from what she required, and quite rightfully she ran away. Moreover, she made more than a merely aimless escape, for she had a destination. She made a positive choice for life-enhancing experience.

It is a beginning, for any human being to leave emptiness, to reject what distorts the inner life, but that is not enough. Like the girl, we must elect something better; we must choose the fullness of life.

The women's movement has matured beyond its beginning. We have discarded. Now we are in a position to create.

## Transitions

Feminists have chosen the path of life. Although our movement began with "limited" goals—the liberation of women from social, political, and economic exploitation, it became obvious very early that we would have to move beyond even those immensely wide boundaries. As our analyses pressed deeper into the nature of the system that oppressed us, patriarchy—the male-defined and male-controlled web of social institutions, we uncovered its very heart and thus its ultimate consequences. In the connections we found between its contempt for women and its attitudes to nature, we could see very clearly a pervasive contempt for life itself, and we understood its terrible outcome: all life at every level was threatened. We were propelled into a gigantic, universally significant task: broadly defined, we must press for the restoration of the integrity, freedom, and survival of the entire planet. Such a task, such a goal, would sound grandiose at best, absurd at worst, were it not true! We need only consider the literature and activities of the feminist movement, their range and scope, to see how much it is true: feminists today are actively involved in the world peace movement, the various campaigns for racial equality, the struggle for ecological balance, the critique of new technologies, the reform of education, the drive for economic justice, and more, in addition to our constant efforts for our own personal liberation. What is more, we know that all these concerns are inextricably interwoven.

In the service of such a task, we must act with strength, courage, and indefatigable energy. We must have power, not *power over*, the currency of the warriors, but *power to*, the force of enablement. Where are we to gather such strength? Where, in fact, have we always found it? In our vision.

Feminism rests upon a vision of life. Beneath the politics and practice of the women's movement is a particular sense of the meaning of life, of how life should be. There is a configuration of values, dreams, wishes, and goals, not only for individuals, but for the world, not only for women, but for all people, not only for people, but for all living things and for all creation.

Finding ourselves increasingly free of the bleakness of patriarchal thinking, including its religion, which is its ultimate expression, we are finding ourselves regenerated. We look back shocked and incredulous at the dark visions from which many of us have escaped. Increasingly cleansed of the deadening, joy-killing mindset, we look afresh at our world, and we are appalled and delighted. We are appalled with the mess of things that patriarchy has made, the violence, the misery. But with the world that is our rightful home, we are delighted: How beautiful is the Earth and all the various species of life upon it; how joyous is nature, physical, concrete, cyclical, ever-changing, time-bound; how wonderful, how deserving of love, admiration, and respect is the body, sibling to all other bodies, source of incredible pleasures, child of time, progenitor of the future; how strong and right is the passion of existence to continue itself, and how absolutely and irretrievably wrong

it is to destroy or defame what is good, pleasing, and truly sublime* in natural existence. How perverse it is to denigrate the Earth,
to fail to acknowledge it as good and decent and able to call us to
live well; how perverse it is to place oneself in opposition to the
well-being of the creatures of this world, to choose misery and
warfare instead of caring, friendship, and felicity.

In broad strokes, that is the heart of feminist vision, forming itself out of our discoveries and our cleansing, moving us to act,
channeling our energy toward our many positive goals, and strengthening our will and determination. The language of the vision is almost embarrassing in its voluptuousness; nonetheless some have
dared to voice it—in poetry, in literature, in philosophy. Why should
we hesitate? Rather, we should be even bolder, say it clearer and
louder. We should, we *must*, put words to our dreams, claim our
insights, build our images of the nature of virtue and the meaning
of existence, tell each other and anyone who cares to listen what
we take to be sacred, honorable, meaningful, absolutely worthy. We
should talk and talk and talk about these things so that from our
exchanges would come visions even more clear, more beautiful, and
more viable, visions leading us to act. Such visions are required
not only for us as individuals but for our communities, because the
function of visioning is to order and direct the lives in its service,
and we know that our societies are in disrepair and desperately in
need of direction. We must even dare to name the name of that
which we deem most venerable, because naming creates power; we
may even worship it; that is, we may grant it *worth-ship.*†

Paradoxically, although it is central to the women's movement,
undergirding everything we do, feminist vision is not comfortably
acknowledged by the movement. For social scientists, political strat-
egists, or for activists on the line, such talk has a disconcerting tone,
altogether too reminiscent of traditional "religion." But, of course,
isn't that just the point? Vision and visioning are born(e) out of
spirit, the rich inner life, and if religion is understood as the tend-

---

*Sublime*: from *sub-limen*; up to the lintel; set or raised aloft. (*The Com-
pact Edition of the Oxford English Dictionary*, New York: Oxford University
Press, 1971. Hereafter referred to as *OED*.) It is revealing to trace the meanings of the spiritual terms to their origins before they were adapted by the
patriarchal religions.

†*Worship*: out of the Old English, *honor*: . . . *worth + ship*. (*American
Heritage Dictionary*, 2nd college edition, Boston: Houghton Mifflin, 1985.
Hereafter referred to as *AHD*.)

ing of spirit, then vision is a creature of religion as well. But why should we recoil from that?

In fact, religion, that part of our lives devoted to the tending of spirit—to its care and expression—is far older and wider than patriarchy. Imagining, imaging, and valuing existed long before the fathers and their father-god subjugated the planet. There was granting worth-ship and acknowledging the holy;* there was pursuing the good, the meaningful, the beautiful; there was sharing veneration long before the patriarchs claimed that space as their own. It is our need and our right to reclaim it.

Yet, sometimes attempts to reclaim it are viewed with suspicion, even contempt. For example, in "Goddess Worship: Toxic Niceness?" a review of two recent films on feminist spirituality,[1] Donaleen Saul, one of the authors, comments:

> At the heart of today's widespread interest in Goddess-based civilizations is a nostalgic yearning for a golden age, approximately 3500 years ago. . . .
>
> To hide behind the skirts of the Goddess and take shots at our male-dominated culture . . . is childish in the extreme. In effect, we are still running to an idealized Mommy rather than truly seeing and feeling the lies, the misery, the games, the crippling acts of destruction that go on within ourselves and in our own homes. . . .
>
> . . . The Goddess fad, like the more hard-edged and arid version of feminism that it is replacing, is, in effect, just feminism drunk on disembodied nostalgia, ritualistic pretense, and New Age ideology. It is not truly interested in real female power. . . .
>
> Well, things do need to change and no one knows this better than the woman who has achieved some degree of all-around maturity. Unlike most Goddess devotees, she is not superficial or self-congratulatory. She has suffered immensely, she bears the scars. . . . She is a warrior. . . . She welcomes her trials. . . .
>
> . . . We need to consciously face the inner war that separates us from our core of being. . . . Such transformation demands everything of us—our bodies, hearts, spirits, our softness and our hardness. The Goddess will not do it for us.[2]

Saul also notes that the women interviewed in the film appear "dull-eyed, armoured, ineffectual, full of unexpressed rage and alarmingly dissociated from their feelings."

---

*Holy*: related originally to the root of *whole*, "free from injury" (*OED*), therefore, free of stain of imperfection, inviolate, inviolable.

It is important to consider this commentary closely because it represents a common attitude. The tone is scornful, the stance aggressive. Assumptions are taken for facts and then reacted upon. The authors speculated about what they saw, but how careful were they to ascertain that they perceived correctly. They might have considered, for example, whether instead of dull-eyed, ineffectual rage, the faces of the women might have reflected centered self-assurance. They might have wondered whether only an escapist, nostalgic yearning for an *ancient* golden age could underlie the interest in goddess civilizations. Indeed, it might be a different kind of yearning—for a *future* golden age, even a personal *present*, that would honor the Female as it has honored the Male. Why is granting worth-ship to a female deity, however construed, however expressed, necessarily a childish escape to an idealized Mommy? It could be a symbolic act of directing attention to the "real female power" that Saul says she respects, a declaration, indeed, of separation from the Mommys (and Daddys!) of our immaturity, an embrace of transformation to strength. In fact, the "goddess" honored in such a ritual might be the very "warrior" Saul describes, the woman, real or symbolic, who embodies and radiates elder wisdom, autonomy, power, and life, the woman whom we might hope to strengthen within any one of us. Rather than a misdirected, childlike dependence on our mommies, worship of the "goddess" may represent a quite wholesome veneration of the "Mother," symbol of generation itself, ultimate progenitor and source of all being.

We cannot fail to empathize with Saul's terrible anger for the injuries caused by a "spirituality" that she has rejected, but perhaps the anger belongs to some other place that it has yet to reach. More problematic for the women's movement is the dramatic misreading of what is presented. In the rituals performed in the film and in the movement the film depicts (WomanSpirit), there is and has always been a call to develop an acute awareness of our potential energy, of our power to act and to change ourselves and our worlds. Never has it been suggested that social action be sacrificed for private peace. Indeed, the opposite is true.

Locating the sacred somehow "out there," away from daily existence, so that worship involves withdrawal from full participation in ordinary life, is a distortion of spirituality. Because feminism presupposes social action, feminist the*a*logians (those who study female deity) have unfailingly maintained that peace comes only from an integration of the private good and the wider good, that effective social action is and must be the inevitable product of inner clarity.

The call is so clearly *for* action and *for* integration. The ardent fear of an anesthetized withdrawal (that doesn't even exist in the WomanSpirit movement) is based on a hidden, erroneous assumption.

Many of us have witnessed and deplored the elements of religion at its worst: the arrogant hypocrisy, the glassy-eyed, saccharine, "toxic" morality, the infantile strategies used to avoid the trials of authentic living, the ignorance, and the intransigence. In fact, it has been such a pervasive experience, so catastrophic in its consequences, that we have come not only to associate these elements with religion, but to equate them. The equation—*religion is equivalent to (or entails) all these awful things*—can form a nearly indelible presupposition in our thinking about anything related to religion or "spirit," so that it becomes difficult to think of religion without it. Because we so thoroughly expect the worst of religion, sometimes we see it when it is not present. Such a misconception is seriously counterproductive for us, because it slows us from taking a direction we need to take.

Feminists have dared to deconstruct our society's world-view; dare we now synthesize a new one? We have already begun to dream visions of the future in diverse ways; some of us talk and listen, some teach, some act in the streets, some create and ponder ideas. Some seek to generate change through theater or literature. Some write stinging poems about social injustice. Others create art revealing female principles, or develop community through dance and celebration. Can we not seek the same goals through other routes, through meditation or ritual or chant, dreaming the grand dream built of imagination, passion, and, at times, ecstasy?

We are learning ever more clearly what is wrong with the patriarchal mind-set and the world it has created. We know ever more fervently what we do not want and what we do not wish to be. For years we have assayed the sins, crimes, and wrong turns of those in power. Early on, that was feminists' first order of business. To make sense of our inherited circumstances, we had to describe minutely the insights and images drawn into focus by our developing woman-consciousness. Set outside of the order of things, displaced as we have been, we are in a special position to do this, and we have done it and continue to do it very well.

To discern what is undesirable and reject it is a crucial early step in progress. The process of purposeful, consciously chosen change often begins in the inchoate recognition of something wrong in the present condition; it progresses to the articulation of what is wrong and proceeds ultimately to a belief that one can and must move from the present to a better place. The struggle then proceeds even more earnestly; there must be change, but to where? Movement at first may be without any clear sense of destination. It is movement *away from* rather than movement *toward*, away from what is known to be undesirable, but not yet toward what is known to be better. Sometimes that is all we have or can have, and it is usually better than no movement at all.

Halting, uncertain, remedial change—progress through trial and error has its utility. A slow, and sometimes even regressive course, it can be productive nonetheless in sum. Each step away from the beginning, each positive step may afford a glimmer, a crucial clue to the character of the place toward which we draw. For every wrong turn taken in learning where not to go, we learn a bit more clearly where we might better go.

At some point, however, the process must ripen. At its best, growth becomes more integrative. In ever-widening circles, we come to understand not just why we must take each isolated step forward, but where the entire enterprise must lead. Finally the time comes to abandon the primitive, piecemeal actions of earlier stages and to adopt a more coherent plan. When it becomes possible to define, in broad terms at least, the ultimate goals of the endeavor, it should be done to clarify and hasten progress.

Feminism and the women's movement is at this point. We have analyzed, described, revealed, and named. Sometimes we have placed our soft, warm bodies before the steamroller of patriarchy and said, "No more." It is time to step beyond, beyond negation to affirmation, from repudiation to assertion. It is time we say to the world and to ourselves, "Here, this is better. This is why it is better, and this is why I believe it."

If we do not dare to propose the proper objects of human veneration, others will happily fill the voids we leave, and they rarely are better equipped or better intentioned than we.

Many of those who seek power over others know at some level that to be living without a vision of life is an intolerable condition. It is to be without meaning, to be adrift, aimless, at the mercy of seemingly pointless physical circumstance, for a kind of primitive materialism appears to become the only context left. So crushing, so bleak is the nihilism of such a state that many would, and often do, choose any alternative that seems even remotely workable, even to adopting visions created by others, visions that may be destructive, oppressive, inauthentic, somewhat meaningful, or patently mad. So long as they introduce structure, purpose, or value in an otherwise measureless world, they can be seductive.

To live honestly and hopefully without vision holds at least the possibility that it may be discovered in the future. It is far worse to live with alien vision, to be forced to dream, or make choices, or act out of a stance not one's own or contrary to one's own. Always the images are askew, the elements ill-fitting. Always there is strain between the self and the prescribed belief system, because it does not emanate from the self but from some other, disconnected place.

To be one's own, a vision must be created by the person out of the ongoing struggle with ultimate questions, out of the interplay between experience and thoughtful reflection. Although our vision may take ideas from others, it must be consistent with our already existing inner reality, validated by more than only positive exchange with the outside world. A vision that is truly one's own does not contradict the total, integrated picture of things one has developed out of experience; it does not negate or discount the self. When visioning is authentic, dissonant information is taken in slowly, processed in harmony with the self, and integrated. The challenge to the inner world would engender growth, not self-annulment. The person trapped in alien vision is committed to a structure out of harmony with essential personal experience and is faced with endlessly choosing between the imperatives of the inner self and the fear of losing the security of the learned system. Tragically, it is the self that is least often chosen.

That is exactly the position in which women have found ourselves in patriarchy. We have been robbed of our right to create our own vision, to construct our own dreams of human living, and we have been expected to accept without question a world-view not only out of harmony with our circumstances, but dedicated to our spiritual annihilation. Here lies the ultimate betrayal of women by patriarchy. More harmful than their economic or social exploitation, more harmful in some way even than their physical violence is the harm done to us by the masters' determination to destroy our freedom to vision, because the shackling of our souls makes possible the rest of our imprisonment. Had they not control over our spirit, they could not bend us to their will. As for the woman battered by her partner, so too for women exploited by patriarchy: emotional devastation and erosion of self precedes and lays the groundwork for material abuse. The lie of traditional religions, that women are profoundly inferior, less divine, serves not only as the patriarchs' justification. It also functions to immobilize us. If we believe it, even a little, the damage to our sense of worthiness and to our spirit can destroy our ability to resist, because resistance to injustice is based on the absolute belief that one is due something better. Like the survivor of battery, we must nourish, replenish the spirit and strengthen the self to alter our circumstances effectively. We must remember, there is a dialectic operating in the relationship of inner self and outward action: To act in the world is crucial. Action influences events. Equally important, action strengthens self. But as feminists have maintained, the inner world controls the outer world. What we believe determines what we do. Healthy action issues from a healthy being.

## *Affirmations*

> [BILL] MOYERS:  What happens when a society no longer embraces a powerful mythology?
>
> [JOSEPH] CAMPBELL:  What we've got on our hands. If you want to find out what it means to have a society without any rituals, read the New York *Times*.
>
> MOYERS:  And you'd find?
>
> CAMPBELL:  The news of the day, including destructive and violent acts by young people who don't know how to behave in a civilized society.
>
> MOYERS:  Society has provided them no rituals by which they become members of the tribe, of the community. All children need to be twice born, to learn to function rationally in the present world, leaving childhood behind. . . .
>
> —Joseph Campbell, *The Power of Myth*[3]

Visioning is the act of a free being—imagining, imaging, and building the possibilities of life out of the realities of one's total experience. Visioning is the product of living at its most lucid, its most liberating, its most alive. Visioning is a quest for and a consequence of vitality.

Why do people require vision? Each of us individually and all of us together in community must cull some meaning from experience with which to order our lives. The pictures of reality that we construct out of our raw experiences, together with the meanings and directions we draw from them, become our vision of Life, not just life in its narrow biological connotation, but in the widest sense, as the on-goingness of all existence. This vision serves as our primary point of reference, through which all other experience is filtered, as well as our focal point, the repository of our ultimate goals. It is our widest and most profound frame of reference, and therefore it is the context within which we make sense out of things. Because it contains our version of how and why life is the way it is, it is also the ground of our values; from our visions we make our judgments about the rightness or wrongness of events and actions, others' and our own. Obviously, the quality of our lives depends upon the quality of our vision.

So, we must make a vision to survive. Such a crucial, formidable task. What drives us to it? Where does it come from? It comes from within us, from the life that is in us, from the unfetterable force of vitality that we are born with and which we struggle so to maintain.

In each of us is a fund of energy that is the very fuel of life. In fact, it is Life, striving to perpetuate itself, to continue. It is in the scream of the newborn struggling for air to breathe and in the stealth of the tiger pursuing its prey. It is in the composite of behaviors that leads creatures to hunt and also leads them to avoid harm; it is in the fear of danger and in the effort to take care. It is what propels us to gather up the necessities for maintaining our lives, not only the lives of our bodies, but of our interior selves. It is in the act of sex and in the striving to know. It is in every expression of the awareness, *I am*, and it contains and comes from the absolute determination to continue to be. This life energy is our umbilicus to Nature, which gave it to us, and it is the source and reflection of our connectedness to all other life, all other creatures, who depend upon it too.

To tap into this energy is to harness the power of being. Like any energy it may be used for good or turned to destructive ends; it may be used by those to whom it rightly belongs, or it may be stolen, expropriated by the treacherous and the greedy; it may run free, seeking its own direction, or it may be walled up and rendered inert.

Energy, being, vitality press to be free, to evolve unconfined. Free though vitality would be, it finds itself always battering against an endless line of blockades, an endless series of forces that push it back, ever back. We are born, each of us, already confined within a narrowness, one that is constructed and put before us by the specific exigencies of our lives and by the particular nature of our surroundings, by our physical world and the people who order it, by our interior world and the options it encounters. What we sense immediately before us, what we must accomplish to survive, how and what we eat and who feeds us, what we are permitted or enabled to learn and who teaches us, what is expected of us in our behavior, attitude, or appearance and how far we are permitted to venture from that career, how many and what kind of creatures we live among and what consequences we may incur for being different—these and a host of other phenomena set us inside a prison of constricted possibilities. Not only physical but experiential and conceptual limitations place us in a social reality formed *for* us rather than *by* us. What is "true" is tendered to us as a given, fait accompli, previously analyzed and interpreted, forced upon our understanding, a commodity already owned and operated. Here is the world, it says to us, this is the universe; this is what you must do in it; this is what is expected and necessary. Here is reality, not just its furniture, but its arrangement as well, not just its past but its future. Adjust yourself! Adjust your body and your mind, your thoughts, perceptions, beliefs, attitudes, feelings, even your fancy. Here you stand; here are the lines around you.

It is a narrow place where we find ourselves early on, before we become lucid enough to question. Marked off for us before we ever choose, before we ever know to make a choice, is the full perimeter of possibilities, binding us within a particular consciousness not only of the environment but of the self. Mapping out a terrain of familiarity and "safety," our narrow place designates even the dimensions of thought that are allowable. In so doing, it tends to fix us, static, absolutely tied to one potentiality, one way, one path, one evolution. To the extent that it is unbroken, unchallenged, such narrowness is the diametric reverse of freedom.

What governs our lives in such a state is expectation, others' and our own, what is set out for us by our given world, and what we come to accept as our boundaries. Not necessarily unhappy, we learn to maneuver within the prescriptions and gain what rewards are possible. Having surrendered the right, perhaps even the ability, to peek outside the walls, not guessing, even fearing what space awaits us, we mistake shackles for choice. We cease (or never begin) to question and struggle, to push beyond the apparent. All but one fixed and predictable universe is denied. Curiosity and spirit recede. Only a certain dull awareness and evenness of temperament may remain.

It may be necessary for the very young and still undeveloped to stay temporarily within such lines. For those still lacking in even basic information, unable to judge or evaluate, a kind of safety may lie within the settlement. (Although even that is questionable.) For all others, to remain permanently or at great length in such a state is a kind of living death, at its extreme not even human, experienced perhaps as painful in some vague way, never fully comprehended, common enough, but nonetheless tragic. Although women are hardly the only ones upon whom such a life is pressed, it has been traditionally assigned to us as our only legitimate province, and feminists have articulated well the character of such an existence. This kind of unfreedom is devastating, life lived within a pen.

It is not the way of a spirited animal to accept a reining in. A creature of spirit, with spirit, is known by its passion for autonomy and respect, its vitality of body and mind, its integrity of kind, its stubborn will, and its lust for freedom. Always it takes for granted the questionableness of walls, and it claims the right to confute them.

The hallmark of the fully vital, fully spirited human life is that it presses constantly beyond its current spaces for tenancy in realms of experience outside familiar existence. Striving to make contact with ever-widening spheres of being, it propels itself after new experience and information. Every awareness that is collected, every new sensation, impression, or intuition and the understanding that they yield is followed by a grasp after more. Every answer to every question asked leads to the next question. Nor is it simple information that is sought; more than mere data, the goal is contact, immediate connectedness with all that is outside the self.

At some level, when we are fully alive, completely alert, we wish to merge with, be part of, come to know, intimately—in the deep mind—the total universe and the processes of being that are our source. The more we come to know life, profoundly, experientially, the more we may consciously connect ourselves and harmonize ourselves with it. The more we understand what is outside us, the better we understand what is within us. We come to know ourselves differently. We are illumined.

Such illumination carries with it a liberation, because it reveals its own configurations of explanations, its own set of imperatives, its own expectations and requirements. These imperatives are not like those imposed on us from without. We do not adopt them; when we find them in their of-courseness, they adopt us. It is a natural and spontaneous relationship between our selves and the universe we find, and in it we are set free: free of alien control, free of the artificiality, dissonance, and inauthenticity of our original, stultifying, ignorance-based narrowness.

It is a normal and constant inclination in all of us, unless we are damaged by rigidity, to seek to place ourselves in relation to life. Were we not very young when we each discovered death and thus life, when we acknowledged our vulnerability, our limitation, and thus the universe? Did we not ask very early on, Who am I? What am I? How did I get here, and why? Why am I in this place and time and not another? Does it have some meaning, or at least, what meaning shall I take from this? In the freshness of our curiosity as children, did we not once lie on our backs under the night sky, look up at the stars, and wonder how we fit into such immenseness? Did we not have some sense of belonging within it and wonder in ever-widening circles how each other thing belonged?

Why do I exist? Why do these other creatures and things, individually and all together, exist? Why do we come and die? How am I to live my life, for myself and in relation to all the rest? What is the best way to live, and how is that determined by the meaning of it all? Is there, in fact, a "meaning of it all," and how am I to know? These questions and others like them are the ultimate questions, in some way bizarre, beyond answers in the usual sense, perplexing and troublesome in the extreme, but not any the less crucial. They appear to us in childhood, simple, perhaps, and selfish; in maturity the questions grow ever wider, increasingly complex and difficult. They may fade into the background at times, but they never disappear, and how we deal with them determines how we believe life should be lived and how we finally choose to live.

The reaching, the seeking, considering this or that experience, adopting and discarding first one solution and then another is the process of life that lifts us into Life, out of the narrowness into which we were born, the ignorant, no-option unfreedom of absolutes—absolutely this way and no other, absolutely bound to this place, this physical, emotional, psychic location, absolutely no way out.

Life, to be life, must breathe. It must change and grow and evolve. To live well, we must travel beyond the confinement of ordinary appearance and press toward a whole range of experiences and meanings that we perhaps never fully comprehend yet know to be vital to us. We want to make sense of the business of existence, and we want to know how we do and should fit within it. It is clear that we cannot "know" these things in the usual way—with data and verification—but rather we must attempt to "know" on some other level, in some other useful way. However advanced or accurate our knowing may or may not come to be, the more we pursue it, the more we are receptive to and come to terms with ultimate issues, the more we confront the totality of life and construct working resolutions to its puzzles, the more we may dare to bring ourselves under the authority of our own judgment, in small as well as in large affairs, hence the freer we may become. Mastery of the self can be reclaimed for the self and brought out of the grasp of external powers.

Coming to terms with ultimate matters is a process each of us must carry on alone, not alone in the sense of isolation, unaided by our communities or out of touch with others, but in the sense of ultimate responsibility for our final conclusions. In the end we must construct our notions of reality for ourselves by ourselves. For us to trust them, our pictures of the transcendent must be created through our own immediate experience and personal confrontations with events. Out of our exchanges with the cosmos, we evolve our structures of understanding and value. Only then have they the force of authenticity. Only when we test the elements of our evolving orientation to life in the most subjective and immediate way can it be sufficiently credible, viable, and powerful to give us the confidence we require to move toward, and to insist upon, self-determination. Nothing else will do. Any construction of reality that is short of such immediacy may suffice to offer us rules to live by; however, as a coming-to-terms, as a source of reconciliation with the inner self and with the universe, a world-view acquired from outside the self is doomed to failure. To the extent that the world-view is external to the self, it does not engage the self. It is alien, it does not connect personal experience with the universe, and it is thus not satisfying.

Although our thinking about these matters may begin sporadically and in disconnected segments, it does not generally remain disjointed, nor do we intend it to. We seek integration; our greatest hope is to discover or to create a wholeness, a total vision of reality that encompasses and includes meanings for all the elements so crucial to us. From the bits and fragments of meaning that we so laboriously collect, we tend to compose an encompassing, organic world-view that functions as the logos of all future understanding, a context against which we place events and ideas to seek their further meaning and direct our response. These are visions.

To create a vision of life is a matter of survival. An individual without a vision, unexercised in the quest for meaning, lives with despair, cynicism, and detachment from others. A society without a vision lives with lawlessness and disorder, because only law that resonates with the social vision has any force of persuasion.

We live in extremely troubling times; we are alive with marvelous possibilities and yet unable to realize those possibilities because we are without ethical moorings. For many of us, our societies have not provided us with adequate visions of life, no ethos from which to generate virtue. It has been said that many of our young (and not so young) lack the ability to transcend the ego, that they have no sense of connection with their communities, their society, or with its future, so they have no stake in contributing.

As a country we are mired in violence, hatreds, ignorance, and suffering. The cities are becoming armed camps. In little towns where people still like to reminisce about times when "we never locked our doors," the installation of "security systems" is becoming a growth industry. "Good" people have rampaged in the streets to save fetuses, apparently oblivious to living human beings starving before their eyes. Americans were said to have rallied out of defeatism, having "won" in the gulf war, delighted with the yellow ribbons of war that should have told them of unspeakable misery. The homeless, we are told, are becoming a nuisance in subways, parks, and bus stations. The sick must raise enough money to buy health care or to die in relative comfort. The public media pander to the worst inclinations of ignorance and reinforce any evil so long as it pays. The professions that could be and should be modeling a different way of life—politics, health care, law, journalism, even education—are no better, only a little more refined. The operative term is "hustle": How much can you get away with? How little can you give and still get the most?

It is no secret that women pay a terrible price in all this. From the "feminization of poverty" to the great backlash, from spiraling violence in the streets and in our homes to the violence of "physical fitness," cosmetic surgery, and reproductive technology, we absorb much of the onslaught. No woman with insight could have watched the circuses of the William Kennedy Smith trial and the

Clarence Thomas confirmation hearing without revulsion, without a deepening sense of alienation from the society that is supposed to be our home.

What we are witnessing is a society in which too many are sick with starvation of the spirit, where some have codes, others rules, but few have a viable, encompassing vision, and most have only the narrowest sense of meaning. In the violence and the cynicism around us is the condition of people who have lost their ground of value and have failed to create another; they cannot find connections to the earth they live on, the people they live with, their future or their past, indeed their own lives outside of the simple, transient action now. They are in despair.

If we want to transform the societies we live in, we must address that spiritless condition, in those around us and in ourselves. And feminists can do it, because we are in a unique position, both a part of, and yet not a part of society. We can do it because we have gotten just far enough away from patriarchy to really see it. And we can do it because we have a different vision, because we can create vision and bring it to others.

Do we have a choice?

## Notes

1. *Goddess Remembered*, National Film Board of Canada, Studio D, produced by Margaret Pettigrew, directed by Donna Read; and *The Burning Times*, National Film Board of Canada, produced by Mary Armstrong and Margaret Pettigrew, directed by Donna Read.

2. Donaleen Saul with Jean Napali, "Goddess Worship: Toxic Niceness?" *New Directions for Women* 20, 4 (July/August, 1991), p. 4.

3. *With Bill Moyers*, edited by Betty Sue Flowers (New York: Doubleday, 1988), p. 8.

# CHAPTER TWO

# Spirit

## *Spirare: The Breath of Life*

To build visions and seek after meaning in order to direct our own lives is a normal and constant inclination of healthy human life at its most liberating. It is the product of vitality, life energy: it is the hallmark of spirit.

Spirit: the center of our sentient, conscious existence, the core and source of awareness, what propels and motivates us, what protects and maintains our integrity, the alpha of self, fully alive, natural, real, very much of this world—the spark or breath of life.

Spirit: according to the *Oxford English Dictionary*, a term derived from the Latin noun *spiritus* related to the verb *spirare*, to breathe. It is defined as "the animating or vital principle in man [*sic*] (and animals); that which gives life to the physical organism, in contrast to its purely material elements; the breath of life."

Most of us first came upon the notion of spirit or *the* spirit, or "soul" when we were very young. Some kind of phantasmal entity residing either inside a living body (our own or someone else's) or apart from a dead body, it was often a source of some terror. Spirits were the part of us that tore off when we died and went either to heaven or to hell or, worse for us, went to wander the Earth, horrifying strangers as other spirits might horrify us. In popular novels and B-grade movies, spirits were depicted as unearthly manifestations, lighter than air, invisible (except to a select few), usually terrifying, although occasionally humorous, and generally sorrowful (because they were no longer living or had not yet reached

21

their appointed destination, or they had learned terrible things reserved only for after-life).

In popular patriarchal religious ideologies, spirit or soul often has had a similar characterization. Here again is the "something," separable from the living human being who owns it (reserved for human beings only, who alone are created in the image of "God"), incorporeal, that is, not of the flesh, actually a counterpart to the flesh, capable of being good or bad, depending on the number and degree of blemishes sustained from the actions (virtuous or sinful) of their corporeal owners. Ultimately there will be final rewards or punishment, a terribly important matter because souls are said to live forever. In almost every patriarchal religion, soul is that part of the person that can or does inhabit the sphere of being where God is, eternal, unchanging and perfect, in contra-distinction to the body's physical or carnal sphere, which is "lower" and in some sense anathema to God.

No wonder we flinch. In many circles, generally among the intelligentsia, *soul* or even *spirit* is a word that is often met with polite but wary silence, or laughter, or even a suspicion of a flaw in the character of the one who utters it seriously. Spirit is not an idea that one easily raises in social or scholarly settings because it discomforts those who, caught between disdain and propriety, do not know how to respond. Because of its history among the patriarchs, for many of us, spirit has become an idea reserved for the undereducated, the weak or dying, or the simply misdirected people of this world.

It need not be so, and because the realm of experience involved is crucial to the quality of our lives, it should not be so. There is another way to think of spirit—which is not mired in the intricacies and illogicalities of contra-natural ideologies, which is suggested by its very origin—*spirare*, to breathe: the breath of life. Here is a meaning that rivets the focus where it belongs—in life.

## Spirit

To speak of spirit at all is difficult in the extreme; to define it may be impossible. Meanings, experiences, perceptions, intuitions—knowings from that region deeper than ordinary knowing may be *ineffable*.* Perhaps because spirit is so dependent upon immediacy, it re-

---

*"cannot be expressed or described in language; too great for words: transcending expression; unspeakable, unutterable, inexpressible" (*OED*).

sides in a place beyond words, and therefore must remain ever "private." On the other hand, perhaps it is simply our neglect that is the source of spirit's alleged inaccessibility; because we have paid too little attention to the tending of spirit's domain, we have failed to create a language of sufficient subtlety and accuracy. Whatever the case, communicating about spirit is fraught with difficulty.

Yet, although we cannot speak directly *of* spirit, can we nonetheless speak *around* it? It is possible to mark off, however imprecisely, some ground in the terrain of spirit and to set landmarks for travelers. We can attempt to set boundaries, that is, we can perhaps make clear where the territory ends, what is not to be taken as the spiritual and what ought not to be regarded as religion.

Here is a good place to begin: What can we say spirit is not? Let us not speak of ghosts. Let us say that it is not that absurdity with which we are all so familiar, the shadow trapped inside a living human body and jettisoned at death. In fact, let us not speak of a thing or entity at all, separable from the physical being, *a spirit*, instead of just *spirit*. Possibly "spirits," souls, or essences exist that survive transitory bodies, (and some believe this is so); in that regard we need make no claims at all. If we use the term *spirit* as a noun, let us do so only for the convenience of language.

Equally misleading is to think of spirit as just a process of our physical being, such as thinking or breathing. Spirit in its best sense does not pertain simply to a body, but to a living being, which includes, but is more than, a body in action.

Spirit ought not to be considered "supernatural," or more accurately contranatural, that is, alien, of a different realm of being, a different sphere of reality than the one in which we live and breathe in this world. Some people posit other spheres of being, and there may be, but we do not know that there are, and again we do not need to say. There appears to us one life and one realm that we do and can inhabit, more or less with spirit.

Spiritual existence, living with spirit, is not an anomalous, aberrant, or esoteric aspect of life, reserved for a special, extraordinary few, or peculiar to a certain kind of community or exceptional activity. The aspect of awareness which we may call spirit or spiritual can exist normally in the lives of ordinary people doing ordinary things, although perhaps it is not always honed or developed. Moreover, it is probably short-sighted or small-minded to think spirit limited to humans only. We do not have "scientific" access to the interior existences of plants or animals, although at times, if we are open, we may have glimpses. At any rate, there is every reason to allow the possibility of advanced experience in other creatures, and there is not conclusive evidence to the contrary.

We are not required to believe that spiritual perspicacity is granted to us by some external entity or personal being, as suggested by the traditional concept of *grace*. It is just as reasonable to conceive of it as a particular refinement of understanding, an integral part of the nature of living and awareness. Like feeling, perception, or thinking, it may be more or less evolved, but it probably cannot be wholly absent.

There is no good reason to believe that spirit lives some separate or different career from its "owner," collecting knowledge, rewards, etc., distinctly apart from and unknown to her or him. That not only "thingifies" spirit; it also diverts us from the understanding that spirit *is* the "owner." Spirit is nothing more than one aspect, one part, of each person's daily experiencing that, like the others, requires attention, nurture, and exercise for development.

If it is true that "spirits" do not live independently of persons, then they do not survive them, have no independent identities or character, and it would seem a reasonable consequence that spirits earn no rewards or punishments external to the lives they reflect and to which they belong. Heavens and hells of any kind, as anything other than symbols of certain qualities of natural life, would be fabrications, logical (or illogical) outcomes of imagining "eternal spirits" welded to transitory, mundane existences.

Because it is possible to suggest what spirit is not, we cannot necessarily assume that we can define what spirit is. In fact, because of its complexity, that may even be counterproductive. Rather it may be more helpful, at least at first, to focus instead on spiritual perspective or insight, on the character of living with spirit.

Although spirit appears to elude ordinary discourse, we are not prevented from any discussion at all, because we are not bound to ordinary discourse only. For ages, peoples and cultures have resorted to out-of-the-ordinary or extraordinary discourse—stories (myths, fables, fairy tales, parables, allegories, romances), poetry, dreams, art, dance, rituals, garb, and many other forms of intra- and inter-psychic communication. Let us then, in that tradition, begin with a series of evocative images and stories (all of which are true).

### Horse

In *Womanspirit*, a university women's studies seminar, I am struggling to lead students to experience at least one sense of spirit. A picture flashes across my mind, and I share it with them.

"Close your eyes," I invite. "See with your inner self; draw a picture in your mind of a spirited horse. Tell the class what you see."

One by one they contribute the details of an image: alone in a vast meadow alive with tiny wildflowers and lush grasses, a beautiful horse canters across the green, its mane flying, its eyes glistening. Its coat shining with health, its muscles bulging, it is the quintessence of vitality, the students say. When it stops, head high, it rears up and snorts. Some of the students picture its legs, others its tail, some concentrate on its eyes. All of them feel its freedom, its power, and its joy. This is an animal that belongs only to itself, and while it can be imagined to ride with others, perhaps to cooperate with humans, even, say the students, to wear a saddle and reins, there is, must be, in it (with it, about it) something that remains unbridled, inviolate, or it ceases to be what we mean by spirited.

Then I suggest: "Now imagine the opposite, a dispirited horse, one whose spirit is broken."

Again the various images are amazingly alike. There is a small, dark place, a stable, dirty and neglected. Within, the animal stands still and tired, perhaps chewing on some moldy straw. Its eyes are clouded and its coat is dull; its tail twitches disinterestedly at a fly. Head down, back swayed, it seems not to notice much or to respond to its surroundings. Several of the students see an old hat perched on the horse's head. It seems, they say, old, perhaps sick.

There is a relationship between the concepts of *spirit* and *spirited*, as the students made clear in this story. Autonomy, vitality, health, freedom, light, connection, awareness, intensity, authenticity are words that rise and form the bridge between the two. In spiritedness are elements of being owned only by oneself, of being true to one's nature, one's kind. Rootedness is acknowledged in the ongoing processes around us, but also there exists a freedom to follow one's own direction. To be spirited suggests a kind of health; dispirited, disease and decay.

People too may be vital or still, may be radiant or dull, may be free or bound. Like the horse, like other animals, we may or may not be spirited. We may choose to develop our life energy, our self-direction, our joy in being, that is, we may live a life of spirit, or we may be bound to a terrible self-created confinement.

At least part of what is included in "spiritual matters" is the endeavor to peel away the layers of fraudulence or misperception from our more authentic selves, so that we may be as much as possible inviolate, autonomous, true to who we actually are or wish to be. Likewise, part of what is included in spiritual matters is the endeavor to discover our world and its place for us also stripped of falsity, so that, like the horse, we may better know how to be in it harmoniously, and therefore joyfully.

### *Flower*

It is a time of great change for W. Her marriage has ended suddenly, and she feels alone in the world with a small baby, with disillusionment, grief, and not a little panic. On the heels of her divorce, she has been fired from her job. She has lost her home, friends, and most of her savings. She feels as if she were dying.

She does not know it, but she is not dying, as she feels; rather she is about to be born, in blood and pain as before, one more time. After the crying time, after the curses and the railing-at-the-heavens time, she bangs back and forth between despair and elation. She digs in her heels—not out of courage; out of no choice. She cannot go backwards, and the present is too painful to maintain; she must move ahead. Ultimately she survives and grows stronger.

Early in this process, unbidden comes to her mind a picture that flashes periodically on and off—a garden, small and scruffy. One flower grows there in a small patch marked off by a midget white picket fence, cracked and weather-beaten. Without determinate color, sometimes pale yellow, sometimes almost red or pink, the flower appears first floundering in the mud, its stem broken, leaves torn, the blossom scraping the ground. At first W. is puzzled by the picture. What is this image, popping up out of nowhere, she wonders, too clouded, too new, too broken, like the flower, to receive the message? Click. *Like the flower* . . . of course. She brings the picture back, this time on purpose, and acts upon it. Lifting the blossom out of the mud, she straightens its stem and props it with a small twig. It responds. In her mind she cleans the patch, paints the little fence, and learns to care for her garden, to water and feed the flower and protect it from weeds and invaders. "Don't step on my flower," W. comes to say, sometimes silently to herself, at times aloud to others, although they rarely understand her full meaning. It hardly matters. Her flower grows, blooms, shouts with color. The weather changes; sometimes rain or wind take their toll, but they do not prevail. She tends her garden.

There is a part of ourselves, the deep connected-to-life at the core, inner part of us, that knows . . . (what it needs to know?) . . . that is of the spirit, that speaks to us, sometimes in what seems like riddles, that yields information and can bring us back to ourselves, if we listen. The inviolate core of our being means to survive, and it struggles after freedom. That core is the spark, spirit. Sometimes, if we give ourselves over to it, the deep part of ourselves will tell us about ourselves. And we should listen. Nurturing the spirit is, in part, listening.

### *Tree*

During an "exercise" at a workshop on feminist spirituality, I tell students the flower story and ask them to close their eyes and meditate upon themselves, to wait, perhaps to receive an image of their own, like the flower, a symbol of the self. A common image is the tree, and it surfaces this time.

Sometimes the tree is experienced as small and slim, living in close space in a forest of other trees, struggling for the light and space in which to grow. But often the tree is felt large and grand, spreading its branches very wide, glorying in the air and sun, granting shade to the territories below. Its roots sink deep into the ground and are cooled by the moist earth and fed by its substance. A woman in the class, describing her meditation, recounts that she was aware of nests among her leaves, birds fluttering in and out, and, of all things, a telephone wire cutting through her branches. It was not a negative experience, she says. As she considered her image, the nests of birds she recognized to be her children, and she was glad to be housing them, keeping them. The wire, at first more puzzling, revealed itself as the outside world, its insistent technology, but it posed no threat to her, for she had grown around it. It had cut through, but it did not impair her.

A strong, enduring symbol, appearing repeatedly in the fairy tales and myths of many cultures, trees were sacred in prepatriarchal religions, and their magic is our legacy today. There stand the trees in the Garden of Eden, all available to the couple except for one, brimming with the potential dangers of the Cosmic, marked by God, source of both life and death. Jesus was said to have been crucified on a tree (albeit dead and not in its natural state), and stories abound in many cultures, ancient Egypt, in China and India, associating trees with god-figures. Western culture celebrates its most emotionally potent festival, Christmas, with trees and logs, as the ancients celebrated their festival of rebirth. In novels and films trees often appear as symbols or portents of good or evil, described or pictured in detail, lending their particular configurations of light and shade to mood and meaning.

On a profound, symbolic level, the tree is a thing of life and a creature of Nature at its most elemental. Grander, more imposing than any other forms of vegetation, it towers above us in size, in sheer resiliency. It is older than we dare hope to be, intimating an imposing independence; it sheds fruit and feeds us, furnishes us with shelter, fuel, or shade and yet is ever renewed. Season after season it appears to die and be reborn. It flashes our world with color and at times overwhelms us with its beauty.

Life, strength, age, power, nurture, endurance, beauty are realized in the tree—and all from Nature to Nature and back again. The tree is of the Earth, sustained by it, sustaining and ultimately returning to Earth to return again. Life loves the tree and is the tree, physical, mud bound, feeding on Earth's stuff, reaching away into air and wind.

To be the tree, to feel its spirit, is to recognize and acknowledge our root in Nature, in the nexus of earth and sky, water and sun, physical and spiritual. We are in relationship with mud, and we are siblings to the greens of creation. To know this, to celebrate it, is to forge connectedness with our Source, sensually, deeply. This gives us greater being; it is an act of spirit.

### Skunk

J. is camping with her family. It is night, and the others are busy with their activities. She is alone in her tent, sitting quietly at a camp table, reading. A small noise attracts her attention. She turns to see a fat little skunk waddle into the tent. "Oh, no," she thinks to herself, "what if . . . ?" She is very still, moves not a muscle, but looks intently at the skunk. It looks back at her. Their eyes meet for a time, each animal assessing the other. The skunk looks away first, wanders unconcernedly around the tent, sniffing at this and that, checking out the assortment of items collected there. It glances one more time at J. and shuffles outside. The other members of the party return. Softly J. calls to them, "Be quiet and careful. Don't disturb her; there's a skunk in camp." Neither quiet nor careful, they raise a din and chase the stranger from their space.

Later J. recounts that after her first moment of trepidation, as she looked into the animal's eyes, she felt at peace with it and knew she had no cause to fear or to act. "We looked at one another, sized one another up and knew that each of us was safe with the other. It was as if for that one moment of the universe our souls were locked together in understanding and union." It is understandable, although regrettable, that the other campers' moment was so different.

All of us animals share this planet, its spaces and resources, its potentials and events. We share material; our tissue is much the same, our blood and organs and structures. We share sensation and feeling—fear, surprise, pleasure, excitement, desire, pain, hunger, need. We share thought. We plan and assess, act, proact, and react. We have families and communities; we communicate, although not always in the same way. We share the life cycle—are conceived, born, mature, and die. We are each and all a part of the all, more alike than different. We are animals, skunks and people, and our beauty, function, and welcomeness is a reciprocal, not a unilateral matter.

To understand our animalness in relation to the skunk and birds and spiders and deer, to know their beingness in relation to ours, is to place not only them but us into context in life, to come to understand better what we are, what life is and may be. By going outside to them, we see inside to our deepest self and then farther outside again. To respect both the sameness and the difference in the other creatures is to both grant and achieve a position in what is ongoing, ultimately to reach out for and glimpse its harmony. Such reaching and glimpsing, such coming to know and acting upon what we find is a quest of spirit.

### Catfish

Spring in central Florida brings R. to visit. Her friends live beside a river "stocked" with fish, and they have invited her to go fishing, something she has never done. It's pleasant, she is told, relaxing. As the story goes, God does not count fishing against one's allotted time on earth.

Her companions are accommodating. Because she is inexperienced, they fix her pole, bait her hook, and cast it into the water for her. She has only to stand and wait. She waits. It is a fine early morning, the sky incredibly blue, the air not yet hot. All around birds are raising a clamor and the greenery is lush. It is country quiet, though not silent, and she feels at peace, happy. They're right, she thinks, fishing is lovely, relaxing.

There is a tug at her line. A nibble. "You have something," they shout, "you have something." Excitement. "Reel it in! Reel it in!" She pulls, she reels. It draws close, toward the bank, and she sees her catch, a large, rounded catfish! "Pull it out," they direct. "Drop it on the shore. She's got one! She's got one!" R. jerks it out of the water, and still holding it at a distance with her pole, drops it to the grass. She is breathless, delighted.

As it hits the grass, from the flopping, agonizing creature comes a squealing sound, almost a shriek (pain? fear? resistance?). Do fish make sounds? She never knew it to be so. R. is transfixed, stupefied. Her companions are laughing, playful. But R. is not any more. Still squealing and flopping, the fish fights desperately against the hook in its mouth. Dragging it (her? him?) along with the pole, R. drops the fish back into the water. "Get it off that goddam thing; get that hook out of its mouth!" R. screams, disgusted, not a little angry. Her companions comply. (No doubt, she thinks to herself, they think I'm crazy, or funny.) They work at the hook for a few moments, pulling and yanking, but it is deeply embedded in the animal's throat and will not yield. Instead they break the line, and the creature disappears into the river.

Fishing. Sport.

As the fish swam away and for some time after that, R. reported, she was awash with competing thoughts and feelings. Primarily, she felt profound regret. I am so sorry, she thought, to have hurt without reason, to have meant to kill for sport, even to think of consuming this creature as food without sobriety and respect. I am sorry, Catfish, not to have realized what I should have known, what the screams and the thrashing told us, that you are a living being, with all that implies, that you feel pain, have young, strain to survive, have a place in creation no less than any other, that you are due the reverence of life.

It is only a fish, she knew her friends must have been thinking. Only a fish. What does that mean? she wondered. That you are less than us? That you are so different from us, so alien, that you do not matter, your needs or your experience? It is a belief among our kind that your kind has no feeling, no awareness, no needs, only "drives," "instincts," and "sensations." Somehow those scientized, sanitized words, belied by the thrashing and squealing, justify our cruelty and lack of vision. There is an arrogance and a narrowness in that, to have accepted such a fiction when we could have, should have, decried it. Such shortsightedness is symptomatic of spiritual immaturity.

For the lesson, Catfish, thank you.

### Celebration

Graduation night the bleachers on the high school lawn are full of people; they are assembled for the celebration ritual. Among the other guests, A., a junior at this small-town school, sits there under the early evening sky, thoughts and feelings merging as she waits. The ceremony has not yet begun formally, but for her it has.

What captures her attention most is the sky—pink, purple, orange, and blue, it is awash with color. The sun, just disappearing under the horizon, adds a luminosity to the hues in the darkening sky. Tonight the sky appears to A. to be at the same time larger and smaller, vaster in its openness, and yet covering her like a dome, a high ceiling or, perhaps, a protective blanket of gauze. There are no clouds, only one small bird, the kind, she thinks, that looks like a V when you see it at such a distance.

She is not aware of the intruding noises, the passing cars or the barking dogs, or any of the usual sounds around the school. In fact, the surroundings all seem to have disappeared, the buildings, the parking lot, the street between, as if this little piece of ground and its inhabitants were adrift in time and space. No individual voices surface, only a quiet buzzing, a tender, hushed hum. Even her chatty teenage friends are silent, and she wonders if they and everyone else may be experiencing the evening as she is.

It is as if nothing beyond this place and time has any real existence. The air is not hot, nor cold, nor moving, and she doesn't feel it; nor does she feel her clothing, her body, or her chair. Conflicts among those present seem to have been abolished, as hostilities are put away for the joy of this passage. There seems, she thinks, an aura of love here. Do the others feel it? She is fixed in the moment, and it seems to have been created just for her and for the assemblage there, as the sky seems to have been painted just for this one event.

An experience that had begun in some foreboding is changing. She had come here acutely aware of the passage of time. Close friends would be leaving her behind. They, as she, are growing older, helpless to stop the flow of their days. In one year's time, she too would be cast out into adulthood, separated from these dear surroundings. Now she feels her fear melting. Not mere euphoria, but a peacefulness brings her integration: all is well, she thinks, all is as it should be. Images of past everyday events—friends mixing at the lockers, early morning conversations before class—shift from sad losses to living pictures fixed in her memory.

The ceremony begins, graduates appear, people speak, hats sail up into the sky, now black and lit with stars. Time passes in a haze, and she and other guests are running to the stage, searching for their special people. She finds hers. They hug, and she is suspended there, at peace, reconciled for a second, for forever. Time ebbs back, but she is not the same.

Sometimes unexpectedly come moments when we seem to open. Typically, we cannot call them forth or make them happen; they come when they come. They are not reserved only for the special or notable times, experiences particularly beautiful or otherwise profound. They come to the old and the young, the experienced and the innocent.

Such times lock themselves within our memory, retaining perhaps forever much of their vividness. Properly attended to and integrated, they change us. But should we fail to recognize the importance or the veracity of such an experience, should we neglect to pay it sufficient attention, we may lose the meanings and the insights carried there.

Such a failure to recognize the value of the moment may be the fault of an ideology that would separate the "spiritual" from the rest of daily experience, insist upon encasing it in a one only mythology called THE religion, and hiding it in a little box called a church. For such a sleight of hand we often discount our own glimpses. "Who am I," we ask, "to claim the venerableness of my moment? I am not *ordained*, made special to God; nor am I in a place made holy, but only in life."

What truths or realities did the sky bring to the girl, absorbed in her spirit on that night? That there is or can be a harmony of purpose among people that makes itself known to us at times? That the passage of time, with its changes and its aging, is not a fearsome, unyielding enemy, but a reality that answers to a harmony of its own? That human beings are, and are seen to be, their most beautiful, most lovable and loving, most at peace when they merge with the beauties of our Source? That as part of the Source, part of creation, A., like her special people, like the rest of us, is a goodness, worthy of honor, respect, and love? That life (with its events) is, and ought to be, good in itself, for itself? This is a message of one's spirit.

### Making Life

Alone and peaceful at home, C. has been sitting quietly for a long while, watching from her window the winter scene outside: trees and hills covered with frost, birds flying back and forth, struggling against the wind. Scuttling across the yard, some dry leaves whirl up in a circle and settle against the fence. As the late afternoon light fades and becomes night, the room inside darkens and disappears, but C. is too rapt, too happily still to move, and she doesn't care to turn on the lights. She is content to be alone with the stars, the silence, and the movement in her belly. Her baby is almost at term and very active, thrusting out a foot, a fist, a foot again. C. likes holding her hand against herself, to feel her life. Incredible, she thinks to herself, to be making out of my body a living thing, a person.

She is corrected almost at once: The night sky, its countless stars and immense blackness, presents to her, connects her with the universe, its timeless processing, its ongoing on-goingness, its being in charge of all that takes place. You are not making a life, It tells her; Life is making this life. You are the vehicle.

Yes, she answers. It was arrogant of me. I do not make life, although I am in league with it. Life works through my woman-body, and I am its willing conduit. Honor enough.

Only in one sense are we things apart from other things. At a different level, all is connection. Each of us, both as entity and as collection of intermixing events, is intimately related to all others, part of, and contributing to, the eternal Process which is Life (which some choose to call Spirit, some choose to call God).

Our task, in coming to know Spirit, that which is "inside" our selves and that which is outside of our bodies, but of which we are a part, is to come to know—to understand, recognize, acknowledge, and experience intimately—that connection.

Substantive morality or ethics is making choices in accord with the recognition of connection. It is acting in such a way that our actions emanate from, are borne of, our knowledge of our connectedness. To live spiritually, ethically, then, involves no straining, because it flows naturally from our celebration of, our felt experience of connection.

We do not, strictly, act upon Life. Life acts through us. As Life creates a child through us, it creates a friendship, a table, a garden, a book. Our consideration in making choices is to ask how we wish life to proceed, what sort of conduit, character, do we wish to contribute to the Process.

### *Attack*

In these times, night in this part of Vietnam is deceptive. The dark of the jungle suggests a kind of safety, a place to hide. Aside from the strictest necessities of life and the demands of war, most tasks are awaiting the daylight. The presence of the men too, collected inside the compound, seems to offer a kind of protection, of number and familiarity. But it is illusory. In fact, there is no safety here, no place to hide.

Asleep in his "hootch," a deep sleep, M. is oblivious to threat. Suddenly . . . Boom! Silence. . . . Then a siren. Men, half dressed, are scurrying in all directions. The siren shrieks out belatedly what they already know, that the compound is under rocket attack. It usually comes like this, at night, the booms and the following silences and the peculiar sounds, precursors to death and chaos. M. runs for the relative safety of the bunker, which offers only partial protection; if a direct hit is sustained, no amount of fortification can protect the men inside.

Huddled one beside the other, no one speaks; they only listen and breathe. Time stands still. As usual at night, all the sounds and sensations of the place are intensified: each man is acutely aware of the night-calling birds and animals, the stench of decomposing swamp and of gunpowder, the noise of breathing, interrupted again and again by the weird sounds and the crashing outside. Bloop . . . (twenty seconds) . . . crash. Bloop . . . (twenty seconds) . . . crash.

At first M. is awash with terror; he feels petrified, turned to stone. He waits, listening to the breathing, measuring the intervals of the hits. The explosions grow louder, the crashing closer. The enemy is "walking it in," to increase the destructiveness, to gain accuracy, to create more terror. They succeed. His dread rises, clouding his brain, and his thoughts go everywhere. "Who made me? God made me." (Boom . . . crash.) "Why did God make me?" (Crash.) "Bullshit. That's a lie; that's not it." (Crash!) (Crash!) Deepening horror, like sickness, sharper terror. It is hard to breathe. . . . Suddenly, at once, calm. "If it comes, it comes. Nothing I can do about it." . . . Puzzlement. . . . "What the hell is going on here? Why are they doing this to me?"

Images rise. M. remembers the war protestors he had seen before he came here. Essentially he had ignored them. If they want to protest, fine. As long as they leave me alone, let them do their thing—they were weirdos and oddballs. Now it occurs to him: "They were right. Why the fuck didn't *I* figure it out?" He thinks of his innocence, his youthful mindlessness, quite gone now. Before, he knew what he was about. Now, he knows he did not. Now, there are only questions, and pain. The most striking thing about right now is the uncertainty. What is going to happen? Who is going to get hurt? For sure someone is going to get hurt. Someone always does when the crashing comes.

The attack is over, leaving a mess, broken machinery, shredded buildings, corpses and parts of corpses. Staring at the faces and bodies of friends, men he knows . . . knew, he thinks, "They were just like me, as young, as innocent and unknowing, and they're gone; but they're beyond it now, finished, in some ways the lucky ones. The others, broken and torn, in pain, will they make it?" The shocking sight of a body with a piece missing, (a piece, he thinks, that took so long to become what it was and will never grow back), pushes him into acknowledging finiteness, mortality, the incredible, fragile vulnerability of the living being.

He has faced death, his own and others', head on, and he is changed. Before, life was forever. Now there is the direct, concrete knowledge that there may be no tomorrow, that in fact someday there will be no tomorrow. He thinks to himself, "Take the wraps off, M. From now on, live, really live. Really do it." Do what? How?

He looks at the neat military rows of bodies, stuffed into black plastic bags, lying in the heat on the tarmac, patiently waiting to be mailed home. "That can't be all," he thinks. "There has to be more. . . . I need to make sense of it. I'm going to put something into this world, some meaning. Fair exchange: I'll take something out, and I'll put something back."

For M., in the midst of this rot, there are intimations of Spirit.

Spirit is a seeker of meaning, a reader and a maker of meaning. Everything in life, even that which does not serve life, is part of meaning, and thus a key to it. When we read the meaning that is there, when we make it, when we allow it to be printed upon our being, we augment our own soul and enlarge universal Spirit.

There is so much butchery in our world, so much barbarism and pain that seems to go nowhere, and life would be better if it never existed. Theories of fortuitous evil-which-allows-us-to-know-good-ness-and-is-therefore-really-good do not serve; in fact they are perverse. Bad is bad, and that is the end of it. How and why do we make the good in us and in our world flourish when all around us the most hideous evil abounds and seems to prevail, that is a question of our spirit. Without that quest, spirit dies, and without spirit, life dies. In the service of that quest, Life finds again, even in the shadows, its meaning and direction.

> It is only when we believe that we are creating the soul that life has any meaning, but when we can believe it—and I do and always have—then there is nothing we do and nothing that we suffer that does not hold the seed of creation in it.
> —May Sarton, *Journal of a Solitude*[1]

## Mandy

In the bitter cold of winter, Mandy, a "mixed-breed terrier" of uncertain origins, seventeen years old, is dying. Her vertebrae have fused, making it nearly impossible for her to walk. Her kidneys have all but shut down completely, and the tumor which is the source of the cancer that is consuming her is bulging larger on her side. Her mahogany-colored fur has lost its luster, and she has grown thin, paper fragile. She seems almost breakable. She is completely deaf, and only her luminous golden eyes still have the shine and penetration they did when we met years ago, in an animal shelter in Buffalo, New York. Then, as is the custom in this peculiarly organized reality, I had paid for her, two dollars for an abandoned puppy, infinitely alone; and I had taken her home with me tucked inside my coat for warmth. She had clung to the safety of a living body and I to her vulnerability, and we had bonded at once. Later, she would keep me warm.

In the years that followed, Mandy, the teacher, conferred with any who knew how to listen—early on about joy, curiosity, enthusiasm, later about sensuality, contentment, and making a go of things.

As she grew older and ripened, her messages deepened. Never the pedagogue, she didn't press; she shared what she knew in the ways that animals do: by choosing or walking away, by modeling a kind of life and a way of being.

Now, in her old age, with infinite calm, Mandy is teaching her final lesson: how to round the cycle, how to end one's time. Unable to walk, she cannot follow her people from room to room as is her pleasure. When she was young, she made it clear that certain things would not be tolerated; among them, she would not be carried. Now, understanding, she has been giving herself over with no resistance, no strain, to the arms that move her from place to place. Unable to approach her dish, she has taken her food from human fingers. Always fastidiously clean, she yields to the constant changing of her blankets, wet from her failing body. There are no apologies, no thank yous. These last cooperations are a trust between us, her final gift to me.

It is morning on her last day. She has passed the night with her friend, the little girl, on the blanket on the floor beside the bed. The two were mostly awake all night, saying goodbye. (The child and the dog understood, or accepted, before I did.) Now, for the first time in two days, on shaking legs, with a supreme and visible effort, she rises, walks to the kitchen door, and asks to be let out. I am astonished at first to see her rise, heartened, and then I realize the portent of her act. It is five degrees below zero, and we both know she cannot survive the cold. I hesitate, but she is clear, and I open the door. Stepping out into the icy sunlight, she walks to the fence, views the street for a moment, and returns to the center of the yard to sniff momentarily at "her spot" (where we had dug a latrine for her in the snow). She moves to the wooden swing where we had spent so many hours and evenings in the summers, taking our private peace. She stands for a short time, the wind ruffling the fur at her neck; then, having said her goodbyes, no hesitation, no hurry, she walks inside. Crossing into the living room, she stumbles and collapses to the rug. For a few moments her breathing comes in short, labored gasps. I lift her, holding her close to me. She lays her head on my arm, and calmly looking up at me, she dies.

We are born, we mature, we grow old, perhaps or probably infirm, and we die. We come into our time in life, and we pass. That is the heart of it. The questions are: What is the point of it? What to do with it? How to make sense of it?

Or is the asking of those questions wrong-headed? Might we perhaps not better ask: What is the point of seeking the point of it? Could we not say, the point of it is itself; or, beyond itself there is no point of it, nor need there be? What we do with it is to live it, and that is the whole sense of it. Does it make life anything less because it does not go on longer or forever?

Mandy was born and lived. She had (I think) no intimations of immortality nor lived as if she did, no inclination to make her mark, leave a legacy, or extend her sphere. Instead she simply was, experiencing her time, her pleasures, and her pains, her interests, needs, satisfactions, and their absence. She had her joys and seemed content just to be. When it was time, she yielded to death as she had yielded to life. And yet she had her immortality, did she not, for she made her contributions, to living, to the Process, to her world.

For such simplicity, creatures have been faulted. They have no souls, it is argued, no minds. Being dumb animals they have no choice, but human beings have the "gift" of awareness, of self-consciousness; for us there is, must be, more.

More . . . or less? We might better take instruction from the "dumb." To impose a "meaning" on life, by the brute force of logic, does that not seem a misuse of awareness? Might not a better use be to become infinitely, intensely aware of the time that we do have, of our place in it and our experience of it? To comprehend life as it is, to harmonize our selves with life, does that not seem a more honest honoring of Being than the twisting and beating of life into the human specifications of traditional theological ideology?

Death will come. It is said by those who study the dying that one generally dies as one has lived. It would appear that the opposite may be equally true: in the way that we meet death, the truths of death, its inexorable realities, in the way we make sense of death, are we destined to live.

## Spirit and Nature

In most patriarchal traditions to live spiritually has the connotation of a life of withdrawal, a life apart from this world, dedicated to an existence and frame of values constructed for another reality. To live under divine direction, in a *state of grace** is to be in con-

---

*Grace*: from the Latin *gratia,* "pleasing," thus pleasing in the eyes of God (*OED*).

trast to a *state of nature*;\* ultimately it is to live against nature, in contention with one's own physical self and with the material world.

Considerable ambiguity surrounds the status of nature in the patriarchal world-view. On the one hand, it is defined as a realm of being created by God (and, therefore, presumably good); and yet, on the other hand, it is lower, baser than His realm, even opposed to His nature and will, and thus evil. Nature contains the delights of the flesh, the needs and interests not only of human materiality but of "animals" and other un-souled creatures as well, and it leads us astray with illusions of power and freedom not granted by the grace of God. Provided to humanity by God essentially as a punishment (after the Fall) and as a training–testing ground for entry into Paradise, nature becomes a temptation and a diversion from God and from piety, thus a snare to the spirit or soul. Spirituality, then, must be antinature or above nature, that is, contranatural or supernatural.

In patriarchy, therefore, to be "good," to live spiritually, we must live in interminable, ever-vigilant conflict with our sensed world and our own physical selves.

If this were the only possible way to understand "living spiritually," we could hardly wonder that people might be repelled. However, as is often the case, the patriarchs have got it backwards. For if, in fact, nature is defined as: the "constitution, character and course of things," the "material world and its phenomena," (*AHD*) the world of "living things" and nonliving things as well, the essential qualities or properties of all that is; if nature includes the universe and its contents, if it includes me, all that I am, and all other being, if nature is all of this, then **to live spiritually (to live spiritedly) is not only not antinatural or supernatural, it is completely, absolutely, self-consciously and purposefully natural in its strongest sense.** For to live with spirit, in spirit, is to be increasingly vital and increasingly aware; it is to be so lucid as to train our minds, feelings, and experience to *paying attention* in the sharpest way to the world that surrounds us, to the realities of which we are a part, and to coming to understand our place within those realities.

---

\**Nature*: from the Latin *natura*, "birth, constitution, character, course of things" (*OED*).

*Nature*: (1) The material world and its phenomena. . . . (2) The world of living things. . . . (4) A primitive state of existence. . . . (5) *Theol.* Man's natural state as distinguished from the state of grace (*AHD*).

Human beings are of this world, this reality, this one inclusive and encompassing reality. Our fortunes and our fate are locked here. We are not alone in this reality but exist here with countless other creatures and forms from which and with which we were derived and with whom we share a future. We are engaged with all-that-is in a connecting and interconnecting process of existence, a life process that is the *ultimate Process*—a network of vitality. All that is, which takes part in this Process and in the stuff of being, shares in the vitality and thus may be said to share in the spirit of life. This Process in its widest dimension may be understood to be Spirit or God.

We are connected, not just with other human beings, but with all living things; not only with living things, but with things which we perceive (choose to define) as unliving. All processes, all, are engaged in the one Process.

Connection is the key to meaning, to the meaning that we seek. As we come to recognize, to know concretely and intensely, at our most primal level, our connectedness with and within flowing reality, we enlarge our perspective, our existential lucidity, and so we enlarge our province and our power, which contributes in turn to our vitality, our spark, and thus our spirit. Yet this is not an enlargement that "takes" away from the rest of creation, that reduces, a power that seizes and keeps apart: recognizing connection leads inexorably to an acknowledgment of interdependence and an understanding of our appropriate position in the network. This understanding ultimately evolves into a decision to harmonize ourselves with the rest, with the cadences of life.

In this context, to choose to live spiritually is to self-consciously seek meaning through the understanding and experiencing of connection; it is to affirm Nature and the natural (reality, being, allness), to live determinedly as part of it, at peace with it, directed by it and directing it simultaneously, granting it worth-ship; it is to acknowledge and focus upon the inclusiveness, the ultimateness of life in process, of Life Process; it is to celebrate Being. It is to accept being in its entirety and make sense of it, all of it, the comfortable elements and those less so, the death, violence, and competition in nature as well as the peace, for in nature, life includes death, harmony includes strife, ever in cycle.

Spirituality, ecology, ethics, morality, science, education, meditation, craft, religion, labor, and politics become entwined in such a spirit-led life. In fact, they are one, only different facets of the same enterprise.

Admittedly, the phrases living *in spirit* or *living with spirit*, synonyms for living spiritually, are ambiguous; they are so on purpose, because their meaning resides in the elusive complexity of the terms. They gather intelligibility as they are experienced in daily life and as they are attended to in thought and contemplation.

To meditate, to reflect intensely, not only with the mind, but with the feelings, the senses, and with the awareness that is beneath, deeper than, "the mind"; *to pay attention*, to listen to what our connected, connecting spirit has to tell us, is to penetrate through the static of ordinary intelligibility to something far more grounded. It is not that spiritual knowing is in a category absolutely different from any other kind of knowledge. We may think of spiritual lucidity as an aspect of knowing, an evolution of awareness at its best, a refinement and an integration of all the faculties of apprehension.

Nonetheless, although such lucidity is a refinement, its cultivation is critical to healthy human living. To tend to our spiritual life is not a frivolous matter; it is not something we can do if so inclined, but something just as easily done without. To pay attention to the ultimate, to place ourselves in context, to acquire a sense of meaning is one of life's essentials, a need.

A *need* has been defined in the life sciences as an element without which the individual cannot survive, without which, or in the degree to which it is absent, a person will sicken and die. Theories of human needs range from the philosophies of the pre-Socratics to current social science. The nature and function of physical needs have long enjoyed relative agreement, because the consequences of deprivation are obvious. Lack of food leads to homeostatic breakdown, tissue damage, and other physical malfunctions that result finally in death.

Considerably more controversy surrounds the emotional needs. However, notwithstanding some debate about the precise definition of need in this context, and exactly which and how many emotional needs should be considered absolutely essential, it is generally held in the social sciences that emotional needs do exist, that they are related to, or are alter expressions of, physical needs, and that individuals deprived of their emotional needs long enough or seriously enough do sicken physically and eventually die. For example, human beings have a need for some measure of contact with others, a degree of stability and predictability in life events, some control over the immediate environment, and mental stimulation. Early symptoms of deprivation may include sleeplessness, eating disorders, hypertension, and withdrawal; later a person may suffer depression or despair, hostility, sociopathology, disorientation, substance abuse, or other serious disorders. Finally, heart disease, circulatory insufficiencies, strokes, and even cancer may lead to the ultimate breakdown.

Most social scientists believe because of the intimate interconnection (or even identity) of body and mind, prolonged deprivation of emotional needs ultimately results in physical disorder. That is, because mental experience is in some sense an evolution of physical phenomena (mind and body are two facets of the same reality), then it is reasonable to suppose that emotional deprivation can result in the impairment of physical well-being.

This reasoning, by analogy, can provide us with an important insight into the influence of our spiritual lives: as the health of a human being presupposes certain minimal requirements of body and emotion, called needs, so too does it require a certain level of spiritual functioning, which, after all, is an emanation or evolution of mental experience.[2] Body, mind, and spirit are integrally related facets of one human life.

If a need is an element without which we cannot survive, then it is not an overstatement to cast spirit in this light, to suggest that we cannot have health in its widest sense unless we pay the same degree of attention to caring for spirit that we pay to caring for body and mind.

Here philosophers and social scientists, especially humanistic psychologists, have provided us with ample language. Meeting spiritual need is associated with growth, expansiveness, vitality, awareness, actualization, productivity, peace, excellence, harmony, challenge, joy, freedom, responsibility, purpose, MEANING. On the other hand, what happens to us when we do not satisfy our spiritual needs, when we suffer spiritual deprivation? When the need to come to terms with the universe is thwarted, the relevant terms are despair, nihilism, depression, boredom, restlessness, meaninglessness, alienation, anxiety, narrowness, strife, loneliness, underdevelopment, malaise, sickness, worthlessness, and death, physical or otherwise.

It would appear that spiritual insolvency, like any other, may take a variety of forms; and like the others, its prolongation must ultimately end in destruction.

What happens to us when we do not use our full capacity, physical, emotional, and spiritual? What happens to us when we do not pursue the spiritual imperatives and we cease to grow, to change, to reach for meaning? What happens when we lose our nerve or our curiosity and shrink from asking the next question, when we neglect to imagine the next larger possibility? What must result if we fail to seek our kinship with the varied levels and forms of existence, if we fail to judge our behavior or morality in the context of wider and ever-widening circles of consequence: from self, to other people, to animals, to more distant peoples, to other kinds of life, to processes beyond our own, to stars and space and time beyond space? We sicken. We shut down. Perhaps we die. We cease to be, to Be, in the strongest, most active, most profound sense of that word. To the degree that we are no longer in process, no longer in evolution, we may speak of feeling alienated, estranged, a stranger even to ourselves. Our lives may feel meaningless, pointless. Rootless, we search for a place, as if no location could be home, no people could be family. Indeed, how could they? If we do not belong to the universe, where could we belong? If being is not enough, for itself, in itself, what small suborder of life could be more fulfilling?

Some substitutes may intermittently fill the void, "highs," games, endless activities, cultural tranquilizers, or private withdrawals. But these do not suffice for health; ultimately we must confront the *need*. We must seek meaningfulness and direction, continually, ever again and anew, and we must have connection.

Most of us recognize that we must tend to our bodies. We have learned that we must nurture the emotions and feed the mind. Yet many would deny spirit, our most evolved human dimension.

Life, lived experience, is an integrated, organic unity, and it must be tended as a whole. No need exists or is satisfied in isolation from the rest. We can deny a physical need to meet an emotional priority or discipline the feelings to create strength of spirit; and yet all are one, for no real splits exist in living process except as we conceive them. We distinguish one aspect of existence from another only to treat them all; it is folly to expect well-being in a person who is not tended in entirety. We may be physically satisfied but emotionally empty, emotionally quiescent but spiritually starved. We may be fed, clothed, exercised, and safe from harm, and yet lonely and afraid. We may be physically strong and emotionally functioning, but spiritually dying.

The symptoms of spiritual deprivation are subtle, but they are not invisible: there is a malaise, a nagging, disquieting, perhaps half-hidden sense of dislocation, sometimes a hint, sometimes a howl of something absent, something that does not quite fit, something that renders everything insipid gray instead of brilliantly colored. If peace and centeredness are the ultimate signs of spirited processing, their absence, dis-ease, marks the opposite.

## Living with Spirit

We could almost say that it is a *secular** vision of spirit and/or spirituality presented here were it not for the unfortunate implication of the term secular itself, which suggests the foregone implication of two opposing realms of reality. There may indeed be *world* opposed to *church*, but it is error, even contradiction, to oppose *world* to *spirit*; one cannot be worldly *rather than* spiritual, for the more intensely, exquisitely worldly we become, the more we are tending to spirit.

What would it mean, then, to live spiritually–spiritedly if spirit were taken to be not other than natural? How would we "tend to the spirit?"

If spirit is the vitality of being, borne of our participation in nature, then spirituality may be conceived of as maintaining the very keenest awareness of that participation and acting out of that awareness. Spiritual perspective is a world-view created out of attention to the character, consequences, and imperatives of our relationship to, and our connectedness with, all other being.

**To live in spirit, then, to live with spirit, spiritually, is to experience our lives, the life process in general, and all of its events, phenomena, and personalities in the positive context of connection. To live spiritually is to make choices and decisions in the light of understanding our part in the intimately interconnecting processing of Being.** Rather than a renunciation of the world, living spirited–spiritually is an affirmation and an acknowledgment of all existence.

How do we come to see, to feel, to recognize our connectedness? How do we come to understand in the deepest sense our participation in What Is? How do we extract from that awareness the truths, the values, and the standards that are there?

We **PAY ATTENTION.**

---

*\*Secular*: from the Latin *saecularis*, "in Christian Latin 'the world,' especially as opposed to the church . . . of or pertaining to the world" (*OED*). "Worldly rather than spiritual" (*AHD*).

How do we come to know the world and nature? Why, we look. With great diligence and serious concentration, we see, take note of, process, and integrate the information. That is true in the sophisticated realm of science, and it is true for the even more sophisticated realm of Spirit. Coming to know about ourselves as children of Nature requires that we come to the enterprise with openhearted honesty and courage, with a willingness to be a friend to the processes of being, to Life in its largest sense—as ongoingness—and to listen carefully to its messages.

This active paying attention is far more than simple passive observation. The goal is not just to collect more information, but rather to garner a different kind of information, more complex, more profound. The intention is not just to function in life, but to find the clues to living well. This kind of attention allows us many strategies: we may sometimes exercise all the faculties of understanding—thinking, feeling, sensing, intuiting, imagining—so that experiences are seen fresh, completely, in all their dimensions, and none of their lessons are missed. Or we may try to clear the mind completely, and allow insight to rise however it will from all the sources of understanding, those conscious and those not. We may harvest the wisdom of others, or we may struggle alone. We may pursue, or we may wait.

Eventually, we must go *within* for final verification. Within each of us is housed our umbilicus to the Process, to Allness, and that is where we somehow come closest to reliable understanding of reality. Perhaps it is because in the silence within we can quiet the noises of inherited conventional belief systems, perhaps because in going to the deep mind, we allow the inner, vital core of being— that part of ourselves nearest the Source—to process and to speak.

When we attend to our silent, inner reality, free of the tug of competing arguments or formulas, we contact our most basic perceptions and insights, our uncontaminated values and authentic wishes. From this inner place come the resolutions we seek to the questions and puzzles we bring. These resolutions are powerful in the extreme. When we grasp them, it becomes so clear that they represent the truest creation of our own being, in touch, as much as we have grown to be, with all Being. For the time, in the concrete personal moment, at least until the contact leads us elsewhere, we have meanings. And upon these insights, because of them, we are enabled to act; we are impelled to act, and the act is not a burden, because it is so completely an expression of our own being.

To be in relation with the world and all reality: to seek to know what to expect of the world and what it expects of us, to make sense of our living and our dying, to understand our latitude and our limits and to be reconciled with these, to act in harmony with what lies outside ourselves and what is within, to *be* fully, this and more we bring to our center, our deep mind, our spirit.

We are rewarded for our in-sight by insight. From the recognition and acknowledgment of interconnection and interdependence comes perspective, meaning, and morality. We learn that we are not in isolation in this world, not as individuals nor as a species, but instead we share a common history and a common destiny. We realize that we must take responsibility not only for ourselves, but for the effects of our acts on the rest of being, indeed, even for the acts of the rest of being, because whatever touches any part touches all. We learn that we must act for Being or we will lose it, either by sin (acts against its continuation) or by default.

To live in the light of this awareness is altering; we experience differently the myriad acts and events that surround us. In the context of new meaningfulness, in the knowledge that each and every action performed contributes its particular character to the whole of the life process, simple actions become significant: how we respond to the touch of a friend, how we order our home, how much of ourself we put into the making of a clay pot.

Conversely, the awareness of our participation in life process, in an ultimate unity, leads us to realize that Life itself acts through us: We build a house—more accurately, Life builds a house through us; we act to change our societies, and Life alters our societies through us. We are Life expressing itself. Any act, any task we perform, can become a meditation on Life if we treat it so. In this way, the concrete, "trivial"* moments of life are *raised*, become *sublime,*† and living—ordinary, earth-grounded (worldly) living—becomes a spiritual, spirit-filled, event.

---

*Trivial*: related perhaps to the term *trivia*; "'Three ways,' a Roman title of Hecate as Goddess of three-way crossroads, where her three-faced images received offerings of cake. . . . The modern meaning of 'trivia' may be related to early attempts to belittle the cult of the Goddess" [Barbara G. Walker, *The Woman's Encyclopedia of Myths and Secrets* (San Francisco: Harper and Row, 1983), p. 1016].

†*Sublime*: ". . . ad. L. *sublimis*, prob. f. *sub* up to + *limen* lintel. . . . Set or raised aloft, high" (*OED*).

### Feminism and Spirit

For women, spiritual lucidity of this depth is critical for many reasons: it stands for vitality, for strength and authenticity, for a life-loving, self-loving potency. That power is in direct opposition to patriarchy's prescription of spiritual domestication. By turning us to a quest for understanding not grounded in external agents or truth systems, inner lucidity affords us a key to freedom from patriarchal consciousness. In giving us a moral ground that is in harmony with our experience, it gives us an impetus for action that translates into very powerful activism.

Spirit, as we have seen, presupposes freedom, something which remains always unbridled and inviolate, a right to will, a right to press to prevail, to direct the self. In patriarchy, however, that vitality, true spiritedness, is proscribed for women in an almost banal truism. Submission, un-freedom, is to be our definitive trait. Indeed, the first principle of womanhood in patriarchy is spiritual necrosis. We must make no mistake about it, the lords of creation want us dead. Like Snow White and Sleeping Beauty when their princes find them, we are to play dead, to *be* dead though alive, asleep except to our Masters' will. Obviously, there is nothing for us in patriarchy, no opportunity for authentic spirituality.

Only insistence upon the life of the self, only the most intense concentration on who we are, inside, by ourselves for ourselves, can counter such an omnipresent hideous intention, and that concentration *is* spiritual vigor.

Patriarchal consciousness is utterly pervasive in Western culture. It informs not only the myth systems of popular culture but also the theories of science, social science, medicine, and all forms of scholarship. It has been shown that an androcentric perspective defines not only the content of accepted knowledge but its modes of definition and verification as well,[3] rendering it a closed, self-sustaining, impenetrable monolith.[4] Where are we to go for knowledge not tainted, not constructed out of the prevailing monolith? As feminists have argued before and in other contexts, we go to experience, to life, where more viable premises and first principles await us and cleaner modes of verification may be found. Although our perception and experience develop in culture and become therefore colored by patriarchy, the twin components of spiritual lucidity (attention to what we see with our deep mind) and confidence in our experience offer us a powerful and progressive cleansing. By liberating our ability to find less contaminated truth, spiritedness, spiritual awareness can neutralize patriarchal consciousness.

Freedom from falsehood is crucial for quality living, but it is not enough. We must act on what we know. We must live better. We have determined that this is a time for action, when we cannot afford to be anaesthetized and diverted from social action. What could be more motivating, more empowering than confident conviction in principles drawn from our own understanding of self and life in the context of connection? When insight is strong enough, we are not only encouraged to act in harmony with what we know, we cannot act otherwise, for if we did the split within the self would be too deep. Between spiritual awareness and spirited action, there is no distance.

Feminism is a spiritual movement, motivated by our passion for freedom, by our respect for all being and for the Earth that houses it, and by our commitment to beauty of soul, individual and collective. We shall not be reduced or impeded by the acknowledgment of spirit. Feminist activism will be enhanced and emboldened by the power of purpose which is engendered there.

## Notes

1. (New York: Norton, 1973), p. 67.
2. This is not a new idea. Abraham Maslow's "hierarchy of needs" expresses the same claim in a different context. Full health, Maslow argued, required the fulfillment of needs at different levels: physical needs first, followed by emotional needs, culminating in the B-needs or "being needs," each level related to and evolving out of the preceding level. Although he might not have been comfortable with the language of spirituality, his self-actualizing needs are directly analogous to the concept of spiritual needs.
3. See Joan T. Roberts, "The Ramifications of the Study of Women," in *Beyond Intellectual Sexism: A New Woman, A New Reality,* ed. Joan T. Roberts (New York: Longman, 1976); and Sandra Harding and Merrill Hintikka, *Discovering Reality* (Hingham, Mass.: Kluwer Academic, 1983).
4. For an interesting discussion of patriarchy as a conceptual monolith see Herbert Marcuse, *One Dimensional Man* (Boston: Beacon Press, 1964).

# CHAPTER THREE

# Religion That Serves

## The First Story—Their Words

My mother had died. On her seventieth birthday, three years into her widowhood, missing her husband and tired of being tired, she had finally let go. I sat alone, uncomfortable, on a rickety wooden folding chair in a small, seedy funeral home in the Bronx. "Guests" sat silently, half listening to a rabbi—part pompous, part well-meaning—as he chanted and intoned in a language neither my mother nor I had learned to understand. (Only the men in our transplanted European neighborhood had been taught to read and pray in Hebrew. The women had been taught how to keep kosher and "make a Jewish home.")

My mother had been **JEWISH**, like so many working-class women of her generation in New York City in the 1940s and 1950s. It was not so much a theological matter, nor even a religious one, in the strictest sense. It had to do with her sense of herself, with her belonging in the Jewish community, with her wholehearted embrace of "yiddishness." In her apartment, beside the photographs of long-forgotten European relatives, artifacts from Israel, plaques of the Ten Commandments and various holy ornaments had festooned the walls and tabletops of each room. She had always worn a Star of David around her neck, and *Fiddler on the Roof* was the only Broadway play she had ever made an effort to see. Never having been educated, she had known very little about the Books, the Talmud and the Torah, except that they were sacred. She could not chant prayers or perform any rituals except for the lighting of sabbath

49

candles, a task specifically assigned to the "woman of the house."
In earlier years she had carried out the laws she knew to the letter,
keeping kosher, minding the sabbath, going to mikvah, although she
had not known why except that God had ordered it so, and that
had been good enough for her. Later, after the death of her parents,
the strictness of her observances had diminished, but never her
commitment to Jewish identity or her absolute belief in God.

Following my father's death, the prescribed rituals had been carried out precisely and without question: immediate burial, closed
casket, the requisite number of men to join my brother in a minyan, chanting the Kaddish, the prayer for the dead. Stark as they
were, these rigors were comforting to my mother. To die and be
buried as a Jew was to take the worst sting out of death, she had
once said. On this my parents had agreed: one of the primary reasons for having children (sons, actually) was to leave behind someone who would see to a proper passing and who would say the
Kaddish when it was time.

I remembered these things as I sat in the late afternoon sunlight,
musing upon the woman who was my mother, missing her (hard as
she had often been to take), experiencing a mix of intricate emotions. I fingered a giant bag of m&m's I was carrying in my purse.
I had bought them for her some days before, planning to mail them
in time for her birthday, as I did each year. Half guiltily indulging
our taste for these candies and giving them to each other for special occasions was a private ritual we had shared; touching them
now evoked poignant memories and sharpened my sense of separation.

I needed comfort. I didn't like having to sit so long in that half-
lit, dusty little room, staring at the box that housed my mother's
body. There were no small amenities, no flowers nor music to soft-
en the bleak setting of the scene; this being an orthodox ceremony,
such things were forbidden. I sought some small solace in the familiarity of the satin cloth draped across the coffin, dark purple with
a golden star, but I felt none. The "eulogy," some *good words* spoken in English about the dead woman by the rabbi-who-did-not-
know-her added nothing for me but a further note of irony and alienation. It seemed rotten to me that after seventy years of being and
doing, the end of one's time should be marked by such barren con-
trivance.

After a time, we left the funeral home and reassembled at a Jewish cemetery in New Jersey, an equally stark, relentlessly depress-

ing place, marked only by plain marble headstones—some slightly askew—by uneven tufts of scrub grass and a scattering of untrimmed bushes. There were few people at the grave site (most of her close friends and relatives having died or moved away from the city): a handful of old women who had recently been her neighbors, her sister, two younger brothers and their wives, my brother and I, and the rabbi. I stood beside a mound of sandy earth, looking down at her coffin, resting now in a giant pit. I had not realized that six feet would be so deep, could look so far. The ceremony began, the rabbi chanted a few lines in Hebrew. Switching to English, he looked around at the party and explained in his everyday voice (which seemed almost a conspiratorial whisper), "Here we would say Kaddish, but we don't have a minyan, so we'll finish." Intoning again, he said, "Let us not tarry among the dead, but make our way back to the living."

Not realizing that the ceremony had concluded and that I was supposed to file through the small row of people and return to the car, I stood there, vacantly, and waited. My brother tapped my arm. "Come on. We're supposed to go."

"Already? What about Kaddish?" I asked under my breath. "No Kaddish," my brother said, taking my arm, "we don't have a minyan."

No minyan. We needed ten men, any ten, to say the prayers, and there weren't enough.

Like the Hindu woman facing suttee, my mother too had committed the unpardonable *faux pas* of outliving her relevant males. I thought to myself, now isn't that a hell of a note! A Jew had died and could not have her Kaddish because she had failed to die soon enough or to produce enough sons. Worse, it seemed to me, a woman had died and could not have her prayers because the number present, being women, did not count for sufficient company to call upon their God.

For a moment I considered rebellion, a scene, perhaps, although I knew it wouldn't change a thing. I was not even to be permitted to stay awhile to say my own goodbyes and make my own unauthorized bidding of the gods. It would be forbidden, of course. In my head I heard my mother's piercing Bronx voice, "Sheila, don't start. Do what you're told!" They had me. Again.

There would be one small act of resistance, though, before I left. For myself, if not for my mother, I would have a "Kaddish" of my own. I reached into my purse and drew out the package I still carried there. Deliberately, tearing open the bag with a flourish, I scattered the little colored candies up and down the giant pit. They clattered noisily, almost happily, along the wooden cover of the box below, and I thought with some satisfaction that they lent a bit of sweetness and color to the place—and to the connection I forged once again with the spirit of my mother.

## Re-ligo: The Link

The story of my mother's funeral is paradigmatic. What happened there and what failed to happen tells us much about religion: what it can accomplish, and should accomplish, when it is functioning well, and what damage it does when it goes awry.

The term *religion* is derived from the Latin *re-ligo, to bind back, to rebind,* which reveals its meaning. In one sense, we may understand binding to suggest a shackling, the kind of bullying by rules and rulers so vividly apparent at my mother's funeral service. Because it exercises illegitimate power over the most profound experiences of life, such binding results in an alienation of spirit and a lost opportunity to confront and make sense of existence. It creates an estrangement among people who are not joined together by their common, intimate sharing of one another's experience, but who instead, being separated from their authentic selves, must remain apart from one another.

At its best, however, religion represents a binding of a very different kind.

> Latin religio meant re-linking or reunion, a restoration of the umbilical bond between nature and man, or between the Mother Goddess and her son–consort, typified by human sexual union. The Sanskrit equivalent was *yoga,* which also meant linking or joining, root of the English "yoke."
> — Barbara G. Walker[1]

So the operative questions for religion are: How am I linked to the rest of life, to the source of life? What is the significance of that link? How do I make use of it, how shall it, should it, make use of me, and what is my duty to that process? How may I take the best out of my bond with life; how can that enhance and beautify my existence, perhaps all existence? How do I and should I understand and direct all the events of my life from the perspective of my profound attachment to the whole of being? What are the ways that I can protect, strengthen, and enjoy the bond?

The function of religion is to continuously cement a conscious re-linking of the individual with the infinite universe. It is to help us acknowledge and make use of the tie that holds us to the Source. The infant takes nourishment from the mother, sustaining its life through their interaction by way of the umbilicus. We as individuals take our spiritual nourishment and survive as selves through interaction with our "Mother," the universe that gave us being. We gain wisdom and perhaps peace because we put ourselves and the events of our lives into the wider context of all being. In doing so, we deepen the dimension of the relationships between ourselves and other individuals and with the community, because all may be seen afresh from the vantage point of the eye of the cosmos and the cosmic. Religion, then, may function as an umbilicus, fastening us to our parent, all being, and carrying back and forth between us mutual influence and awareness.

The rites and rituals of religion are meant to be conduits of meaning: from the inner life, to more concrete daily awareness, and back to the spirit.

A ceremony of death
should carry the symbols of the cosmic (the Star, the
    Ankh, a deity, a crescent moon)
to our inner mind,
so that it can co-mingle with our very real
    confrontation with death,
in order to color that experience with a wider
    understanding and meaning,
so that our inner being may reconcile itself to life
    process, can unite with it and be made whole again.

The death of someone significant to us is an extraordinary event in our lives and potentially dis-integrative. To meet death in a way that affirms life is a complex task for mind and emotion. Not only must we deal with the raw sense of loss, we must also integrate a whole array of everyday changes the death will have upon our lives.

On a deeper level, because we are faced with death in such an immediate way, we also must come to terms with our own death and other coming losses, with death in general, and with the fragility and impermanence of life. We must consider once again "the meaning of life." One more time, we must reassess our orientation to being, of which death is a part.

To manage such a powerful event well, we require strategies to pull things back together for us, within ourselves, between ourselves and meaning, and between us and our community; we must re-sociate. Part of the work is rational, cognitive. But the most powerful portion of the experience centers in the emotions and in the spirit, and there the healing must take place, in the deepest, central core of our beings. Fragmented by an event that tears apart all our carefully soldered relationships and psychic structures, we need to reestablish or remodel our connectedness, our "friendship" with life. Providing us the materials to achieve that is a major function of religion and their rituals.

To accomplish the purpose of integration and healing, rituals must speak to our felt condition and in our own tongue. My mother's burial was barren to me not for want of enough men (or even people) to carry on the prescribed observances. Rather, the ceremony failed to pull together for me the disparate elements of the event— my absent mother, the dead woman, the people present and not present, the place, my feelings, my thoughts, the fact of death, the fact of life, the cosmos—and present them to me in some sensible bundle. It failed absolutely to touch the woman who had died (more accurately, to touch the woman who had lived); it failed to speak of her and for her to those connected with her. The surroundings were sterile, not because they were poor or ugly, but because they were alien to her and to those present. What had that stark little storefront room to do with the life (not just the death) of this person? Had she ever been to that room or to one like it? Did it hold anything of her or hers? Was it a place she might love, like, or relate to in any way? In fact, given choice, she would never have entered there voluntarily. The incantations were meaningless, not simply because they were in a foreign language, but because they had little to do with the life the woman had led, her days, her dreams. Indeed, because they had never really been connected to the lives any of us had led, they could not evoke even the sense of the extraordinary that they were meant to. By defining the situation in terms of the missing males, the ceremony had discounted the women present; it therefore had negated us, all of us, including the one being buried, separating us from the proceedings, the deity, and the wider community. In so doing, it severed the bonds that should have been cemented. For those who came seeking meaning and solace, there could be only fragmentation.

In the end, at the burial of my mother, in a space that was totally alien and therefore alienating, the only voice of Spirit left to me was the symbolic sharing that had bonded us so many times before. In words that were my own, the candies we both savored, I spoke to my mother, to the gathering, and to myself as well.

Scattering the candies was an act of religion. It is this kind of speaking, and everything that surrounds it, this kind of connecting and everything that surrounds it, this kind of marking of a life-changing event, and everything that surrounds it, that forms the core of religion, done well.

Death, of course, is not the only "moment" in life that is critical to the spirit. Various rites of passage are very familiar: vital biological events, such as birth or death, or those more obviously socially constructed, such as reaching the age of majority, retiring from work, or completing periods of training. Every society recognizes its own collection of milestones, and they are assigned meaning and value through particular activities and symbols. A person is raised to a new level of authority, for example. There is a ceremony. Now one may wear special clothes—a certain cap, a feather, a color. A title may change—chief, Madame, professor.

When an event or experience is given special recognition, when it is set apart by reverence or celebration, when members of the community are asked to bear witness, in these and in other ways, the event is *marked*. It is designated as an important occurrence to the individual and to the community. The raw event is given meaning, even granted "reality" by the symbols attached to it. Because it is focused upon, formally "spoken," the awareness of the event is sharpened in the consciousness, brought into the foreground of thought, so that it can be dealt with in the particular way determined by the society.

Just how much marking contributes to the meaning or reality of an event may be seen more readily when compared with events or moments for which marking is denied. Just as events may be brought into existence by marking, it is equally possible to drop them from existence or distort their meaning either by not marking them at all or by giving them a false marking.

Responses to the Vietnam war provide a perfect example of this process. Much has been said about America's changing attitude to its part in the war and how that was reflected in its treatment (or nontreatment) of returning Vietnam veterans in the 1960s and 1970s. No marching bands welcomed them home; no stars were placed in the windows of the mothers of the dead. For two decades, there

were no memorials in the U.S. capital to acknowledge those who
struggled there as veterans of other wars had been acknowledged.
The absence of these symbols and the collective silence of the country spoke volumes about ambivalence, anger, and shame, and left a
destructive mark upon the survivors and upon the society. For the
nation, the war became a "non-event." Unmarked, in a sense it was
erased, left ambiguous in the social consciousness, and thus there
could be very little coming-to-terms, for the society or for the survivors.

> As a psychiatrist who has worked with Vietnam veterans, I know all
> too well the long-term effects of wartime traumas. Ten and fifteen
> years after the events, there remain nightmares, fears, depression and,
> most fundamentally, failures of loving in veterans of combat. The
> timelessness of the unconscious does not bend to political realities.
> National treaties mark the beginning, not the end, of the psychic work
> of mastery.
>
> Primitive societies intuitively knew the value of cultural ceremo-
> nies that marked the end of hostilities. Rites of passage were provid-
> ed for the soldiers and the society to make the transition from the
> regression of combat to the structure of integrated living. These rit-
> uals acknowledged and sanctioned the otherwise forbidden acts of
> war. They thanked the soldier for his protection, forgave him his
> crimes and welcomed him back to life.
>
> Our failure to provide such a cleansing for our warriors and our-
> selves has left our culture struggling for closure. It has as well made
> the task of intrapsychic mastery so much more difficult for the indi-
> vidual soldier.
>
> — Harvey J. Schwartz[2]

The building of the Vietnam memorial in Washington, D.C., the
burial of an unknown soldier of that era next to the others in Ar-
lington Cemetery, parades in many cities, and other activities late
in the 1980s represented the delayed marking of the-war-now-final-
ly-acknowledged-to-be-a-war, brought it back into national consciousness, and allowed individuals to reintegrate it in their lives in
a meaningful way. No one who has been to the Wall, seen the re-
membrances placed there, seen the people fingering the carved in-
dentations, grief stricken, but relieved at last to be no longer unseen—no one who has seen those things can doubt the power of
the mark.

All markings have force, but those markings which are said to
connect with the Ultimate are particularly powerful. To make a

promise before a judge of the land, surrounded by leather-bound volumes housed in mahogany, in the old marble courthouse in the county seat is impressive. The judge, to be sure, represents not only the people of the state, but the force of law and tradition and the granting of social approbation. Yet how much greater is the force of validation when it represents not only society, but God! To make a promise *in the temple* signifies that the promise has particular meanings because it places itself in relation to the Infinite. The vow is made not only to oneself and to the community, but to the eternal, to deity, which represents society's most fundamental mores and its hopes and expectations for the future. What is more, it is expected that the deity will respond with like for like—promises kept for promises kept. The whole fabric of the event is altered: There are additional responsibilities, expectations and prohibitions; attitudes and emotions are invested here that do not exist in other contexts; and this promise is perceived differently even by those outside the culture, even by those who are not believers, because they comprehend the implications of the religious element.

Of course, things other than life events may be marked. Designating a day to honor Martin Luther King Jr. not only honors the man, but what he stood for. Having such a celebration says as much about American culture, history, racism, and law as it did about Dr. King. That is why it meant so much to those who pressed for it, and why it was so equally resisted by its opponents. Obviously, markings are as meaningful and as consequential in their absence as in their presence, for if the presence of the mark denotes acknowledgment, response, and importance, consider what the withholding of a mark signifies.

For women, the violence done to us by absent or false marking is commonplace and crucial. How many of our most profound life experiences are lost in silence—menarche and menopause (both of them a coming-of-age), rape, the moving on and moving out of our children, taking to ourselves a close friend? How many others are distorted or perverted, turned upside down by no marking or the wrong marking, no words or the wrong words? A purification ceremony at the close of each menstruation, assuring that the woman will return to her men "cleansed" and harmless, common in patriarchy, is the wrong marking. Rather there should be affirmations of femaleness, celebrations for the bringers of life. After rape, secrecy and shame are the wrong "words"; what is required is some dramatically transforming reassertion of absolute, *inviolate* dignity and power, a communal "naming" of the vileness of the wrong, a ceremony of outrage, retribution, and compensation. In a reality constructed by men for men, no words, no ceremonies, no constructive markings have ever been permitted to evolve for women's life-altering moments.

*A gathering assembles itself around a dinner table dressed for a feast, covered with flowers, wonderful foods, sweet-smelling herbs, and incense. The girl who has just had her first menstruation is seated at the head of the table, dressed in what she loves best, adorned with ribbons and flowers, surrounded by the women close and dear to her. There is laughter, play. From each one present she receives women's gifts. Finally it is her mother's turn. The woman gives her daughter a jewel with red beads or stones, marking the blood, celebrating the sign of femaleness, welcoming her into the family of women. The daughter returns a gift, honoring the birth, honoring the line. They are very proud.*

*In a darkened classroom the only light comes from a scented candle placed on a desk in the center of the room. A group of students are constructing a woman's ceremony by giving their teacher a "croning," a ritual to celebrate her becoming a "crone," a woman of maturity, wisdom, and consequence. The teacher is given a white robe to wear, signifying youth, beginningness, purity of intention. To symbolize her gifts to them, a sweet drink is poured into a silver cup, and she is asked to bring the cup to each woman, standing in a circle, and offer her a sip. Then she is blindfolded and led gently around the circle of students, as each one in turn takes her hands, rubs perfumed lotion into them, and thanks her for something she has given them—new insight, compassion, humor, permission to be powerful, and so on. When the circle is completed, a tinkling bell is sounded, the blindfold is removed, the white robe is replaced by a black one, signifying maturity, fullness, power. They all share some cookies and drink and laugh together. There is affection among them, acceptance, validation, but even more. There is a collective granting of respect to certain abstractions, learning, the sharing of knowledge, caring, maturity, aging.*

In women, aging is rarely venerated. Quite the contrary. The gifts we may receive with age, uncelebrated may become invisible; maligned, they may be denied, lost. In honoring those gifts in their teacher, the students are making an equally strong statement about their own futures, their expectations for themselves and for other women.

What happens to powerful experiences that go unmarked or unremarked by the communities where we make our psychic homes? In our deepest selves and in our awareness, what is their status, and what is the consequence of their going unnoticed or of their being inverted? Are they erased? Are they distorted? Do they toxify?

That women's uniquely female "moments" go unmarked or falsely marked is no accident, but one more reflection of the fact that the "world's great religions" and the patriarchies that created them are not of us nor for us.

How are we to respond to patriarchal religion's contempt for our lives? Do we simply reject the religious altogether and opt for purely social, secular markings? Does that meet our needs? Isn't there an insufficiency in stipulating or recognizing meanings that do not go beyond the social order? The relativity of social norms always leaves the force of their conviction incomplete. We must make some attempt to reach a truth that lies beneath the social form and lends it veracity. Anything less will leave us feeling incomplete.

Let us take for example an adoption. If no religious ceremony exists to mark an extraordinary new relationship with a child, a parent may go to court, swear an oath, rename the child (a powerfully symbolic act). A party may be arranged or a special dinner. These are social rituals, and clearly understood they may be significant. But is this sufficient? Are these acts truly equal in power to religious ceremony? Without some processing at a very deep level of what the adoption is—what it involves in the very widest sense, not only for the child, but for the community, the family, the parent, *for parenting itself, for one's whole reading of the nature of things*—is everything said that needs to be said, is everything marked clearly enough, deeply enough?

If we are spiritually strong, each of us may find our meanings by ourselves, make our own peace with life-events, and create our own markings; sometimes we do that very well. Of course, at some level we must do this for ourselves even when positive sacred ceremonies exist. But how much more powerful can it be to join with others in our affirmations and join all together with some symbolic connector to ultimate being.

## *Religion: The Acting Out of Spirit*

In its simplest sense, religion is the acting out of spirit. That sentence is ambiguous. It can be read in two ways: religion is what we do when we act on the basis of, make choices and decisions dictated by, the fruits of spiritual knowing; or religion is a kind of acting out, a putting into practice the ideas and insights we glean from spirited inquiry. Both senses are intended.

When we tend to our spirit, when we cause and allow to flourish the natural vitality in us, when we strive for ever-increasing understanding in ever-widening circles of connection and consequence, we create and augment within ourselves not only insight but power, power which is both energy and potency. By its very nature such potency is not held within the flimsy boundary that is the edge of self; it is expressed, pressed into the world. What spirited experience makes of us and reveals to us changes and colors what we do and also what we allow or invite life to do to us. Religion becomes, then, a double enterprise. It is at the same time each and all of the things we do that are expressions of spiritual awareness and also all the things we do that are aimed at nurturing and stimulating a spiritual orientation.

*In solitude and quiet, on a dreamy, winter walk, a woman becomes acutely conscious of a bit of sunlight; she enjoys its warmth and light and considers how much she has always prized the sun, the tempering of the weather it brings, and the lifting of feelings. She may note how when its time lengthens it brings the fields to life, and how the animals and insects seem to thrive more in its care. Perhaps she moves to musing upon the sun's part in the natural order, how the smallest change in the earth's position in relation to the sun or to the clouds effects a pronounced change in the earth's condition, warmer or cooler, illumined or dark. She is reminded of the beliefs of the ancients and can better understand, more concretely, why they would have considered the sun to be divine, a representation of the godhead. Perhaps, in her own time, she too comes to grant it worth-ship. In its magnificence, its incredible sustaining power and beauty, its succor of the earth, to her too it reflects the Allness, the Process, its ongoing interrelatedness.*

Such musings are of the spirit. Grounded in experience, fed by thought and feeling, they move out beyond their origins in evolving circles—from self to event, to the connection of self and event, perhaps, to the context of both, to the nature of the context, and other selves, other beings, and on and on . . . Pursued freely, untrammeled by insistence upon foregone conclusions, such contemplation enlarges in every dimension. It connects us within—feeling to thought to feeling—and without—self to life to cosmos. It affirms what I am, where I am, that I am, in my moment, my place. It yields new, qualitatively different knowledge.

The woman beneath the sun is connected.

*It is she and the other creatures which are flourishing beneath the sun; it is she and the sun, both children of Nature, who depend upon Life as life depends upon the sun.*

Such seeing can bring direction.

*If it is good, if there is joy or pleasure in living so peacefully beneath the sun, must she not do what is possible to ensure its continuing?*

To do so would be an acting out of religion.

If, following from that experience, the woman crafts a clay pot and portrays upon it an image of the sun, to remember or capture the moment, to honor the sun, or to express it to others, or to encourage it in others, then that is an act of, an acting out of, religion. If, following from that experience, she opens her curtains to the sun so that it can pour into her rooms, if she peoples her house with plants to remind her daily of their kinship in Nature with the sun, if she is more or better mindful of the creatures of the Earth who, like herself, thrive beneath the sun (and so are like herself), then these are acts of religion.

Simple though such insights and connections may be, and superceded by others far more complex, farther reaching, they exhibit one aspect of the relationship between spirit and religion, the consequences of spiritual lucidity upon our behavior. On the other hand, if the woman purposefully sets herself to sit alone outside beneath the sun, to experience its effect and ruminate upon its meaning, her object being to induce or to encourage insight and awareness, that too is an act of religion, the evolution of spirit by action. Every act that flows from spirited awareness and every act designed to stimulate such awareness is part of what religion is.

## Religion: A Total Reaction Upon Life

William James said of religion that whatever else it may be, it is one's "total reaction upon life."

> Total reactions are different from casual reactions, and total attitudes are different from usual or professional attitudes. To get at them you must go behind the foreground of existence and reach down to that curious sense of the whole residual cosmos as an everlasting presence, intimate or alien, terrible or amusing, lovable or odious, which in some degree everyone possesses. This sense of the world's presence, appealing as it does to our peculiar individual temperament, makes us either strenuous or careless, devout or blasphemous, gloomy or exultant, about life at large; and our reaction, involuntary and inarticulate and often half unconscious as it is, is the completest of all our answers to the question, "What is the character of this universe in which we dwell?" It expresses our individual sense of it in the most definite way.[3]

The religious perspective is total in several ways: for one thing, it involves the total person, all the faculties of knowing, including thinking, feeling, and receiving (what we are given through our animal connection with nature), and all that we are, including memory, personality, and attitude. We bring our whole being, character, personality, conscious and unconscious life to the business of Visioning, for what we are seeking is a "spiritual" home, a place in which to *Be* in the profoundest sense.

Because it involves the total person, the reaction James speaks of must be total in the sense of entirety and of unification. Our response to what we experience on this level is a composite, including our beliefs about existence, our expectations, and our evaluations. But these pieces of the composite are also of one piece, interlocking; they form a governing pattern, a personal tone—whether we are expansive or contracting, trusting or guarded, outgoing or removed, proactive or adaptive.

And finally, we respond to life in its totality as well. All of what life presents to us, all the events, phenomena, and images it provides us, are taken together as a unitary configuration.

The religious component of awareness is marked by a largeness, by an essential and defining element of our consciousness, which is trained upon the universe in its completeness. It is this component, this holistically oriented, integrating mechanism of thought that, ideally, becomes our "center," what is referred to when we speak of becoming centered, of centering in, or centering down, or going to one's center. Developed and honed, strengthened by attention and exercise, it is this part of our being that becomes the source of our thoughtful, considered life, of our understanding and our values, of direction, motivation, judgment, and action. It functions as a kind of conduit or clearinghouse, absorbing wider and more complex segments of information from the universe, processing them through our perception and experience, through the fund of spirited knowledge already present in us, and passing that knowing through to our lived, visible behavior.

If spirit, the "breath of life," is that part of us which quests after vitality, after freedom and the lucidity that grants freedom, if spirit is the part of us that quests after meaning and meaningfulness, which inquires, seeks, processes and thus creates "knowing," religion is the binding of that knowing with action. Like spirit, religion too is a process, a dynamic activity, a verb,[4] the outer, visible manifestation of the deep mind, which in each of us is our ineffable, inner existence.

Centering and its process exist in some form and in some degree of evolution in all of us, perhaps rudimentary and more a matter of potential in our youth, developing later only with purposeful attention. Spiritual development, like physical development, is a choice and a task, not a happenstance. Thus, for one who elects to grow spiritually, the enterprise becomes pervasive and encompassing. This is not to say spiritedness is diverting, that is, derailing, as when one is led away from life to be engrossed in withdrawal. Quite the contrary. One carries this honed acuity concretely into life; there is a keenness about life and for life. Rather than *div*erted, one is *con*verted, in the best sense of that term. (Convert: from the Latin, *con-*, together, with union + *vertere*, to turn. Therefore, to turn with, to come together with.) In life-loving religion, conversion begets and is a coming together with life.

Religious living both produces and is grounded in an attitude that says: Life, the whole process of being, including both what is comforting and what is terrifying, is good and meaningful, worth living and worth living well. If I come to Life straight on, if I approach the Universe positively, honestly, openly, and respectfully, it will embrace and instruct me, and I will be at home.

Returning again to James, we find a valuable and subtle characterization of religious consciousness: The religious "constitution" is "actively positive"; although serious and solemn, it is tender, emotional, and joyful. There is an "acceptance of the universe . . . with enthusiastic assent . . . a mood of welcome . . . cheerful serenity . . . happiness in the absolute and everlasting." Spirited living creates a resilient mind and temperament in which a sense of a "higher happiness holds a lower unhappiness in check."[5]

Have we come to a contradiction? Religion is a kind of binding, and yet creatures of spirit resist a reining in. Positive religion must empower and not overpower to bring about liberation. How can an enterprise that binds be construed to be liberating?

Whether or not we may wish to be bound must depend in great measure upon that to or by which we are to be bound. Quite reasonably, we do not wish to be bound to or by externalities, to or by alien standards created by alien agents. Contrary to the principles of patriarchy, no glory resides in humbling oneself to extraneous power. Warriors may submit ecstatically to their chiefs, but for the spirited, such gladsome submission does not appeal.

To be bound to others by others is slavery. To be bound by nothing to nothing is nihilism, the ultimate nonbeing, the ultimate absence. On the other hand, to be bound to powers and standards which are not alien, self-wrought rather than foreign, is neither submission nor abdication; it is expression. To act in accord with the verities of my own most serious inquiries is to act in accord with my own nature. To be bound to myself by myself, to reality and existence gleaned from truth as I have found it, to be and act in harmony with my own understanding is the opposite of being reined or ridden; it *is* liberation. There can be no greater freedom.

Nor does this represent the freedom of the disconnected. It is not that I cut myself adrift in some totally subjective, ultra-egoistic float of passion and interest. Rather, it is that at least part of the verification I have for all the knowing that I adopt as my own is self-based. I acknowledge and assert that in the end, I am the final arbiter of belief.

## The Heart of Religion

It is cliché (although true) that "religion" covers vast territories and that it functions in many ways. It is a complex of activities and experiences, a composite. Nonetheless, we should not be led into thinking that religion is anything one wishes to call religion; that would reduce it to nonstatus, for an enterprise that could include anything would have no particular character at all.

Like spirit, religion does admit of some description, although not definitive, and it is possible to articulate at least some of its elements outside the patriarchal context. Also as with spirit, religion is more easily approached from the nether side, that is, from the perspective of what it is not.

Contrary to the history and many of the traditions of martial patriarchy, religion does not have to be "an institution," a highly formalized and organized array of lore and legalisms, buildings, books, rules, rulers, and tax collectors, or ordained elites gaining power over a loved, but wayward flock. It is not necessary that there be dogmas, regulations, activities, and structures created outside of an individual and imposed thereon. Nor is there by necessity a delineation of reality prepackaged by a central committee and affixed to an individual early in life, before the age of reason, before the possibility of thoughtful consideration.

Likewise, religion need not be a matter of gaining power over the self by the self for the purpose of shielding oneself from honest, difficult encounters with reality. Not a crutch, a retreat, an opiate, as has often been charged, positive religion should be neither self-delusional nor escapist, offering hiding places from the rigors of necessity or shortcuts from the struggle to grow in spirit and to come to terms with existence.

Religion that serves life could not be opposed to, or apart from, nature. It is not supernatural, counter-natural, or unnatural. The living out of religion in its best sense ought not to propel us into conflict with our own being or character, our own nature or the Nature in which we live, the concrete, material, physical world. It therefore must not aim either for the obliteration of natural human impulse or the denial of the animal element in human nature. It cannot or should not seek to separate people from the other creatures or kinds with whom we share life, pretending to raise us "above" them or granting us precedent or dominion that is not rightfully ours.

It is not the proper end of religion to contract life, to limit experience and feeling, to pinch our possibilities to a nub, crushing our capacities and abilities until we are left with a mere vestige of what might be, with the limp and colorless dregs of passion, joy, exuberance, will, and fire.

Religion, done well, does not reduce.

Done well, religion expands. It expands our sense of self, helping us to see ourselves as independent and inviolate as well as connected and interdependent; it expands our sense of other selves, other creatures, species, and kinds, their spirit and their realities; it enlarges our awareness and understanding of our world and our universe. Expanding awareness, lucidity, it enhances power, our own, not the *power over*, which we come not to need or want, but *power of*, and *power to*. It empowers: It develops our strength and our ability to meet life. It leads, therefore, to an amplification of life-enriching capacities.

Because a major aim of religion has always been to gain for an individual a sense of peace with what is, religion must move to harmonize—self to self, self to others, self to life. Only the deepest kind of understanding or wisdom can accomplish such a goal. Not fictional, then, or beguiling, however reassuring, religion must be courageously honest, curious, and searching. It must above all be reasonable, not only rational, for logic speaks to only one aspect of human awareness; it must be credible to, and consonant with, all forms of knowing—emotional, sensible, intuitive, or experiential.

The practice of religion must be integrative, inclining as it must to harmony. Acts that set us apart from parts of ourselves, that split rather than join, cannot be in the province of Life-serving religion.

It is for this reason, this integrative element, that joy, pleasure, fun, delight, play, laughter, euphoria, excitement, ebullience, passion, and light-heartedness are proper ends of religion. These qualities and feelings indicate integration. They reflect harmony within the self and reconciliation with what is. They are visible manifestations of inner work done well, of a collation of the inner and outer world. They indicate an acceptance of the self and an affirmation of the reality in which the self resides, however short self and reality may fall of the ideal.

The opposites of these characteristics—misery and all its company, suffering, self-effacement, strain, and self-denial—can never be seen as goods, as ends in themselves and are never properly sought by religious activity. Suffering is to the spirit what pain is to the body, a symptom of disorder, necessary perhaps, but requiring correction.

An interchange some years ago with an elderly, rather street-wise and experienced aunt was instructive to me in ways we did not then predict. We were at home, and I was struggling with a tool, unable to get its parts to interlock. In frustration and pique, I banged away at it, trying to bend it to my will. She watched me drolly for a few moments, then quietly took the tool out of my hands. After some examination, she turned the sections around, refitted them, and snapped the pieces easily into place. Handing it back to me, she looked me directly in the eye and said softly, "If you have to force it, it's wrong."

That principle has remained with me, and it applies to more than just tools. When parts are made to fit, "if you have to force it, it's wrong." Pain, conflict, and strain, the suffering borne of struggle, are a consequence of the forcing of parts.*

Perhaps the greatest indication we have of the error of patriarchal religion is its wholehearted embracing of misery. *"For discipline,"* they say, *"for the strengthening of the spirit, for God or His prophets in remembrance and imitation of His own agony. Offer it up,"* they say. *"God knows what He's doing. Offer it up. For chastisement,"* they say, *"to cleanse you. Offer it up."*

Yet for all they say, the patriarchs, the martial ones, if we pay attention to what they do, what they require, if we cut through the rhetoric and look straight at the reality, we see plainly an accent on all that is dolorous, dark, and punitive: People are not good; they are sinful. Natural life is a veil of tears, a training ground only for a better world to be. Industriousness and labor are signs of virtue; fun is vice. Pleasure, particularly physical pleasure, is evil. Seven deadly sins lie always in wait for the incautious heart. Self-interest is wrong. Struggle is the sign of piety. Laughter has no place in church. Sacrifice is the ultimate gift. Celibacy marks the highest calling; abstinence, except for procreation, stands close behind. Tears, and more tears. God moves in mysterious ways. He asks Abraham to sacrifice his son (a reasonable test, you understand), and willingly He offers up His own.

Here is the beautiful young man, The son (sun?) of life, the dear dead god, portrayed again and again in his agony, beaten, humiliated, murdered, hanging, blood spilling onto his face and oozing from his wounds. Here are his special followers, his select, always in black, in perpetual mourning. Here is the honored devotee, murdered, martyred, hacked or torn to pieces. There might have been so many other symbols, so many other ways to remember, so many other lessons to make central to the story, so many other stories to tell.

Health, which is "soundness," "general well-being" (*OED*), "free-

---

*Conflict*: "1. A state of open fighting; warfare. 2. A state of disagreement and disharmony; clash. 3. *Psychol.* The opposition or simultaneous functioning of muturally exclusive impulses, desires, or tendencies. . . . Lat. *conflictus* . . . to strike together: *com-*, together + *fligere*, to strike" (*AHD*).

dom from disease" (*AHD*), contravenes pain. When one functions well, ideally, there is not pain, but its opposite. That is what is meant by functioning well, by health. Pain serves only as a sign, to alert the creature to tend to its needs lest there be irredeemable damage.

If it is so for the body, that pain is but a warning, a sign of physical disorder and a cue to re-order, it is no less so for spirit. Pain—suffering, struggle, anxiety, and dolor are not to be sought, induced, or precipitated, but recognized to be signs of disorder, signs that the individual needs to "work," needs to come to terms, to reconcile, to seek the reestablishment of harmony within and without.

Nor should we believe that the creation of suffering or struggle is even the best path or inducement to learning or growth. History, experience, and even social science have shown us that positive, not negative, modes of training are most productive. It is not self-denial or "mortification of the flesh" that directs us to spirit, but the wholehearted enjoyment of spiritual experience and lucidity. How more spiritually enhancing is music, art, dance, play, meditation than self-mortification?* That suffering is not a proper end or path for religion is not to say, however, that struggle, pain, and discipline have no place in the life of the spirit. Making our way through life, maintaining relationships, changing our habits and perspectives, coming to understand ourselves, learning new skills and gaining insights, establishing and reestablishing life directions, making moral decisions, and so much more, all involve confronting and coping with dilemmas and their conflict. Just absorbing the exigencies of life, its uncertainties and its tasks, includes suffering and anguish. Conflict and suffering are normal parts of normal living, and growth rarely happens free of pain.

Spiritual living does not hide from suffering or avoid pain at all cost. It uses it. We must meet pain when it comes and endure what suffering must result from striving after quality life. We must come to understand and acknowledge the place of sorrow in existence and come to terms with it. We might even gladly submit to some anguish as a sign of personal growth in the same way that we might accept the aches of our body when we exercise for increased

---

*Mortification*; from *mortify*: "1. To cause to experience shame, humiliation or wounded pride; humiliate. 2. To discipline (one's body and physical appetites) by self-denial and austerity. . . . Lat. *mortificare*, to kill: *mors*, death + *facere*, to make" (*AHD*).

strength. Life-loving religion recognizes the inevitability of pain that comes from struggle, the necessity for struggle that leads to becoming. Life-loving religion must offer wholesome solace and support for spiritual suffering as medical science develops remedies for its physical counterpart, but it never embraces pain, never invites it or turns to it with admiration, never makes of it a fetish as the patriarchs have done.

Living has its ugly elements, and spirited living properly strives to prevail. It has often been said of religion that its chief aim is to lead an individual to some measure of transcendence, the ability or capacity to "rise above" or "go beyond" the ugly, the difficult or "mundane" circumstances of daily existence.*

Transcendence is a complex idea that can be interpreted in many ways, some positive, others destructive. We must ask just what it is that is to be transcended, how it is to be accomplished, what purpose would be served by such a "climbing over," and to what or to where we would climb.

If what is sought in transcendence is escape from the "trivialities" of daily necessity, removal from the travail of lived, concrete existence, then such a goal would seem an error, for it would involve removal from life itself, in other words, it suggests death. In fact, this is exactly the sense that traditional patriarchal religion holds out to its faithful as the supreme desiderata: transcendence over the pains and uncertainties of "this world" by flight or removal (of one sort or another) to another world. On earth (while living), one climbs over to the kingdom of "spirit," gaining a sort of dematerialization through the obliteration of physical desires; later (in death), one hopes for the ultimate removal to the ultimate other place, Paradise. In this case, transcendence signifies defection from life, a kind of suicide, hardly a positive aim.

In the best sense of transcendence, we do not seek escape from "trivialities" or even "immanence," (the ongoing, commonplace events of daily life), but escape from banalities, the meaninglessness that comes of narrowness, the petty parameters of ignorance and small perspective. In this case transcendence is a more than reasonable goal and coherent with life-serving religion.

Relief from what is pointless and insipid in existence is not accomplished best by a sleight of hand or by turning one's back on life. Quite the contrary, it requires an active, intense involvement

---

* Transcend: "Lat. *transcendere*: *trans*, over + *scandere*, to climb" (*AHD*).

in life. It is accomplished through the purposeful creation of meaning that comes from placing all events and experiences into context and coming to know them as elements of the "unseen order." It comes from being able to see oneself and one's world as fitting into the Process of Processes, in which everything participates. That is the heart of transcendence, to be lifted into a wider, more encompassing perspective. That is also religion.

> Were one asked to characterize the life of religion in the broadest and most general terms possible, one might say that it consists of the belief that there is an unseen order, and that our supreme good lies in harmoniously adjusting ourselves thereto. This belief and this adjustment are the religious attitude in the soul.
> — William James[6]

## Religion: A Home for the Primal

> Now if one thing is certain about all human beings, it is that they communicate their inner life in symbolic terms.
> — George Boas[7]

If the substance of spiritual experience is ineffable or unutterable, it is so only when we attempt to speak in the wrong language. The content of spirit, like that of the inner psyche, is best communicated through symbolic language. Spirit and spirited religion speak through imagery, through shape and color, through signs and metaphors, through stories that tell other stories, myths, fables, allegories, fairy tales, poems and "histories," and through rules, rites, and rituals—all representations of verities that elude direct expression. Like poetry and art, religious communication is holistic rather than linear. It answers to a different rhythm of comprehension and requires different forms of verification from ordinary intercourse. Like poetry and art, religious meaning is perverted when subjected to literal translation. Religion, poetry, and art are one; they fill the same human need and intention. They form a sphere of consciousness compatible with linear consciousness, yet separate. What results when the two languages, the two spheres, are confused is absurdity.

Many of us became disenchanted with religion early, often because we were repelled by a whole series of exchanges with the schemas of religion and their apologists, a whole set of theorems and presuppositions classifiable under the heading: Nonsense. Silly stories were told, rites performed, dogmas advanced, rules prescribed, explanations and evidence given, all with a straight face and pious urgency, and they were promulgated as absolute, literal truth. We were expected to receive without question these absurdities in perfect solemnity and silence. We could not do it.

If spirit is integrative, religion cannot present us with materials that our rationality must reject. Suspensions of logic and acts of the will not withstanding, in the strictest sense, Tertullian was probably wrong: healthy people do not believe in the impossible because it is absurd.

It is true because it is impossible.
I believe what is absurd.
—Tertullian, Christian Philosopher,
  2nd and 3rd centuries, A.D.[8]

In fact, it is conceivable that Tertullian did not mean to say in the strictest sense that we believe absurdities; it is possible that he was speaking of belief and truth in a different sense, and he was referring to realities of a different order.

When we explore the work of the best philosophers of religion, the theologians who created the material upon which most of contemporary religion is based, we do not usually find the gross contradiction and simplicity of mind that characterize popular beliefs. A metamorphosis takes place when the ideas of the great thinkers are translated into systems and schema for "ordinary" people. Undoubtedly, many factors are involved in this shift—politics, power, incompetence, ignorance, economics, craziness, and who knows how many others.

What happens in the space between careful thought and popular absurdity? Among other things, there is a misreading of intention and a crossing of languages. Was religious talk or spirited talk ever meant to be taken literally, in the same way that we talk of tables and chairs? The Old Ones, who first told tales of trees and snakes and floods, of matings between gods and mortals and the demigods that were their fruit, who first talked of Beings-greater-than-which-nothing-could-be-conceived, very likely spoke of these things in a language and conceptualized them in a dimension, unlike that of their daily comings and goings. This dual–double conceptualization was understood by speaker and listener alike. The difference in logics was purposeful. It posed no contradiction because the languages and the realms they represented were not meant to occupy the same mental space (or they coexisted there comfortably), and therefore they did not compete for ascendancy.[9]

The deep mind, that level of consciousness most primitively (primally) intimate with the fundamental realities of life, hears and speaks in terms and modalities different in character from our ordinary, material exchanges. Often when Life speaks to us, when the world beyond the cognitive talks, it tells us things as it does the other species, and if we are to hear, we must listen with more than our human faculties alone. When we respond, we must use a mode appropriate to those other faculties.

We communicate the content of the deep mind through different modes; we communicate spiritedly within ourselves (transcribing and exchanging awarenesses between one part of ourselves and another), with our material environment and its processes, with other people individually, with others communally, and with the past and future. We chant or sing or intone. We speak different languages. We dance or clap or beat rhythmically with a drum. We paint pictures in our minds, with our minds:

*I invoke a beautiful woman, floating in the clouds, Mother of Life, now young and lithe as I remember Her in my childhood, now dark and stooped as She was at the death. I call Her forth when summoning the Infinite. I speak of Her to others, I call Her the Mother, I am respectful, and they are awed, and together we remember to reverence the Source of life.*

Just as dreams present us with otherwise inaccessible data or knowledge through symbols and combinations of ideas (often seeming bizarre, rarely linear or "logical"), so does the exquisitely intense level of awareness that is spirit.

Spirit seeks meaning behind meaning; it trades in abstractions of abstractions, with elements of reality contained not only in many spheres of daily life, but in many dimensions, across time, through space never experienced, peoples never seen or never born, possibilities only imagined, events only guessed. Spirit burrows to the hidden core of self, to awarenesses prior to language, perhaps before, certainly outside of, memory, to the kind of knowing we share with the other species, the primal, the animal comprehension inherited from Mother Earth. It works with meanings that may not be composed of straight lines of logic, with meanings that may not appear in discernable segments of data connected clearly to other discernable segments, but in entireties, in whole chunks of apprehension at once. There are no accurate words for these awarenesses, only special symbols, complex metaphors.

> The symbol awakens intimations speech can only explain. The symbol plucks all the strings of the human spirit at once; speech is compelled to take up a single thought at a time. The symbol strikes its roots in the most secret depths of the soul. Language skims over the surface of the understanding like a soft breeze. The symbol aims inward; language outward.
> — J. J. Bachofen[10]

Elucidating Bachofen's thought, Joseph Campbell says, "And the message of the symbol is not a mere thought or idea, but a way of *experience* which can be understood only by responding to its summons."[11]

Primal symbols and metaphors may look like and combine like ordinary terminology, but they are misused if they are treated or understood as ordinary terms for ordinary discourse. Spirited, primal consciousness is the consciousness of extraordinary meaning; its language is composed of metaphors of metaphors. Only in this way can it be understood and can it maintain its veracity.

Unlike dream talk, fortunately for us, spirited communication contains a second, collateral dimension: reciprocity. In dreams, meaning usually flows in only one direction, from the deep mind to the upper level of awareness, but spirited knowing flows back and forth, from the deep mind to the surface and back to the primitive layers of awareness. We can purposely and consciously stimulate the deep mind by presenting it with profoundly evocative symbols. A mantra, a lighted candle, an image of a woman hurling thunderbolts and carrying snakes in her hair, a tinkling bell, the graceful movements of a ritual dance, the color green—all are associated with powerful meanings and can nourish the spirit. When we utter the words or meditate on the images, their meanings are transmitted downward, coaxing that level of awareness into life, encouraging it to send insights in return. Even more than dream consciousness, spirited consciousness is dynamic and ever-expanding.

In religion this language of symbols and the awarenesses it represents are trained on the infinite and the ultimate. Because religion is an acting out, it externalizes, it finds ways to make visible and verbal what would ordinarily remain invisible and ineffable, hence the metaphors, the analogies, the images and effigies, the ceremonies, and all.

For human convenience, to facilitate relationship with the unfathomable and abstract; to give channels to our feelings; to tell others about them and to hear then assent; to petition Nature, the Intractable; to commune with and be part of in our minds what we are already part of in our being; to render sensible the insensible, to make meaningful the bewildering; to locate and identify the alien objects of our most possessing fear, love, or need; for the sheer joy of it or in our anguish—for all of these reasons and others, we grasp at the Absolutely Real with our minds and render it present with our "hands." Only when the primal is thus made comprehensible in conscious human terms can we have cognitive, practical intercourse with it.

Encounter the Allness, the Oneness, the Process of Processes, Life in its completeness, Ongoing Being, Infinite Meaning. For comfort, assign it a symbol word—perhaps *God*. Does analogy lend insight? Select one, suited to the purpose, tied to primordial human experience and fecund with possibilities: a tree, a cloud, a mountain, a person. Select well, for the image provides a meaning and direction of its own. The image may very well come to have a life of its own as well, independent of its creator and, perhaps, independent of its model.

> Myth is the exegesis of the symbol. It unfolds in a series of outwardly connected actions what the symbol embodies in a unity. It resembles a discursive philosophical treatise in so far as it splits the idea into a number of connected images and then leaves it to the reader to draw the ultimate inference.
> — J. J. Bachofen[12]

The process is complex. Metaphors without end are possible, and countless abstractions may be symbolized, as many as are required or desired. Left purposely vague or minutely defined, the metaphors may be manipulated into whatever configurations or appearances are suitable for the intended purpose.

The Allness which is God-which-is-person could have been born a flower or an eagle or the number one; good, bad, or neither; great and triumphant or enmeshed in conflict; each representation bears different possibilities of meaning and consequence. The combinations are without limit; their potential elaborations equally inexhaustible, determined solely by the intention and turn of mind of their creators. Forces of nature or Nature itself, emotions, events, or ideals may find their way into concretization and may interact with others, in growing complexity.

## Communicating and Excommunicating the Primal

Words, as we know, do not constitute the only language. The complex experiences of spirit can be expressed in many symbolic forms: pictures and images, sculpture, music and movement, dress, protocol, complex procedures and repetitive acts, rules, kinship expectations, and more. Words, objects, rites, rituals, chants, stories, songs, status, and statues—all may be symbols for what cannot be uttered in ordinary language because it exists "at the prime," at the first or most profound level of awareness, beyond common speech.

Religious language, verbal and nonverbal, amounts then to a kind of "signing"; its characters represent *primal* conceptualizations. Simple metaphors are fashioned to meet a complex need and a potentially salutary purpose: to render accessible a realm of meaning that would otherwise be impenetrable, too elusive for ordinary human understanding. Which character or metaphor is adopted is determined by the preference of the individual or the group based on how well it represents the concept intended and how it resonates within experience. The critique of such metaphors, therefore, must be based not on cognitive evidence, but on the relative accuracy with which the term or image captures the experience it is meant to portray. Its material "truth" is not at issue. It matters little, even if it could be determined, whether Buddha, the human, lived and walked and performed the acts ascribed to him. What is important is whether and to what degree the idea of the Buddha captures the concept and meets the needs for which it was created. It makes little sense to ask whether God or a god exists, not because it does not exist, nor, in fact, because it does. *Exists* in the material sense is not the appropriate concept to apply here. *Serves* or *suffices* would be better terms. Does the concept *God*, however it might be defined, serve the need that is felt now, at this moment, by this person or community?

This is slippery business, to be sure. It is not that words like *real* and *unreal*, *true* and *false* are meaningless. Rather, they must be radically reinterpreted in each context. Of course, such interpretations and reinterpretations carry risk.

The advantages of religious signing are clear. It allows us to express and communicate crucial experience that would otherwise remain unspoken. The dangers, however, are even more obvious. The fluidity of meaning entailed by such complex symbolizing lends itself not only to adaptability, but to confusion, and that in turn can be fertile ground for manipulation and, in the wrong hands, for oppression.

As dynamic entities, alive in their way, the meanings of symbols may shift and move as do the experiences they represent: Going to my altar, rattled, scattered, needing strength, I close my eyes and hear myself thinking, "Let me have courage." At one time, I experience, I feel, I create a listener to my petition, the Mother, and She is brimming with power, more than sufficient for Her work and mine. At another time, it is my Sister I make to listen. For me She is no less the Universe, but like me She is limited in strength, limited in options; in fact, it is the very boundedness that we share that yields the comfort and support I require. At other times, neither Mother nor Sister, nor Father, nor even Nature itself listens, but rather the Silence, White Noise, the Allness, and if I can receive It, It is as meaningful, as instructive and strengthening as the Person I might have created or encountered.

I create my symbols out of the alphabet in my mind, out of my experience, my need, and intention, but they are not always the same; and I do not always create them consciously. Sometimes my symbols take me by surprise, catch me off guard, even throw me off center. Once, under hypnosis, I had an image of being on an icy, snowy plain and seeing the face of a wolf looking down at me intently. I had the distinct thought that the wolf was caring for me, that she was my mother, and that I owed her love and respect. Indeed, I did feel love for her. Later, I could not interpret the image; I did not know what to make of it except that I felt it intensely and I believed it had important meaning. Should symbols present themselves as if they had been created elsewhere, they must be culled for latent meaning. Perplexed, I might wonder, what am I saying to myself? What is Life telling me? What do I know that I have not raised to awareness? What do I believe that needs correction, refinement, or reflection?

Of course, symbols can be misread for many reasons: parts of myself in living conflict with other parts, signs incompatible with one another, shifts in insight I had not noted, subtleties of feeling may all create confusion within me.

If I become careless in my reading or misreading of metaphors, I may fail to understand or remember what I am about—that together with Life, I am the author of my signs, that they serve me rather than the other way around, and that they must be treated with careful attention and respect or they may become unhealthy, weak or, worse yet, contaminated. Symbols improperly used may create more blindness than light. Metaphors, standing very close to material realities, may be mistaken for material realities, their mythic, "fictive" character forgotten.

If confusion within the self is a danger, it is no less so among people. Communication of ordinary ideas is replete with the risk of misunderstanding; in this regard, it is as though we suffer the torments of Babel! Left to our own devices, perhaps, with perfectly good will, we might resolve the plague of confusion, within ourselves and between us. Add one morsel of malevolence, any inclination toward manipulation or control, and only the strongest or luckiest can resist the evils that can arise.

Whole communities as well as individuals can create religious symbols. Representing not only personal attempts at life resolution but communal experience, communal consciousness, spiritual metaphors emerge not simply from individual members of society thinking and creating independently, but from the group as a whole, responding inter-collectively to circumstances of its existence. These religious signs become expressions of the collective ethos. Frequently they carry the mind-set of the prevailing power elite. As such they are returned to the group and now imposed upon all, as part of the group world-view, through socialization and enculturation.

People tend to fall in love with their symbols, to reify them, and thus to idolize them. Frequently they forget or choose not to acknowledge the fictive nature of the symbols they themselves have created. For public symbols created by and received from the community, in patriarchy especially, it is an article of faith that the fabrication not be acknowledged.

For minorities, eccentrics, or outsiders, the imposition of religious meanings to signs can be particularly catastrophic because there is a strong possibility that the signs will not fit their lives. If the signs do not fit, if they contradict, nullify, or omit personal experience, they not only fail to serve, they demolish spirit. More than any other oppression, spiritual chauvinism chokes. Because experience of the spirit is more profound, more life-defining than any other, spiritual enslavement is more debilitating than any other.

In patriarchal societies, of course, this is exactly what happens. The signs evolved by the power-carriers have become universalized, reified, and made exclusive: "I am the Lord, thy God, . . . thou shalt have no other God before me" (Exodus 20:2–3). People, even those disfranchised by the patriarchal system, have been trained to lionize the prevailing signs, to disparage all others, and to criminalize difference. When women, deeply dispossessed, are made prisoners by signs that are not our own, it engenders resistance to new signs forming within ourselves which might set us free.

## Women's Spirits and Men's Religion: The Signs Did Not Fit

Sunday morning. I had slept in. Relishing a day with few obligations, I let myself wake slowly, opening one eye, then the other, measuring the amount of light that was seeping into my room from behind the window shade, trying to judge how pretty a day was waiting for me and how quickly I should rise to meet it. Deciding to poke, I lay a few moments longer, then turned drowsily toward the table near my bed to check the clock. As I moved, I became aware of a warm wetness between my legs and beneath me. Like a properly housebroken puppy, I reacted at once: Oh, no! My period. I wasn't due yet. What a mess! Oh, damn!

I whined and crabbed and clucked as I had seen my mother do a hundred times before, years ago when I had lived in her house. Always, when she had "the curse," she would sit in the big kitchen chair beside the stove and, rocking back and forth, she would hold her stomach and groan. When I "came around," I had not felt as much pain as she had, but, like a dutiful daughter, I did what was expected: I grunted and grimaced and complained, displayed the proper disgust for all the necessary apparatus—belts, pads, pins, and such—and maintained a level of secrecy that would have impressed the CIA.

At 15, when I had my first period, I was pleased, proud to be a woman at last, an adult, one of the girls. I could telephone Jeanie and Marian and whisper that I had "gotten a letter from a girl friend," just as they did. (In the 1950s, young women didn't even utter the words among themselves, among close friends.) I could refuse to take a shower after gym class (in 1955 everyone knew it was dangerous to get your hair wet when you were . . .), and I could (blush) find excuses not to go swimming with the rest of the gang.

My mother too had been pleased. After all, I had been "late," older than usual, and she had worried that "oh-my-god-what-if-Sheila-couldn't-have-children?" Still living out of her roots in the small Austrian village where she was born, she had called every aunt, cousin, and woman friend she knew to spread (very decorously, of course) the good news.

To mark the event, my mother delivered the requisite lecture: "Now, Sheila, this means you're a big girl, and you have to . . . uh . . . be careful. Not that I mean you aren't good . . . I know you're a good girl. But, you know, this means, uh. . . ." A new tack: "We keep the napkins here, on the top of the closet in the back, behind the toilet paper" (where the men of the family never ventured). "This is the belt that holds it on. It goes here like this, around here, under there, pinned to this, and when you change, you wrap the old pad in toilet paper, like this, then in newspaper; fold it several times so it stays closed. Don't leave it in the bathroom waste basket because it will *smell*." (Worse than . . . ?) "Take it to the big garbage pail outside behind the garage and close the lid tight." (So it can't get away?) . . . and don't let your father or brother see. If you need to buy a new box of pads, go to the store when Mrs. R. is there, not Mr. R., and ask her for Modess when she's alone." Mrs. R. had indeed been discrete, giving and getting in hushed tones, wrapping the box in a paper bag and placing that one in a larger one, disguising as best she could that so distinctive package. Her efforts rarely succeeded, and I was always left to hide it as best I could beneath my coat, lurking along in the shadows as I hurried home and into the house (by the back door, closest to the bathroom). It was a far less funny drama then than it is now in memory.

Soon after leaving my mother's house, I had relinquished most of the charade, the ceremony of hiding, the outward groaning and apologies—at least in my head. Yet more than twenty years later, in my own home, quite alone, here I was, daughter of Miriam, the daughter of Esther, a daughter of patriarchy, responding to stimulus as prescribed, following the proper cues: "Ugh, what a mess! Oh, the sheets are ruined (?). I've got to get to the bathroom. Omigod, what if I get blood on the rug? It'll never come up. Ugh. Ick. Damn."

Cupping one hand between my legs, I hobbled to the bathroom and the safety of the tile floor. It was a gusher. Dumping my nightgown in the tub, I went to the business of cleaning up. What first? The potty or the sink? The sink. Clean your . . . ugh . . . hands. They're full of. . . . I reached for the faucet with my "cleaner" hand, watching the other (for signs of decay?), making sure not to touch anything. I looked down. My hand was covered with red. I stopped. I just stopped. I looked. Standing there, naked, blood trickling down my thighs, not staring or inspecting or analyzing or anything complex, I just looked.

Time shifted, and I was in another bathroom in another day, during my married-to-L time, flushing the red down the toilet. I was pained, grieving and disappointed because the red told me that I wasn't pregnant, again, and I wanted so much to be. Every red said no.

Red and pregnancy. Red and babies. They meant each other. They mean each other.

Flash. Lightening bolt. Back to Sunday morning, to red in my hand. Red and pregnancy. Red and babies. Red and Life! Blood and Life. They mean each other. I looked again. I looked anew. This time I did inspect. Blood. Darker, thicker, slightly viscous, but blood. I smeared it between my fingers, raised it to my nose to smell. No "stink." Nothing that needed to be "deodorized." Just blood. The same stuff that spills from the rest of me when my skin is opened. If I cut my hand, would I squeal and grimace and guard the floor from pollution? From the stuff of Life? I am disgusted with the flow of Life, because it comes from between my legs, from my own vagina?!

A parade of obscenities marched through my head: the pads in the top of the closet, in the back, behind . . . the drugstore embarrassments, the synagogue humiliations, my mother sharing her secrecy, my father who (very decently) never spoke of it, my "orthodox" uncle, refusing my handshake in the synagogue, pulling back his hand from my contamination—taboo, taboo. The blood of Life, reviled, ridiculed.

I started to cry, almost to wail, almost to howl. Some measure of feminist consciousness had been part of me even in my childhood, to be crystallized years later as a politic, but this, this level of experiential recognition was different—deeper, wrenching, powerful in the extreme.

I cried, first pain, then relief, then rage, fury. "You bastards," I hurled, "you fuckers, you sneer and growl and make your damn rules. How dare you?"

How dare they malign FEMALE, how dare they malign the symbol of Life, the source, the center, the beginning? How dare they try to separate me from me, from a portion of myself that is uniquely female, that marks me as woman? To hate this is to hate me, to hate the womanness of me, to hate women, to hate what we are, let alone what we can do. We, women, collectively, make life. We are Life. And they revile it? For what? For themselves, for their hatred of us, their fear of us, for their inability to match this capacity, for their need to control and direct it . . . us, for their own self-glorification, for power for themselves and the power of their gods, for God . . . the Father . . .

Thunderbolt again. God the Father? Fathers don't have periods, they don't make blood, and they don't make babies. They partly make pregnant, but they don't make babies. Not never. Not no time. Not no species. Women make babies. We make Life. Earth makes Life. Universe makes Life. Life makes life. God, if you are to have one, would not be a father; it would be a MOTHER! *God is a woman*, damn it, like me. She's a sister, my sister. We're alike in this. We make living things. If you want a deity, try this one on for size: God the Mother–Sister. That had a ring to it. It certainly rang my bell!

I started to laugh (to hell with crying). I laughed and laughed and laughed some more and never gave a damn that I was bleeding all over the floor.

Not their words. Mine. Not their experience, Mine. Not their consciousness, Mine. Not their awareness, Ours. Not their (S)spirit, Ours. Not their signs, Ours!

Where in all their books could we find signs for this?
Not possible. You had to be there.

### Religion: Why Speak the Word?

For many feminists, memories of religion are memories of alienation and servitude. For those of us who fled, religion had functioned as the worst kind of binding, as an unfriendly master we had been expected to serve and revere. Our religions and the people who administered them told us how to behave and what to think, how to make judgments, what to choose, and when to defer. The authority of religion over our conceptual lives and our behavior was final and absolute. In its rigid exclusivity, its nice demarcations of social groups, it proposed to determine who was friend and who was enemy, whom we might seek out and who must be shunned. (These are good people, those are bad; these are right, those are wrong; these are "ours," those are not.) As source of all Truth, religion was primary arbiter in matters of conscience and morality. (Thou shalt not disobey thy parents—even if every fiber of life and thought judge them wrong; thou shalt not enjoy thy body—regardless of how sane it seems to do so; thou shalt not doubt God or priests or book—for this you will suffer death or hell or both or worse.)

Even more than "God," religion ruled; ours was to serve and thus to garner our due measure of approval, respectability, security (such as it was), and self-esteem. Not to conform ourselves to religious expectation was to invite rejection, slurs on our "reputation," and not a little physical risk.

A bumper sticker on the rear of a pick-up truck parked outside a tavern in southern Missouri proclaimed in bold letters:

God said it.
I believe it.
And that's the end of it.

I felt cold when I saw it, because it undoubtedly implied something to the effect of, "and I and we believe better than you, and if you don't think so, keep your mouth shut, because if we catch you alone, we're gonna beat your ass!" What is more, in my memory such violent insistence on conformity applied even more to women than to men, and the punishment for deviation was far more severe.

It has been suggested, even by those who are very positively oriented toward spirituality, that it would be more judicious for a project like this book to avoid the term *religion* altogether and opt for some more neutral term that would be less offensive. They argue that the hostility many people, especially feminists and other activists, feel for religion would contaminate both the ideas I wish to preserve and the chances those ideas might have for a fair hearing.

In fact, it is a strong argument. Many activists often have a negative knee-jerk reaction to the very idea of religion. Although this
is an inappropriate response, it is understandable and hard to
counter; and it makes the task of encouraging a reconsideration of
religion extraordinarily difficult.

Yet there is an equal risk in abandoning the language of religion
precisely because of the history and the associations it has developed. Could it not be argued that religion *as religion* must not be
relinquished just because it carries such authority, just because of
the respect it engenders, because of the magnitude of its themes?
For centuries unknown, the most crucial elements of human existence have fallen under the purview of religion—the setting of values and ideals, the design of primal metaphors, the arbitration of
morality, the call to the deep mind, the dispensing of sacred rites.
For the most of the population these things are still centered in
religion and will never be seen anywhere else. Are not these aspects of life far too significant to ignore or to leave in the hands of
the twisted, the ignorant, and the power-hungry? Not to "take over"
religion in mean spiritedness so the thugs will not have it, but with
all authenticity, we must face these matters and cleanse, clarify, and
refine these ideas, because they reflect a rich and vital portion of
human experience that does persist, will persist, and should persist.

Because what properly belongs to religion profoundly and per-
vasively affects our lives, and because it holds positive possibilities
for society, the power that religion as religion carries must be tapped
and turned to human good. If the term religion evokes associations
of awe, reverence, and respect, then that is the very best reason to
use it in the service of Life.

I am reminded of an incident that took place several years ago
at a conference on feminist scholarship. A professor of literature,
also a Roman Catholic nun and a director of a women's studies
program, had delivered a paper on sexism in literary criticism. The
piece was insightful and was very well received by the audience.
During the discussion period that followed, the professor revealed
a more radically feminist orientation than she had in her paper.
Perplexed by the combination of a strong feminist consciousness and
an equally committed Catholicism, the students abandoned the subject of literary criticism to question the woman, to challenge her
about her religious identification. She stoutly defended that identification, arguing that for her the sacraments were ultimately important, more so than the matter of who administered them. Dismayed

and not a little frustrated, one young woman asked, "How can you tolerate remaining in a church so populated by sexist oppressors?" "It's *my* church," the nun answered. "Let them leave. Why should I?"

The incident raises a vital feminist issue, that of the "proprietorship" of ideas, or knowledge. Who, if anyone, *owns* ideas? Are squatters' rights to be granted to those who get there first and lay claim to them by usage? If religion and many of its terms and concepts—*sacred, holy, sacrament, deity, worship, grace*—have been kidnapped and pressed into service by the ultimate pirates, must they languish forever in captivity? It is said that possession is nine-tenths of the law. Surely that principle does not apply to ideas!

The feminist nun was defending her right to the use and interpretation of certain concepts that were meaningful to her, the idea of the holy, the sanctity of sacrament, the relevance to her life of Jesus, in fact of Christianity, particularly Roman Catholicism. Regardless of whether we experience the sacred as she did, the force and the reasonableness of her presupposition are clear: the religion, if not the power structure, is no less hers because it has been (illegitimately) appropriated by others.

We may make the same analysis of all religion. It does not belong to the patriarchs, no matter how strong their claims to the contrary. Why should it be surrendered to them? Why should we freely grant them this one more larceny without resistance?

Just because we are appalled by the errors of the "world's great religions," we must not commit an equally egregious error. We must not allow the assumption that patriarchy's treatment of religion is the only possible treatment. To do so would be to commit the androcentric fallacy: the error of treating masculinist perspectives as universals.

Rather than quit religion, we need to recover it and to create for it a different and better treatment than it has been given—one in which life and humanity are served by its content and not the other way around. We need to construct a sense of religion that serves people, and not one in which people are the servants of priests and books. Service to people's living needs is the proper and probably original intention for religion. Patriarchy's religions become catastrophic when the adherents commit terrible sins: they steal people's spiritual birthright; they gain power over people by lying, they appropriate their energy and their goods; they manipulate human affairs in order to gain the vilest political ends; they abuse trust and exploit the weakness of those who come seeking help.

It is not the exercise of power over individuals that is the province of religion, but the empowerment of individuals to define and gain their own liberation.

## Notes

1. Barbara G. Walker, *The Woman's Encyclopedia of Myths and Secrets* (San Francisco: Harper and Row, 1983), p. 850; following Joseph Campbell, *The Masks of God: Oriental Mythology* (New York: Viking Press, 1962).

2. Harvey J. Schwartz, M.D., quoted in Lynne De Spelder and Albert Strickland, *The Last Dance* (Palo Alto, Calif.: Mayfield Publishing Company, 1983), p. 329.

3. William James, *The Varieties of Religious Experience: A Study in Human Nature* (New York: Collier Books, 1961), p. 45.

4. Mary Daly, *Beyond God the Father: Toward a Philosophy of Women's Liberation* (Boston: Beacon Press, 1973), pp. 33*ff*. Daly refers to God as "the Holy Verb, to be."

5. James, "Lecture 2," *passim*, pp. 47-56.

6. Ibid., p. 59.

7. "Preface," J. J. Bachofen, *Myth, Religion and Mother Right*, translated by Ralph Manheim (London: Routledge and Kegan Paul, 1967), p. xii.

8. "Credo quia absurdum est." Rendered: "The fact is certain because it is impossible." Quoted in H. A. Wolfson, *The Philosophy of the Church Fathers* (Cambridge, Mass.: Harvard University Press, 1956), Vol. I, p. 103.

9. See, for example, Jamake Highwater, *The Primal Mind: Vision and Reality in Indian America* (New York: New American Library, 1982).

10. Quoted by Joseph Campbell, "Introduction," in Bachofen, *Myth, Religion and Mother Right*, p. xiv.

11. Ibid.

12. "Symbol and Myth" in *Myth, Religion and Mother Right*, p. 48.

# Part Two

# CHAPTER FOUR

# A Feminist/Pagan Testimony

## *Confession*

I am a Pagan, I said to myself with some surprise. Years ago it came as a thought unbidden, the realization that what I had come to believe might have a name, Paganism. It was not an unpleasant thought at all, but it bewildered me. On the conscious level, at least, I had only the sketchiest notion of what a Pagan was; what is more, like most other people in Western culture, I was beset with all the usual stereotypes and associations.

My grandmother's telling and retelling of the ancient stories from the Old Testament provided the earliest images I had of "pagans": evil peoples, not among God's Chosen, who worshiped women and idols, who cowered before false and fantastic deities in the likenesses of beasts, who were led by cruel temptresses ("priestesses"), who practiced unspecified but vile abominations, and who sacrificed living children to the fire.

In my head were Tarzan stories and B-grade movies that provided additional images—half-clad, blood-crazy natives, chanting and twisting to banging drums. In college, "explanatory" notes in the margins of literature texts conjured up pictures of satyrs and demigods, of weird mythological beings, and the wonderfully imaginative but dubious events of mythical times. The total effect was an image of Paganism that included aboriginal ignorance affixed to sexual excess, affixed to cruelty and violence, affixed to total otherness from civilized society and the One True God.

Such a singularly negative image of Paganism, having existed in popular lore relatively unadulterated for centuries, was largely present in my own understanding; yet oddly, somehow what was important and positive in Paganism had managed to survive in me as well, at least at some level of my awareness. Peaceful afternoons in the Egyptian rooms of New York's Metropolitan Museum of Art had left their mark upon me. So had the ancient myths of Greek and Latin literature, the art of Crete, the "Venus" figures of prehistory. The tales of the European "witches" had always held for me not horror, but fascination and appeal: I did not believe a word of the calumny; I was drawn to the magical, uncontrolled women going about their ancient activities. I grieved for their murder. I took it personally. Perhaps it was their opposition to everything I experienced as oppressive in the traditional religions that made them call up for me the feelings that later became part of my Pagan sentiments. Perhaps it was their supposed familiarity with nature's gifts, their skill at midwifery and herbal medicine, perhaps their religious ceremonies held outside, at night, timed with the cycles of the moon. Perhaps it was the portrayal of them being on intimate terms with animals, whom I had always respected and loved.

Why, from what source, came the idea that I was "Pagan"? Did the images precede, or had the sentiments come first, the visions and values that make the world meaningful for me? Perhaps they were there from the beginning, and later I came to realize that they had a name, a history, and that they were shared by others.

The adoption of the identity, Pagan, however it came to be, was nonetheless experienced as important and pressing: I set out to find with greater clarity what Paganism was.

I began by scanning the "word books," which proved to be close to fruitless:

*American Heritage Dictionary*

pagan n. 1. A person who is not a Christian, Moslem, or Jew; heathen. 2. One who has no religion. 3. A non-Christian. 4. A hedonist . . . Lat., country-dweller < *pagus*, country.

*Merriam Webster*
The same.

*Roget's International Thesaurus*[1]
pagan n. 984.20

(unbeliever 485.4; 989.4)

(idolater 991.5)

984. Heterodoxy, Sectarianism

20. pagan, heathen; non-Christian, non-Mohammedan, non-Jew, gentile, infidel, paynim [arch.], *giaour* [Turk.], Kaffir [Moham.]; zendik, zendician, zendikite [all Moham.]; henotheist, pantheist, polytheist; animist; unbeliever etc. (irreligionist) 989.4; idolater, etc. 991.5.

What was here was only a whisper of what I was seeking. Worse—this image seemed to come inside out, like the reflection in a mirror: non-[Patriarchal], infidel, henotheist, animist, hedonist . . . Paganism was a negation: it was *not* one of the "world's great religions," *not* believing, *not* faithful, *not* religious. Moreover, Paganism was represented as sin, and I clearly sensed virtue.

I queried those of my colleagues who might have known something about it, those in literature, history, ancient language, classical philosophy, but they only repeated what the word books had said and reiterated the definitions that appeared in the margins of their texts. Another round of investigation proved to be futile.

The further I searched the clearer it became that Paganism as a serious, living orientation, worthy of respect and even philosophical debate, had succumbed to the suppression of the ages. In the early 1970s, when I began my search, some pagan religions were practiced by only a very few (mostly reviled, frequently secret) scattered groups, or they were studied by a diminishing number of esoteric scholars.

Just a few years later, by the mid-1970s, I found myself in company with others. Apparently what had happened to me, in me, had happened to others; the forces that had brought me to this turn in my life were at work in other quarters as well. Gender scholars, feminist theologians, women activists, poets, philosophers, psychologists, anthropologists and others began to talk about, write about, and meditate about "the Goddess," who predominated in ancient traditions. From then on there was rapid development in discovering and recreating a world-view that would be called Pagan.

Yet even now affirming a Pagan perspective is difficult. In popular society Paganism as an alternative to traditional religion is fraught with malignant associations and met with derision or fear. Those who dare to profess it openly or even suggest affinity with it (by polytheistic tendencies or interest in female deity) are advised by friends to change their language or risk offending. Enemies, of course, are nearly hysterical with anxiety; of late, Satan (a child of Christianity) has made a comeback.

Yet Paganism ignored is a powerful resource lost. It conceives of people and gender quite differently from an androcentric world-view, and it is a far more salutary philosophy of life than any of those widely approved today. Further, against the backdrop of this ancient and profoundly different orientation to life, the patriarchal mind-set and its consequences become sharply visible.

## Heritage

One tradition has it that the *pagani* were the bumpkins of Rome. (In Latin the word *pagus* denotes a village or country district, *Cassell's Latin Dictionary*.) Living as they did outside the city, removed from political power and fashion, country people were less apt to adopt whatever religion currently prevailed in the state; they were more apt to keep to the "old ways," grounding divinity in nature instead of in people (as did the city elite), and so they appeared ignorant and unsophisticated. As Christianity established itself in the Roman Empire and tolerated no other religions, the *pagani* or pagans came to be seen not only as ignorant but as obdurate, and therefore anathema.[2]

Following this tradition, the evolution of the term Pagan has established a threefold meaning: (1) Pagans are outsiders, removed from the seat of power and to some degree in opposition to it. They are the ultimate "others," the not-Christian, not-Moslem, not-Jew, not-whatever established ideology prevails. (2) Because of their "otherness," Pagans are reviled by the "insiders" of the community, as heathens or worse. (3) Pagans are country dwellers, not necessarily living physically in the country, but living there spiritually. For Pagans nature and its processes manifest the eternal truths and are, therefore, the seat of the sacred.

Of course, this history represents only the barest introduction to Paganism, for it is a richly multifaceted orientation that allows for a wide range of interpretations. As understood today, Paganism is religion in all its dimensions: it provides a representation of reality, a world-view, and an orientation to life; a ground of values and morality; a metaphor for meaningfulness; and a home for all the stories, celebrations, dramas, and rituals that people may use to petition an otherwise intractable reality. What is more, Paganism is a particular kind of religion, for although it has extraordinary tolerance of diversity, it has a distinctive, definable core: It is life-loving, and it is positively rooted in concrete, this-worldly existence.

Paganism as it appears in feminist circles is a call to the fullness of life, a call to embrace with zest and anticipation all the goodness that this world, this existence offers—beauty, pleasure, kindness, laughter, loftiness, creativity, friendship. Contrary to the licentiousness it is believed to profess, it does not deny the need for restraint, responsibility, obligation, and other forms of discipline, but views them as servants of joy and harmony, not as ends in themselves.

To be Pagan is to celebrate this world, this reality, all of it in totality, the enduring and the transient, the wonderful and the terrible, creation and destruction. It is to find the eternal truths manifested in what is present to us in this world, without the need to posit exotic realms of being and authority above and radically separate from us. It is to believe that the "mundane" and "trivial"* events of concrete life contain and reflect the wonders and mysteries of Spirit. The divine, the deities, reside here with us, in us. If we would know them, we need to pay attention to what is around us and learn to live in harmony with the world we inhabit.

More even than a love for life, Paganism is a "falling in love" with life. In all the wild intensity that phrase connotes, in that degree of feeling and commitment, is all the depth and dimension for which the spirit yearns. To be in love is to be a little crazy with the beloved, to delight in the delightful, but also to come to terms with the ugly, not to pardon imperfection or to give it free ground, but to accept what cannot be changed so that we may not lose the whole.

Paganism is a call to *be*, to assert and cherish the will to survive, not only in others but in the self as well. It grants respect to the children of Nature as worthy in themselves, not because they are the reflection or servants of some alien power, but because they are a part of the power of All-being. Self-hatred is wholly abhorrent, as is the thesis that humanity, in its stumbling imperfection, is somehow irredeemably stained. What sin there may be that is done by humans requires human reparation, but wrong-doing does not

---

* *Mundane*: from the Latin *mundus*, world (*AHD*). Trivial: from the Latin *trivialis*, of the crossroads, hence, ordinary (*Cassell's Latin Dictionary*).

demonstrate a universal magic flaw, only the mistakes or offenses of ordinary people. Autonomy and pride stand side by side in Paganism with humble respect for life and all its creatures.

Paganism values diversity. Order rests on integration rather than on control or hierarchy. Because reality presents itself in multiformity, truth is perceived to be polychromatic. No incompatibility resides in cherishing both spirit and body, experience and reason, immediacy and transcendence, change and eternality, self and community. Deity may be characterized as a whole collection of Beings, metaphors for the profound realities of existence, or as Being Itself, the Process that contains all process(es). The dualities that torment the patriarchs present no difficulty for Pagans, for in this world-view dualities and pluralities form not oppositions, but glistening possibilities. In place of the quest for One Absolute and Supreme Truth, which is a self-inflicted delusion, Pagans prefer to accommodate ambiguity and flow. The straight line is preempted by circles, cycles, and spirals.

Ethics and morality for Pagans are ultimately grounded in living experience, not in abstractions externally wrought and imposed. Nothing could be more monstrous, in conception or consequence, than lodging rightness and wrongness in disembodied logic. We are kind or honest because we care, love, or empathize, that is, because we *feel*. Although intelligent reflection helps us to understand the consequences of our actions, without the subjective *experience of connectedness* with others, no rational or irrational gymnastics, no legal obligation, short of force, can induce a person to be fundamentally decent. In values, reason serves feelings. The essential question for ethics, then, is how to induce a culture of caring.

For Paganism, as for some other religions, no chasm separates religious life from material life. Conflicts between spiritual existence and material existence (which essentially are facets of the same reality) must be resolved not by limiting one or the other, or giving precedence to either, but by integrating and recognizing their oneness, by subsuming both under one reality, which is the wholesome experiencing of life for the self in connection with all.

To be Pagan is to be

Life-affirming
Earth-loving
Bound to the Mother
Joyous
Animal-knowing
Celebratory
Enchanted
Tolerant
Magical
Natural
Immediate
Ecstatic
Self-loving
Harmonious
Sensing
Integrated
Connected
Mystical

In love with cycles and seasons

## Notes

1. *Roget's International Thesaurus*, (New York: Thomas Y. Crowell, 1946).

2. See "Paganism," in Walker, *The Woman's Encyclopedia of Myths and Secrets* or Margot Adler, *Drawing Down the Moon: Witches, Druids, Goddess-Worshippers and Other Pagans in America Today* (New York: Viking, 1979), p. 9.

# Worth-Ship

## Invocation

Goddesses and Gods:  Nameless Ones,
　　Guardians, Keepers of Life,
Goddesses and Gods:  Who hold the sacred words,
　　Who speak in magic tongue
Goddesses and Gods:  Friends and Furies,
　　Known and not yet known,
Goddesses and Gods:  Spirit and spirits,
　　Hear me.
　　I call upon You.

I come to the stillness and call upon You.
I come to the Dark and call upon You.
I come to the Light and call upon You.
　　I form Your names.

My lips form Your names.
My blood forms Your names.
My dreams form Your names.
　　I come before You.

In yearning I come before You.
In power I come before You.
In reverence I come before You.
In service I come before You.

　　Mother,
Your daughter entreats You to this place
Your friend and sister entreats You.
　　I come to speak Your worthship.
　　Bliss this task.

With Your wisdom, bliss this task.
With Your beauty, bliss this task.
With Your presence, bliss this task.

　　Be here.

## Exorcism

Malignities
    Malefactors:
Woman-killers,
Self-killers,
    Be gone!

Sins of the Narrowness,
Sins of Mars,
Sins of the Father(s),
    Be gone!

Be we cleansed
    of your hatred,
Be we cleansed
    of your madness,
Be we cleansed
    of your blemish,
Be we cleansed.

    Deformities
We will suffer you no more.
    Get you gone!

## Prayer

Spirit of Life, come into me.

Spirit of Courage, come into me.

Spirit of Beauty, come into me.

Spirit of Power, come into me.

Spirit of Love, come into me.

Spirit of Joy, come into me.

Spirit of Knowing, come into me.

Spirit of Peace, come into me.

Spirit, come into me.

Mother/Sister, come into me.

That I may be quiet.

That I may hear.

That I might speak with Your voice.

That I might be a conduit for Spirit.

# Musings, Memories,
## and Messages

## *Witness*

Testimony, at last. A chance to witness. I have been so looking forward to writing the "poetry," the speaking from the soul. I have been waiting for the freedom, the joy of speaking out loud the Names and the Visions so long restrained by academic etiquette: Caution, Professor, remember what you are. Toughen your objectivity; brace your "rigor"; keep your qualifications up, or they'll have you. Don't overstate, don't understate, don't misstate. For that matter, don't state at all. It isn't done. It is not the business of professors to profess. And a woman? Not her place. Not her place at all.

But this *is* my place. Here in these pages I am my own, and I can dance to my own rhythms. It is for me to decide what "biases" to answer or answer for, what offenses truly offend, what convictions stand or stand convicted. Those who read this book do so by their own choice; they may enter this space or go at will, so I may furnish it as I choose.

And I choose Goddesses and Gods, songs of the Earth, conferences with the Mother, moments loving her loving me.

## Meditation: Inspiration

*There has been so much anticipation of this time, this writing, yet there is only silence. For days I have sat at this desk, "clutching," staring down at blank yellow paper, this intimidating, reproachful, empty pad. Much as I press, it will not yield. It fairly dares me to speak.*

I pick up my pen and scribble, *blue marks on yellow, nothing more: words, words, words.*

*Wrong. It's all wrong, not at all what I had in mind. Scribble some more. Scratch for the words. Struggle, strain. But it's wrong. Again wrong. Tear it up, start again. Tear it up, start again. Crumple the yellow paper and drop it all around. The floor is a garden of garbage.*

I pace the floor, the knot in my stomach tightening, the knot in my head even more. *Sit down. Try it again.* I feel blind, clouded. I cannot see the thoughts for the words. *More scribbling, more garbage. How does my garden grow?*

Out of frustration, vexation, the knot in my stomach (head?), I think to myself, perhaps I will take some time off. Even through the guilt—deserting the work!—I am prepared to admit that this is (I am) not working.

Outside, yellow July is spilling itself over the landscape, over the lawns and the field across the street, atop the roofs, and on the lacy weeds and wildflowers. The air is warm, luxuriant, and irresistibly inviting. Day after day I have been at war with myself, battling to keep to my desk, to resist the summer, to work. Longingly, I have watched the children and the dogs, even the dizzy, buzzing bugs, wanting to be where they are.

What the hell, I think, nothing happening in here. Just half an hour, I lie to myself, just a little while.

I surrender to the day, haltingly, almost grudgingly, feeling like a sinner.

Outside I go, into the yellow heat, taking my pad and pen with me, *just (to expiate the sin) in case.* The chair in the back yard, slightly tattered, listing to one side, provides a familiar couch. I lie back, my face to the sun, delighted with it despite myself. The sky is absolutely bright, shimmering. Sharp, intense, the colors present themselves, blue, green, brown, yellow. Here and there birds skitter along the grass with their goofy two-legged hop or perch on the roof tops whistling out their messages and answering others. Bees and flies rocket themselves through the air, buzzing in and out of the bushes. Crickets call a steady hum, varying only in rhythm and intensity. The breeze, the rustling leaves, birdsong, and insect voices play to one another in wonderful cacophony (and yet it is quiet, still).

At last I let go—of head, of hard-place, of reason, and of will. The creatures' voices mesmerize me into succumbing, and I join them in my creature self. Creature-knowing rises in me. Like the rabbit and the deer, transfixed, utterly still, listening to the words of twig and scent, I understand.

She comes for me. Bug and bush, heat, wind, light, they are Her voice. They speak of Her, for Her; they whisper and I hear: She croons to me, as my grandmother did years ago, "Be quiet, foolish child, be still and listen."

I become still. The sun floods in on me, making love to me with its heat. The air radiates nourishment, and I take it in, gratefully.

After a time, (S)spirit calls mind. My eyes open(ed), I pick up pen and pad and begin to form words. Inspired,* I write and write and write, but I do not speak—She does.

She (the Mother, the Source, She who is Life, All Being) breaths upon me with Her creation (Her Be-ing), and I take it inside as it takes me. We touch, She and I; we are in league, in communion (co-union). Because we are inside one another, there is no space between us, no distance between my being and Hers, my spirit (core, center, self) and Hers, the truth of me and the Truth of Her. She is revealed.† The veil is pulled away, the curtain, *my* curtain, born of *my* blindness (She is always visible); the covering that stood between us has been drawn back and I can see.

---

*Inspiration: "Stimulation of the mind or emotions to a high level of feeling or activity." Inspire . . . from the Latin "*inspirare*: *in-*, into + *spirare*, to breathe."
—transitive: "Archaic. a. To breathe upon. b. To breathe life into" (*AHD*). *To instill the vital, animating spark of vitality.*
—intransitive: "To inhale" (*AHD*). *To bring within the spirit, the breath of life, the core of lived being.*
†Revelation: " . . . a dramatic disclosure of something not previously known or realized. . . . *Theol*. A manifestation of divine will or truth." Reveal . . . from the Latin "*re-* (reversal) + *velare*, to cover" (out of "*velum*, veil") (*AHD*). *Velum*: "a covering, awning, curtain" (*Cassell's Latin Dictionary*).

There is often such a rift between


doing    and

being.



We are taught:

to "be" (to have a right to be), we must first

"do" (accomplish, meet obligations, complete

tasks and expectations).



What ***doing*** of any value can be wrought by a creature who ***is***
not?


To *be*, completely, to experience myself and the moment

fully, is to be integrated, grounded, alert.

From such *being*, flows such *doing*.



Time is too precious to consent to slavery.

## *Meditation: The Mother Calls*

Trance time again. The Mother calls. I feel myself drawing to Her (being drawn?). Welcome. She is well come. Always it is welcome, this joining, this floating in to Her.

The common world retreats as real-life rises. This plane of plastic and metal appears increasingly bizarre in its not-life. Feeling alien in it (alienated?), I dangle between the worlds. Uncertain. Hesitant.

. . . Surrender.

Mother Life, I seek You. Find me. Touch me. Teach me. I would be found. I would know you.

(She is never silent. Rather, I am deaf.)

It is Power time. I am in my Blood. She breathes into me. Gratia. Gratia.

## *Seeking Spirit*

How difficult it is to speak of Spirit, so elusive, so fragile. Must we, should we come to it dragging our usual freight—methodologies and systems, nice distinctions, tight arguments, our little black bags of scholars' tools? If we come to it arrogantly, banging away, might we not crush what chance there may be at understanding?

Perhaps clarity would be better served if we were more willing to leave wider spaces in our thinking, to be joined later with bridges built of other stuff than "thought."

Perhaps we lack the trust: trust in our language to be a guide and not an inquisitor, trust in our reason to be a comrade and not a tyrant, and trust in ourselves to take in wisdom without the illusory safety net of "proof."

## Soul

Soul is in some sense another way of saying self, only from a different perspective: the focus is on our being in the world relative to all other beings and to Being itself.

Life has (is) a soul.

To apprehend the Soul of Life we must let our own deep-knowing move into it; it is, after all, where our own souls already reside.

From time to time we must waive our ordinary boundaries and allow ourselves to trickle out beyond our human pores, to flow like liquid into Hers.

We will not drown; we will not be extinguished. Each of us will keep our integrity, a-part, but integral, necessary.

## *Faith*

Faith.
Forms: feith, feyth, fayth, faithe. "See also Fay" (*OED*).

> Fay. Out of the Old French *fae, faie*, the Portuguese *fada*, the Spanish *hada*, the Italian *fata*, the Latin *fata*, the fates. (*OED*)
> fay . . . noun. A fairy; elf. From the Middle English *faie*, out of the Old French *fae*, enchanted, out of the Latin *fata*, the fates. (*AHD*)
> fay . . . noun. Obsolete. Faith. Out of the Middle English *fai*. (*AHD*)
> fey . . . adjective. Having visionary power; clairvoyant. . . . Appearing as if under a spell; touched. Out of the Middle English *feie*. (*AHD*)

Fayth. Obsolete.

> Perhaps. Perhaps not.

"Faith," the established (establishment) dictionaries said (very properly) out of *fayth*, out of the Old Language *fae*, enchanted. . . . linked with captivation . . . possession . . . magic spells. . . . "Fey" . . . touched . . . under a spell . . . having visionary power. . . .

> Although the modern word *faith* can be traced back to ME *fey*, there appears to be no etymological connection between *faith* and the modern word *fey*. Wickedarians, however, inspired by similarities in sound and by our own Wicked word sense, Bespeak hitherto unheard connections.[1]

> [Wickedarian: a "wicked" woman, that is "beyond patriarchal 'good' and 'evil'; characterized by Original Integrity; . . . actively participating in the Unfolding of Be-ing as Good."[2]]
> — Mary Daly

> . . . hitherto unheard connections . . .

When I am in fayth, have fayth, I am enchanted (*sung into* a spell) by what life is—real, beyond real, magical, suffused with glistening, exquisite beauty, yet filled with awe-full events and purport. When I am in fayth I believe that to be alive is dear and filled with meaning. It matters whether I try to understand or experience beyond myself. It matters whether or not I try to live well, or virtuously, or whether I live at all. It matters how I influence the world around me and how I am influenced by it.

When the spell is cast, I am touched. I am possessed by a Sorceress, and I come to Her seeking guidance: "Take me deeper; make me fey—give me power to see." I am hungry to feel the Truth and to be (Be) with it, in it; I am hungry to join with it.

But there is not always enchantment. I vacillate at times between fayth and futility, pointlessness. When I am without fayth, life is a rubble—existence only, insignificant events floating in an absurd progression of time.

With an act of incredible will, I elect the meaningful, or I do not. I must choose.      I alone?

May I always choose the singing, the incantations* of fayth, the enchantment.

May it be granted by Life more than it is denied.

---

*\*in-cantare*: from the Latin, to sing into *(Cassell's Latin Dictionary)*.

Presence, Lifeness,

I come before you seeking nourishment. I am hungry;
feed me. I am empty; fill me.

I come seeking grace.*

I would be *pleasing* to the universe, in the universe, that is, in harmony with it; and then, since we shall be in harmony together, I
with the universe and it with me, it will be pleasing to me, and
there will be fayth.

---

*Grace*: from the Latin *gratus*, pleasing *(Cassell's Latin Dictionary)*.

In scribing the words Elemental feminist philosophy I intend
to Name a form of philosophical be-ing/thinking that
emerges together with metapatriarchal consciousness—
consciousness that is in harmony with the Wild in nature
and in the self. . . .

Elemental philosophy *is* of the world. It is for those
who love and belong to this world, who experience Be-
Longing in this world, who refuse the horror of Self-loss
implied in dying "with Christ" to the Elemental spirits of
the universe.

— Mary Daly[3]

## Credo: A Beginning

Life is worth the living. Pain and evil are real, but beauty, joy, love, and pleasure exist in enough sufficiency in this world to keep me here. The alternative to this life is not-being, and while I do not fear death, I do not desire it either.

Being, the Allness that is, is meaningful in and of itself. It requires no dependency upon external agency, no assignment of purpose from without to give it meaning. Being means itself. It is its own context.

Should I at some time choose to use the word god or the name God, I would not mean a being, or a person, or an object, although at times, for my own experiential reasons, I might decide to conceive it or construct it that way. Except poetically, therefore, I do not wish to speak of a Supreme Being or of a Creator or of One-Who-Does-This-or-That or of One-Who-Might-Be-Petitioned. Instead, what I mean by God is not a thing at all, a being out there, but rather it is a certain kind of *experience in me*, and yet more than only in me; the concept of God (or godness) is a way of conceiving connection with the ongoing activity of Being, of all that is. When I experience godness, I am focused on the entirety of Life, on its wholeness and interconnection in time and space. I am aware more of its sameness than of its divergence. I sense depth. I sense the ongoing, ultimate reality that lies beneath what I experience, reality that is *of* life and yet *more than*. . . . When godness prevails, it is in this context that I see my sights, ask my questions, choose my acts.

To utter the word/name God says more about me and my state of mind or feeling than about what is outside of me, in the universe. It is more accurate to say that I am in godness or god-knowing or god-being than to say that I am believing that God exists.

To be *in Spirit*, to be in the presence of godness, is to train our attention on the Wholeness, whether in the external dimension or in the internal dimension. It is to move with interior awareness to the Reality which underlies all.

Perhaps to "be in the Spirit" is not so much a matter of knowing God, but rather a matter of apprehending through God-knowing eyes.

Life can be understood in two ways: The smaller, but not lesser, sense is life as we live it, each creature individually, transiently, in our limited time. The other sense of Life denotes the ultimate Process of Processes, the Allness, the ongoing totality that contains both life and death, that has meaning and yet is beyond meaning. We participate in both. How we live influences our exchanges with each, even though ultimately being is beyond choice.

To seek what is good in life, to seek to be happy, is a choice (it is also a choice to opt for misery). Happiness is not accidental; it must be created. To make ourselves as happy as possible, so far as we are able, and to create an environment in which others too may be happy is a lofty, spirited task.

Loving God is loving Life is loving the earth-bound physical universe, the planet, and its events. In the seasons and cycles, in the coupling of animals, in the terrible rumblings of the Earth, in the process of birth-into-death-into-birth-again, in all—the beautiful and the terrible—is lodged the purpose we seek to lend meaning and grandeur to our coming and going. These constitute the Context, the Allness of which we are a part.

My life is shared with all other beings, who are my family. Together we share the Universe, which is our home. In the connection among us (which is so close that it houses our common soul), in our intimacy and relationship are found truth, love, meaningfulness, and deepest pleasure. Therein is Spirit (*spiratus*—the breath, the center of Life). To hurt any other, without need and sobriety, is to wound both the Spirit and our own self. That is sin.

There is good and evil in human life, and we can frequently discern the difference, although it is sometimes very difficult. We decide a thing is good because our spirited core assents to it and calls it beautiful. Life, as it is lived and may be lived by all the beings of this world, holds the ultimate measure of our actions. Life alone is Teacher and Judge. Goodness is what I do in service to the preservation of Life. Evil is the harm I do other beings. It is my sisters and brothers in Being who will grant me praise or blame, who will teach, reward, or punish.

Damnation or redemption is grounded respectively in our perceiving ourselves isolated from, or in communion with, All Being. Through our behavior toward others and toward ourselves, it is we ourselves who elect which we shall have.

To love life, I must love and honor myself, I must be wholesomely self-ish, for my self is my core, my center, and it is through my center that I am attached, as by an umbilicus, to the center of all Being. I celebrate my self. I celebrate what it is to be female, to be human, to be animal, to be me. While this implies no derogation of any other creature (for the wonderfulness of self is not incompatible with the wonderfulness of another), it asserts that no other being is, or has the right to claim to be, preeminent over me, no other being has the right to harm me or to blight my existence. It asserts that my own desires, interests, needs or cares, tempered by my coexistence with others, constitute one proper ground for virtuous decision-making, for action.

Celebrating self is celebrating selves; my being, their being, my feelings, their feelings, my good, their good. What better ground for morals could there be?

I celebrate all of myself—mind, body, reason, sensuality, emotion, spirit. I say *yes* to who and what I am as well as to what I can be, may be, wish to be. I utterly abhor and reject any philosophy that measures me against perfections not of my nature and then bewails the falling short. I forswear self-hatred and self-demolition.

To know godness requires a knowing that is not merely human knowing—in the mind or even in the experience, in the simple, surface, human sense. We are human, but not only that. We also are animal, and in our animal selves we have access to a kind of knowing that we share with the other animals. At times, when my human self is quiet, I glimpse my animal lucidity, the knowledge I sense in the hare or the deer. To refuse my animal self, wherein I am so closely attached to What Is (to God), to fail to pay heed to my knowing, which is sharper and deeper and more powerful than my logic, is to turn my back on a precious resource and a splendid route to Truth.

One goal of spiritual life is to "transcend." This does not mean to "cross over" into a realm of existence cut away from concrete existence or from the immediacy of daily life. To remove myself from the familiar and warm elements of worldly life would be to cut myself adrift and lose my original mooring—not a desirable goal at all. If I am to transcend, then I shall cross over into another realm of *understanding*, another realm of perceiving and assessing the comings and goings of my daily life and of others. To transcend is to place the events of our lives into context in wider and ever wider circles of meaning and value, circles that connect the present with the history of Life and the future of Being, the present place with all others, this center of experience with myriad others.

Context is the key to meaning. To link where I am with the farthest possibilities is to have all creation in between for a ground in which to be.

The One and the many


are One


and Many.


Monotheism is a regression in human understanding.

Ritual



is




play with a spiritual
purpose.

## Self-Blessing Ritual

This ritual should be performed before doing any magical work.

Begin after sundown. Prepare your altar with two white candles anointed with van oil or blessing oil or your favorite ritual oil. The altar is dressed in white, the chalice is filled with half wine and half water. Sprinkle salt on the floor and stand barefoot upon it.

Light your altar candles, saying: "Blessed be thou, creature of fire." Light meditation incense or peace incense.

Dip your two forefingers into the chalice; touching your forehead, say: "Bless me, Mother, for I am thy child." Dip your fingers again and touch your eyes, saying: "Bless my eyes to see your ways." Dip again and touch your nose, saying: "Bless my nose to smell your essence." Dip and touch mouth, saying: "Bless my mouth to speak of you." Dip and touch breasts, saying: "Bless my breasts, formed in strength and beauty." Dip and touch genitals, saying: "Bless my genitals that create life as you have brought forth the universe." Finally, dip and touch feet, saying: "Bless my feet that I may walk on your path."

Take a little time before extinguishing the candles. You shall experience a surge of energy and lightness of heart. Blessed be.

— Zsuzsanna Budapest[4]

Magic, magic . . .


> What is it to be a Seer?
> To look with God's eyes.

> What is it to conjure?
> To act with what is found thus.

## Mantra Meditation

It was the sweet, flush time of earliest summer, of pale greens and delicate afternoons. Happy and at ease with myself and the world, I was taking my days in comfortable cadence, as they directed.

On that particular day it was lightly warm and pleasant. I had opened the windows of my apartment so that the breezes could brush through the rooms and carry in the gifts of the season—fresh air, the scent of wet earth and grass, the sounds of life in the open. In preparation for my usual afternoon meditation, I lay on my bed, eyes closed, breathing deeply, releasing the tightness of muscles and mind, repeating my mantra, allowing myself to slip down (or in, or away or . . .). Not readily relinquished by the outward self, my consciousness tripped stubbornly around, like a youngster reluctant to come in for dinner, and I was intermittently aware of the sounds and smells of the outside: young leaves rustling on the newly green-ing trees, children and birds going about the business of setting up a racket; off in the distance a dog barking out an excited, high pitched yapping; across the hall a door slamming shut. On my legs I could feel the heat of the sun, still strong in the sky, and the green perfume scent of new mowing, intoxicatingly heavy, kept teasing my thoughts back to the surface. The intensity of life surrounded me, providing the couch, the ground, for my meditating self.

Continuing my mantra, focusing more sharply, breathing slower and deeper, I began to sink—down into that space where the body feels loose and light and seems to float away, leaving only . . . the interior (?), where thinking spills out of the mind's windows in every direction and trickles away, where awareness shifts. But even as I continued to sink deeper into the stillness, the outside sounds remained, receding for the most part, but swelling now and then, as if trying to lure me back to ordinary sensibility.

The letting-go, the surrender of meditation often frightened me, the sinking, the sense of mind and body floating, of some of me drifting away. This time, my fear and resistance were particularly intense. I could feel my surface self slipping off, out, and I wanted to pull back, to stop. (Control was always such an issue with me.) I knew, or at least I had been taught, that I was not in danger, that I could call myself back at any time, and yet I feared, what if . . . ? What if I could not call myself back; what if I lost myself?

Foolish, I thought then to myself. That is foolish. Keep going, don't stop. Concentrate, keep saying your mantra; let go. It was as if there were two of me, quarreling over the moment, quarreling over ownership of my soul: one of me frightened, trying to run, to draw away, to grasp the safety of ordinary awareness; the other insisting, determined. The battle continuing, the meditation progressed deeper; my terror as well as my determination mounted.

Suddenly, in an instant, a heartbeat, the terror broke, vanished, and was replaced with a profound euphoria, an awareness (sense? feeling?) never experienced before or since. Although I lay upon my bed and could not have moved physically, I felt my body drop in space (a foot or two? a mile?), and I made no move to stop it, to catch me.

Deep in meditation, an element of me remained on the surface, still aware of my surroundings. I knew where I was and what I was doing, and I could reflect: that I was on my bed at home meditating; that I was experiencing a nameless joy, more than joy; that I was accepting this extraordinary event willingly, surprised, but not at all afraid or confused. The summer outside my window came to the foreground again and connected with the event. The breeze, the grass, and all were part of the insight forming within that joy. For a "moment" there were just the exquisite emotion and the living season. Then—an awareness? a thought? an insight—a knowing. Not a voice, not even an idea, but a certainty presented itself to (in) me, not a line of logic, one datum connected to and following another, but an understanding, immediate, wholly, at once: All is well.

However it may sometime appear from my peculiarly small vantage point in existence, Life knows exactly what it is doing, and time and events are proceeding exactly as they should. The living things growing and being outside my window are close to me. The plants and animals are siblings; with me, they are children of the same Parent, Earth; and we are all particles of the universe, part of the living Process that binds us together. There is no end to this belonging, only cycle and change. Death is illusory as death, a final discrete event. Rather it is only change, part of a cycle, a turn and return. There is nothing to fear.

Surfacing from my meditation, I lay quietly on my bed for a time, reflecting. Soon my sense of ordinary time and location returned. With it came my surface rationality and all of its murky confusion, all of its incessant drive to analyze and nail down. My science-trained, logic-trained, philosopher-trained, academic scholar-trained mind stole back into control and began to "make sense." What was that, I queried? What (in my psychology? in my biology? in my . . . ?) could have created that experience?

Yet, never, not for an instant, then or now, have I ever repudiated the importance or truth of that experience; there never has been a moment's doubt of its veracity. Never has the certainty diminished that somehow, for a moment, I had a glimpse of (Reality? Allness?) it-is-so-ness. Whatever "it" was, whatever created or precipitated that "awareness," I know that it was sound, and that its message is trustworthy.

Since that afternoon I have been different, in how I perceive myself, in my understanding of the boundaries and not-boundaries of existence, and in my relationship to the universe that I inhabit and share. Never since that time have I feared death, as I did before. Even more important, far less do I fear Life.

Peace

is not

absence of strain,

nor is it even acceptance of what must be.

It is a union of    understanding and choice.

## Deity

What is it to speak of Deity?
Is it not to speak the sign for all that is beautiful and meaningful
in life? Is it not to speak the sign for
That Which Must Be Sought
That Which Must Be Preserved
in all our actions and our products
that which requires our most singular attention
and our fiercest devotion?

What is it to address Deity?
Is it not to call upon all that we believe to be most valuable, most
important, and most Real? Is it not to address that element in our
own self that knows the sacred and touches the sacred, so that we
may bring it to the events around us? Is it not to declare that we
are about to fix our attention on what matters most profoundly?

The word *God* can no longer claim to be a metaphor, though quite likely it was at the beginning. Filled with male images through the centuries it has done its work well in spinning out political, social, and economic structures of control and dominance. The maleness is so well established in cultures and mentalities it is responded to almost universally as revelatory, whether one is religious or not. Indeed, whether one is in church, or synagogue or another institutional religious order matters little. That is why the challenging of and shattering of this male image is the task of every citizen . . . every human being—not just the overtly religious. All, even the most common masses of people, have been too well indoctrinated to leave room for change, the calling into question, breaking that which is in tight control. A metaphor opens up new space and ushers in a new reality—iconoclastic first and then epiphanous action.

— Nelle Morton[5]

## Matriarchy

Matriarchy, in a womanist sense, is not patriarchy in a dress. It is not a mere transposition of the face of Mars onto the form of Venus: woman with a sword in her hand, finally in charge, taking revenge, stomping upon the Earth, stomping upon the Other.

Matriarchy in a womanist sense is quite literally the "rule of the Mother," the ascendancy of the Mother's way.

# Categories of Opposition in
# Matriarchy and Patriarchy

|  | *Matriarchy* | *Patriarchy* |
|---|---|---|
| 1. Nature of Deity | God is Female. Union of divine female and mortal male to produce superior being. | God is Male. Union of divine male and mortal female to produce superior being. |
| 2. Grounding of ethics | Ethical system based on blood tie. | Ethical system based on abstract principle. |
| 3. View of matter and material world | Material creation the model for all creation. Reality and value found in the material world. | Reason the model for all creation. Reality and value found in the spiritual world. |
| 4. Meaning of death | Death terminates material existence, which is the only real existence. | Death is the entry to spiritual existence, which is the highest form of existence. |
| 5. Meaning of life | Time is cyclical, renewing itself endlessly. Meaning of life found in terms of life itself and contribution to its renewal. | Time is linear, moving toward a goal. Meaning of life found in terms of contribution to the goal. |

*Selected Secondary Ritualistic Concerns*

| *Matriarchy* | *Patriarchy* |
|---|---|
| 6. Moon and lunar calendar Night precedes day | Sun and solar calendar Day precedes night |

|     |     |     |
| --- | --- | --- |
| 7. | Settlement and soil | Nomadism |
| 8. | Lower | Upper |
| 9. | Left | Right |
| 10. | The number two and evenness | The number one and oddness |
| 11. | The mother names the child and inheritance is through the mother | The father names the child and inheritance is through the father. |

— Carol Ochs[6]

Ethics is grounded in blood. Value is found in this world, where our existence is anchored. Death is a natural event, ending our time, but time moves in circles and is not the enemy. The dark is sacred, and the night is holy. The earth is where we find the divine, our Mother, Life.

Why should such ideas so frighten and anger the patriarchs?

## God the Mother

walks among Her children, the creatures of the earth, blissing them, feeding them, teaching them to Be.

Are the children mindful of the Mother? Do they heed her, that She not be dishonored? Do they guard Her, that She not be torn? Do they speak Her name, that She not be betrayed? Are they vigilant, lest She be lost to them forever?

Eternally patient, She is eternally present, even when they fail to attend Her.

The air is filled with Her perfume; everywhere Her beauty reaches for the light, even when the children fail to see Her.

She brings them fruit and candy, pleasures that they might delight, lessons that they might learn, solace that they might rest, wisdom that they might prevail, even when they fail to receive Her.

Like all things beautiful, She is vulnerable to harm. After all, the Mother is the Sister and the Daughter of our ways.

Dea, Femina, Mother Goddess;
Source of Being and Being itself;
She who provides, She who is lush and ripe and
        gives forth;
She who prevails, who endures:
    She Is.
We reside in Her; eat of Her; rest upon Her;
        come to sleep within Her.

She is the Sacred.

## Why do I call upon God the Mother and not God the Father?

I call upon the Mother

Because I am a woman, and God is my child as I am Hers.

Because I am a woman, and Her name reverberates in my being in a way so different from His.

Because I am a woman, and His People have treated Her children with such meanness that they almost cannot speak Her name— they almost cannot speak their own names.

Because I am a woman and She is Woman, and I love Her in me and me in Her.

Because I am a woman, and my heart flies out to Her (who is Woman) and to Her kind.

I call upon the Mother

Because I am a woman, and if I cannot clothe all that I deem holy in female form, I cannot myself be holy. If God cannot be Woman, I cannot be God. If I can call only upon the Father, if there be no choice but to call upon the Father, then I am never to be for myself; I shall never grow to fullness, to lushness, to maturity. I cannot be Mother, I shall always be daughter–child, supplicant.

I call upon the Mother

Because I like the way She teaches me. I like Her way. I like that She is sisterly. I like that She is beautiful and clever and strong. I like that She dances in circles. I like that She shows Herself. I like that She frees me. I like Her way.

I like how She teaches me.

Because the conjuring of Her leads my mind to the women I have loved: the playmates of my childhood years, all giggles and lis- tening; the sisters, understanding without words; the faces in the gatherings, surprised to hear another share their secrets and speak to them of their power and beauty; the servers in the little breakfast shop—growing older, growing tired, growing lame, but laughing, playing, feeding me in body and spirit; the Lady-dog, content to be, menacing none but those who men- ace; the golden daughter, all perfume and response;

and because they direct my mind to Her
and because She is they and they are She.

Because His conjuring leads me not, but bows me.

Because She is yes-ness and He is no-ness.

                              I call upon the Mother
Because She is Earth, and I am Her child,
    flesh of Her flesh, bone of Her bone, and I owe Her honor.
To love Her is to love me; to deny Her is to deny myself. To turn
    from Her is shame; who disparages Her besoils the self.

*"I who am the beauty of the green earth and the white moon among the stars and the mysteries of the waters, I call upon your soul to arise and come unto me. For I am the soul of nature that gives life to the universe. From Me all things proceed and unto Me they must return. Let My worship be in the heart that rejoices, for behold— all acts of love and pleasure are My rituals. Let there be beauty and strength, power and compassion, honor and humility, mirth and reverence within you. And you who seek to know Me, know that your seeking and yearning will avail you not, unless you know the Mystery: for if that which you seek you find not within yourself, you will never find it without. For behold, I have been with you from the beginning, and I am that which is attained at the end of desire."*

. . . . . . . . . . . . . . . . . . . . . . . . . . . . . . . . . . . . . . . . . . . .

People often ask me if I *believe* in the Goddess. I reply "Do you believe in rocks?" It is extremely difficult for most Westerners to grasp the concept of a manifest deity. The phrase "believe *in*" itself implies that we cannot *know* the Goddess, that She is somehow intangible, incomprehensible. But we do not *believe* in rocks—we may see them, touch them, dig them out of our gardens, or stop small children from throwing them at each other. We know them; we connect with them. In the Craft, we do not *believe* in the Goddess—we connect with Her; through the moon, the stars, the ocean, the earth, through trees, animals, through other human beings, through ourselves. She is here. She is within us all. She is the full circle: earth, air, fire, water, and essence—body, mind, spirit, emotions, change.

The Goddess is first of all earth, the dark, nurturing mother who brings forth all life. She is the power of fertility and generation; the womb, and also the receptive tomb, the power of death. All proceeds from Her; all returns to Her. As earth, She is also plant life; trees, the herbs and grains that sustain life. She is the body, and the body is sacred. Womb, breast, belly, mouth, vagina, penis, bone, and blood—no part of the body is unclean, no aspect of the life processes is stained by any concept of sin. Birth, death, and decay are equally sacred parts of the cycle. Whether we are eating, sleeping, making love, or eliminating body wastes, we are manifesting the Goddess.

The Earth Goddess is also air and sky, the celestial Queen of Heaven, the Star Goddess, ruler of things felt but not seen: of knowledge, mind, and intuition. She is the Muse, who awakens all creations of the human spirit. She is the cosmic lover, the morning and the evening star, Venus, who appears at the times of love-making. Beautiful and glittering, She can never be grasped or penetrated; the mind is drawn ever further in the drive to know the unknowable, to speak the inexpressible. She is the inspiration that comes with an indrawn breath.

The celestial Goddess is seen as the moon, who is linked to women's monthly cycles of bleeding and fertility. Woman is the earthly moon; the moon is the celestial egg, drifting in the sky womb, whose menstrual blood is fertilizing rain and the cool dew; who rules the tides of the oceans, the first womb of life on earth. So the moon is also Mistress of Waters: the waves of the sea, streams, springs, the rivers that are the arteries of Mother Earth; of lakes, deep wells, and hidden pools, and of feelings and emotions, which wash over us like waves.

— Starhawk[7]

Eve: The first woman, the wife of Adam. According to *Genesis* 3:20 she was so named because she was the mother of all living beings; but the Hebrew word . . . for Eve may have meant "serpent," and her name thus has been associated with the primitive myth that all life originated in a primeval serpent.

    — *The Oxford Dictionary of the Christian Church*[8]

# The Mother of God

Can Notre Dame de Chartres be the same as Nuestra Señora de Guadalupe? No Catholic would hesitate to kneel and pray before either image: "Holy Mary, Mother of God, pray for us sinners, now, and at the hour of our death." Yet the usual anthropologist, arriving as it were from Mars, for whom theories of diffusion are anathema and all cross-cultural comparisons methodologically beneath contempt, would be in danger of returning to his planet of pure thought with two exquisitely separate monographs: the one treating of a local French, the other of a local Mexican goddess, functionally serving two entirely different social orders; Our Lady of Chartres, furthermore, showing the influence of a Gallo-Roman Venus shrine, of which the evidence appears in the cult of the Black Madonna observed in the crypt of the present (twelfth to sixteenth century) cathedral, whereas Our Lady of Guadalupe is clearly of Amerindian origin, having appeared in vision (or so it is alleged by all native informants) hardly a decade after the overthrow of Montezuma, on the site of a native shrine, probably of the great serpent-goddess Coatlicue. All of which, of course, would be true, and yet, not true enough.

Let us press the question further: Can the Virgin Mary be the same as Venus-Aphrodite, or as Cybele, Hathor, Ishtar, and the rest? We think of the words of the goddess Isis addressed to her initiate Apuleius, c. 150 A.D., which are cited at the opening of *Primitive Mythology*:

> I am she that is the natural mother of all things, mistress and governess of all the elements, the initial progeny of worlds, chief of the powers divine, queen of all that are in hell, the principal of them that dwell in heaven, manifested alone and under one form of all the gods and goddesses. At my will the planets of the sky, the wholesome winds of the seas, and the lamentable silences of hell are disposed; my name, my divinity is adored throughout the world, in divers manners, in variable customs, and by many names.
>
> For the Phrygians that are the first of all men call me the Mother of the gods of Pessinus; the Athenians, which are sprung from their own soil, Cecropian Minerva; the Cyprians, which are girt about by the sea, Paphian Venus; the Cretans, which bear arrows, Dictynian Diana; the Sicilians, which speak

three tongues, infernal Proserpine; the Eleusinians, their ancient goddess Ceres; some Juno, others Bellona, others Hecate, others Ramnusie, and principally both sort of the Ethiopians, which dwell in the Orient and are enlightened by the morning rays of the sun; and the Egyptians, which are excellent in all kind of ancient doctrine, and by their proper ceremonies accustomed to worship me, do call me by my true name, Queen Isis.[9]

— Joseph Campbell[10]

## Mother River

The Mississippi River is beautiful just north of St. Louis. Magnificent, craggy gray bluffs, more than 200 feet high, border its eastern edge. Caves and rock platforms, partially hidden by greenery, form an intricate pattern of lines and colors in the face of the cliffs. At the base, a scattering of huge boulders, jutting out at different angles, conjures up shapes of animals, long disappeared. Further north, rock formations have fashioned what appear to be faces on the walls of the cliffs. Tradition has it that the native people who lived in this region before the Europeans came believed that the faces belonged to individuals who had displeased the gods and whose spirits, therefore, had been imprisoned in the rocks forever, as a punishment and as a warning. High on the roof of the bluffs, eagles have made their nests, and during certain times of the year, they can be seen from great distances along the water. They have hidden their homesites well, for although they can be seen circling very near the trees and platforms, from the river they are rarely seen to light.

On the opposite side of the river it is very different; there on the flatlands are cottages and clubhouses raised on stilts (to protect them from periodic flooding), harbors and worksites that run right to the water's edge. Buildings, campgrounds, and farms dot the landscape with patches of human color and industry.

In the water and along its banks on either side, sandbars, islands, and marshy places provide sanctuary for every kind of river life—woods animals and water creatures—frogs and snakes, ducks, birds, bugs, and crawling things too numerous and varied to be identified. Here hatch the tiny flying things that travel two by two, attached, as if in tandem, as if making love in flight, as if teaching by example what the river is about.

People too animate the river. They live there, work, fish, play, travel, and transport. Barges and houseboats, big cruisers, sailboats, and little speedsters form an endless line of movement in each direction. Somehow, different as they are, they manage to share the waterway, accommodating each other as needed. During the steaming days of summer, it is the people who seem to give definition to the river; everywhere their noise and purpose cover up the more essential scene. The creatures, quite sensibly in hiding, are not seen nor heard. Instead one hears horns and buzzing motors, voices calling to one another, dogs, and babies, and radios. The crossing wakes of all the boats raise an unnatural chop in the water. Tents and camping gear, towels, and picnic baskets form a veritable city in the sand.

A novice to the river, seeing these things, might think that the humans had control here. Those more experienced, "river rats" they call themselves, tell it differently. "The river's beautiful," they say, "but she's a mind of her own. She'll have you in a minute if you don't take care. Why, I remember once. . . ." They each have stories to tell, about a time some years ago, when . . .

. . . when the river decided one way or another to reassert her authority, perhaps because someone forgot who was in authority, or someone neglected to give proper homage, or just because she, the great river, wanted to. Every year on the river, someone dies, or disappears, or "has a close one"; people make mistakes, forget that they are in the presence of divinity, and she replies.

In her power times, the Mississippi can rise up, and no amount of frantic, human effort can keep her in her banks; she just floods, covering streets and houses and farmlands and all, until she's good and ready to return to her bed; and everybody sees and comes to gawk and marvel and remark. But she speaks as well in secret, surreptitious ways. Just for play or mischief, she can conjure little circlets of current or sudden changes of depth, twenty, thirty feet, or more. Sometimes a branch cracked off a rotting tree fixes itself into the dirt, right midriver, just below the surface, and waits there for an eye not quite sharp enough or a hand not quite fast enough.

Storms seem to come up faster on the river—one moment a grayish ball in the sky, far in the distance; the next, a whole-world-darkening blanket of color just overhead. The winds seem to blow more menacingly loud through the overhanging branches and the open water. The lightning falls closer, more visible, cracking branches and sending them hurtling downstream. When the thunder bangs and the sky lights, everything—boat, creature, and leaf—everything, reaches for cover. In minutes, the river is vacant. It is as if she says, "Begone; get out of here! I've tolerated your small silliness long enough, and I'm out of patience"; and she sweeps the pests away.

Not only potency and awesome strength evince sovereignty on the Mississippi. There are quiet, peaceful times of perfect beauty— also the river's will; times at night when all that is heard is the slosh and splatter of water licking the shoreline, or the slapping back down of a fish, emerging from the dark in a great curved leap, or the magnified sounds of night, the island birds and the rustle of animals making their way through the thicket. At these times perhaps one sees nothing but absolute black in every direction, except for a star here and there or the occasional glow of a distant harbor. Peaceful too is sunrise, when the river birds rise to search out breakfast, and twilight, when hues of mauve and purple streak a horizon, glowing pink.

She is never the same, the great river. Everyday she shifts—bend, turn, bank, bottom, current, and all. And she is never different. Nothing, neither human nor natural, alters her essence or ruffles her fundamental peacefulness, the endless, ongoing surety of place and time. She is Earth.

Through the river, the Mother speaks clearly, because She is the river, and the river is Her child, among Her first born. The Mississippi is alive, and it teaches the Mother's ways. Dwarfed beside her cliffs, her world-sweeping sunsets and vast skies, her wild, life-challenging manners, we become her pupils, her neophytes. She calls us to silence, to listening, to lucidity, and grants us sometimes an almost unbearably poignant sensitivity. This is the domain of Spirit. It is sacred space.

Transgression here is that much more a sin.

Just above the Illinois town of Alton and across from Elsah Landing, a river stop established more than 200 years ago, stands a tall, slender white statue, clean-lined and modern, the shrine of *Our Lady of the River*. The Lady is represented here as Mary, the Virgin. Hands clasped upon her breast in eternal prayer, she stands reverent and serene in silent vigil, her body absolutely still, static; her head, veiled modestly, bowed in quiet humility, capped by a halo. (At night they light it up.)

On some occasions, river-religious times, I have fastened my attention upon her shining image glistening in the sun or lit up by the incandescent light aimed at her from below. I have walked to her feet from the little harbor nearby, looked up into her face, her sightless eyes, and tried to make connection with my Lady, the Mother, but I have rarely been successful, and I have never been at ease.

Once the lady before me was the Great Mother, Ancient Ancestress of all the peoples, Source and Sustainer, She Who brings forth and Who destroys in Her time. Once She was the Queen of Heaven, Morning and Evening Star, fearsome and proud, commanding respect and honor.It was said that She made the rivers to flood, the grain to grow, babies to be born, and the earth to flower or withhold, at Her pleasure. It was said that She had a lover, that together They shared in the act of Life, and that through Their sexing all life came to be and was imbued with divinity.

Now, like the beings entombed upon the face of the bluffs, She stands a captive, imprisoned in the image of this pathetic woman, Mary the Virgin, daughter of the Patriarchs, shadowy descendant of the Goddess, dethroned, desexed, robbed of vitality, brought down before Her own son, bowed now before all in silent submission, trussed up in robe and veils, as if prepared for sacrifice.

There is a joke on the river about the statue. With great amusement, people note that seen from a distance, especially from the side, the statue doesn't look like a lady at all. Rather, it resembles a giant, erect penis, shining in the sun.

Oh, Mother, what have they done to Your name? How filled with grief and disgust must You be at this slander. Mother, I am sick at the sight of Your image so caged and defamed. I come to worship, but I feel only shame and anger. I can think only of your vindication. How shall we both be freed? How shall we all be freed? Why do I feel with such insistence that somehow the task is mine?

## The Doe

At Southern Illinois University at Edwardsville, in the main foyer of the administration building, just inside the huge glass facade, there stands one of the university's "art holdings," a sculpture of wood, metal, leather, and rope—a deer, dead, brought down by a hunter's weapon. Trussed up by her four legs, she hangs upside down from a tall wooden tripod. Her one visible ear hangs limply off to the side, a poignant touch; she appears eviscerated, ready perhaps for skinning or butchering.

The piece was acquired years ago from the student who created her as part of his thesis project. It is hard to know what he might have had in mind, a reproach for those who kill (for food?) without sobriety, or perhaps he meant only to recreate a pleasant memory, an image of outdoor afternoons and manly camaraderie.

Now there is just a dead deer hanging upside down in the administration building, and although most passersby recoil from her at first, for the most part she hangs there with little notice. Sporadic attempts by small groups of women to have the body removed have received no serious attention; the men in charge, through the Office of University Something-Or-Other, have stood firm, as if each move to open the question only redoubles their resolve to reinforce their authority to decide the matter.

She hangs there, my Mother/Sister, slaughtered, upside down, torn, bleeding her gentleness to the polished floor. Everyday the powerful and the would-be-powerful glide past her, insensible to her pain, oblivious to her debasement. She hangs, but they take no notice.

The women saw, her sisters; they petitioned, again and again, politely, as women should, judiciously, as women must. (They should have come by night and stolen back their kinswoman's body.) They made appeals: "Please, cut my Mother down. We are all dishonored by such disregard for Her sanctity."

"It is art," the men replied, peevish, exasperated.

"It is art," the men explained, impatient.

"It is art," the men insisted. "And we paid for it. Where are we to put it, now the money's paid?"

And they turned their backs, and they turned their minds, and still she hangs there, bleeding.

For us all, it is a place of death.

Marduk killed Ti'amat, and Jahweh cursed the Holy Snake. Thus has it been for eons: they come against Her, shame Her, slay Her, refuse Her even sacred burial.

**Mary's Virginity**. The belief that the Mother of Jesus was always a virgin. Three stages of virginity are professed in this belief: Mary's conception of her Son without the cooperation of man, giving birth to Christ without violating her integrity, and remaining a virgin after Jesus was born.

The Church's faith in Mary's virginal conception of Jesus found its way into all the ancient professions of belief. In a text dating from the early second century, the Apostles' Creed speaks of "Jesus Christ . . . who was born by the Holy Spirit of the Virgin Mary." The biblical basis was traceable to the prophecy of Isaiah (7:14), which the first Evangelist applies to Mary: "Therefore the Lord Himself shall give a sign. Behold a virgin [*halmah*] shall conceive and bear a son and his name shall be called Emmanuel [God with us]." From the beginning, Christians understood the passage to refer to the Messiah, since the sign had been fulfilled. Matthew thus interpreted the term in recalling the Isaian prophecy (Matthew 1:23).

All the Fathers affirm Christ's virginal conception by Mary. At the turn of the first century, Ignatius of Antioch spoke of Jesus as "truly born of a virgin." Starting with Justin the Martyr (c. 100-65), ecclesiastical writers uniformly defended the Messianic interpretation of Isaiah, as given by Matthew and confirmed in the Gospel by St. Luke.

Christian tradition went a step further. Not only did Mary conceive without carnal intercourse, but her physical virginity was also not violated in giving birth to Christ. When the monk Jovinian (d. 405) began to teach that "A virgin conceived, but a virgin did not bring forth," he was promptly condemned by a synod at Milan (390), presided over by St. Ambrose. Her integrity during the birth of Jesus is included in the title "perpetual virgin," given to Mary by the fifth general council held at Constantinople (553). Without going into physiological details, ancient writers such as Ambrose, Augustine, and Jerome employ various analogies—the emergence of Christ from the sealed tomb, his going through closed doors, penetration of light through glass, the going out of human thought from the mind.

Mary remained a virgin after Christ was born. Denied in the early Church by Tertullian and Jovinian, the doctrine of virginity *post partum* (after birth) was strenuously defended by the orthodox Fathers and crystallized in the term *aeiparthenos* (ever virgin) coined by the fifth ecumenical council (second of Constantinople). From the fourth century on, such formulas as that of St. Augustine became common: "A virgin conceived, a virgin gave birth, a virgin remained."

— from John A. Hardon, S.J., *Modern Catholic Dictionary*[11]

Mary conceived, they say, without carnal intercourse. (*Carnal . . . fleshly . . .* from the Latin word *caro*, flesh. . . . In today's lexicon it has a distinctly smutty sound; the early fathers of the church deemed it filthy: "carnal"—full of sin, of vice, degradation, and punishment.) In conceiving without benefit of fleshly intercourse and in giving birth "without violating her integrity," Mary was virgin. "Her integrity during the birth of Jesus is included in the title 'perpetual virgin,' given to Mary by the fifth general council held at Constantinople."

Her integrity—before, during, and after—was not violated. . . . Now there's a bizarre thought, that a woman's "integrity" should rest upon her being antithetical to what is natural and common to women; how perverse to insist that this woman's integrity rests upon the denial, for all her life, of her sexuality and her body's truth.

It is a marvelous device, really quite stunning, an ideal to serve the patriarchs in their profoundest need and in their deepest fear. In this one person, Mary, are realized the twin, incompatible visions of woman: sexual receptacle/sacrificing Mother and eternally "pure," untouched, and untouchable virgin. She receives the seed, carries, and bears; she suffers, serves without reservation, adores, protects, and nurtures—and yet she is completely free of the physical realities of body, without blood, lust, will, or stain of pleasure.

Hail Mary, consummate mother, totally desexed, integrity intact.

In the worship of the female deity, sex was Her gift to humanity. It was sacred and holy. She was the Goddess of Sexual Love and Procreation. But in the religions of today we find an almost totally reversed attitude. Sex, especially non-marital sex, is considered to be somewhat naughty, dirty, even sinful. Yet rather than calling the earliest religions, which embraced such an open acceptance of all human sexuality, "fertility-cults," we might consider the religions of today as strange in that they seem to associate shame and even sin with the very process of conceiving new human life. Perhaps centuries from now scholars and historians will be classifying them as "sterility-cults."

 — Merlin Stone[12]

Christianity has turned Aphrodite into a slut.

— Fritz Marti
Personal letter
April 12, 1985

They have their vision, the Fathers, the synods, and the councils. I have mine.

I love to imagine the Goddess sexing. I see Her marvelous great body, all sinew and steel, electrified with pleasure, curling and stretching, reaching for touch. She howls and grunts, and the world shakes. She climaxes, and the stars shoot around the heavens like Chinese sparklers, colors swirl, lightning bolts fall, and all the animals run for cover. She laughs and is delighted.

No fragile, lifeless creature wrapped in paper-white skin and tepid blue cloth is my Lady. She is not thin and frail. She radiates color, fiery warmth. Her flesh is full and firm, Her body hard from action, Her hair wild and free. She has a will, my Lady, a power and direction fully Hers, of Her, in Her. She is all life, my Lady, vibrant, passionate, untamed, and when She sexes the universe applauds.

Inanna opened the door for him.
Inside the house she shone before him
Like the light of the moon.

Dumuzi looked at her joyously.
He pressed his neck close against hers.
He kissed her.

Inanna spoke:
      "What I tell you
      Let the singer weave into song.
      What I tell you,
      Let it flow from ear to mouth,
      Let it pass from old to young:

      My vulva, the horn,
      The Boat of Heaven,
      Is full of eagerness like the young moon.
      My untilled land lies fallow.

      As for me, Inanna,
      Who will plow my vulva?
      Who will plow my high field?
      Who will plow my wet ground?

      As for me, the young woman,
      Who will plow my vulva?
      Who will station the ox there?
      Who will plow my vulva?"

Dumuzi replied:
      "Great Lady, the king will plow your vulva.
      I, Dumuzi the King, will plow your vulva."

Inanna:
      "Then plow my vulva, man of my heart!
      Plow my vulva!"

At the king's lap stood the rising cedar.
Plants grew high by their side.
Grains grew high by their side.
Gardens flourished luxuriantly.

      — Diane Wolkstein and Samuel Noah Kramer,
      *Inanna: Queen of Heaven and Earth*[13]

*When I sex, I am perfectly alive. All is sense, and feel, and will, and want, and get, and give. I have no parts, only center, which is amplified, flourishes, takes control. When I sex, time evaporates, space and place collapse. Self moves elsewhere, outside of ordinary consciousness. When I sex I am truly with the Goddess, joined with all the wild things, they who came before me and who will follow. I see them, and I know inside them, for they are me.*

*I alone exist, I and the All; I am the All—in the Vitality, in the Life Power, in the pleasure, its sign. There is a knowing: this is good and true. This is being, integrated and borderless.*

*When I am there, sexing, living it well, there is almost no thinking, but in my remembering, when I recall it, sexing is a very softness: lips, small resilient cushions of tissue and taste, padded and pliant, catching my own, moving with a delicate plasticity, smooth . . . like skin, smooth as glass, only warmer, smooth as water looks—still and silent in the river at night, smooth like satin stretched over a bed of marshmallows, nearly as sweet, but in a different way, savory . . . like the smell of sex . . . nothing else I know is like the scent of human body, mixture of warmth and process, mix of stay-on-the-senses perfumes, mix of hair and breath and soap and sweat . . . and touch . . . I love to touch, to play my fingers, lighter than a moth-wing, over prickling flesh. I like the feel of it, the sense of it. It makes me laugh to give such pleasure; it is strength, power . . . to be so soft . . .*

*I love to be touched, to feel the infinite luxury of fingertips or palms against my back, across my breast, between my legs, within my hair, to feel the crackle of so much sensation . . . such indulgence of the self is a nourishment—of flesh and soul.*

Sexing is a me-ness, a boundless celebration of self. And yet,

*there is another . . . I feel his heat . . .*

> Though at first the Goddess appears to have reigned alone, at some yet unknown point in time She acquired a son or brother (depending upon the geographic location), who was also Her lover and consort. . . . Known in various languages as Damuzi, Tammuz, Attis, Adonis, Osiris or Baal. . . . Wherever this dying young consort appears as the male deity, we may recognize the presence of the religion of the Goddess. . . .
> — Merlin Stone[14]

*I feel His heat, His vitality and His strength, moving to its own need.*
*He is bright with passion. . . .*

> Untamed! untamed!
> Stag and stallion, Goat and bull,
> Sailor of the last sea, Guardian of
>     the Gate,
> Lord of the two lands,
> Ever-dying, Ever-living, Radiance!

The image of the Horned God in Witchcraft is radically different from any other image of masculinity in our culture. . . . He
is gentle, tender, and comforting, but He is also the Hunter. . . .
He is untamed sexuality—but sexuality as a deep, holy, connecting power. He is the power feeling. . . . Our God wears horns—
but they are the waxing and waning crescents of the Goddess
Moon, and the symbols of animal vitality.
    — Starhawk[15]

*He is bright with passion, my consort, my brother, the panting Bull . . .*
    *I feel him stretched against me, skin upon skin, heat upon heat,*
*want upon want, and I take him into me, swallow him with my body,*
*as he presses harder, loses himself, his hips taking a motion more than*
*human . . . more even than animal. . . . We sex, bringing ourselves*
*exquisitely close, each of us acting for ourselves, and yet not only for*
*ourselves. In the intricacy of sharing, selves get lost, dissolve, do not*
*matter, and then even doing gives way, leaving only being . . . feeling*
*. . . and one fundamental consciousness—it is mine (perhaps it is his*
*too). Human self retires. Animal self, deeper self, emerges—vital, gor-*
*geous, linked-to-prime, linked-to-Dea me-ness. Please me, (I) she says,*
*pleasure me, feed me, give to me; lost is awareness of the other body/*
*self pleasing itself at that very moment.*

Sexing, as I experience it, is a Life-ness. In the foreground, all is
music and delight. In the background, far more. Always, beneath the
doing is a Knowing: Here is sanctity; we move in a mystery of Being, an exalted act, paradigmatic of all creation. Thank You, Lady,
for the joy in the Act of Life.
    Sexing for the love of it, for the pleasure of it, in celebration of
body, is a good-ness, as much an act of communion, a ritual of Allness, as the taking of the Eucharist or a touching of the Holiest of
Holies.

Golden calf (. . . the Hebrew word translated "calf," would be more properly rendered "young bull"). An object of worship set up (a) by the Israelites in the wilderness (Exodus 32); (b) by King Jeroboam I (937–915 B.C.) at Bethel and Dan for the worship of the Ten Tribes (1 Kings 12:28).
— *Oxford Dictionary of the Christian Church*[16]

Bull. The biblical title translated "God" is *El*, originally the title of the Phoenician bull-god called Father of Men. As the "supreme god of the Semitic pantheon, El was worshipped throughout Syria alongside the local gods, or Ba'als, one of his titles, indeed, being 'the Bull'" [*Larousse Encyclopedia of Mythology*, London: Hamlyn, 1968, p.74]. Like Zeus the Bull, consort of Hera–Europa–Io the white Moon–Cow, El married Asherah, the Semitic sacred Cow. He was identified with Elias or Helios, the sun. He was still the Semitic Father of Men in the time of Jesus, who cried to him from the cross, calling him Father (Mark 15:34).

Nearly every god of the ancient world was incarnate sooner or later in a bull.
— Barbara G. Walker[17]

Golden Calf. The image of God that Aaron made at the foot of Mount Sinai to please the Israelites, who were tired of waiting for Moses during his stay on the mountain (Exodus 32). Even if the Jews did not worship the calf as an idol, they were forbidden to make any representation of Yahweh (Exodus 20). Moreover, bovine images were associated with obscenity. That is why, on descending from the mountain, Moses was angry with the Israelites and told them, "You have committed a grave sin" (Exodus 32:30).
— *Modern Catholic Dictionary*[18]

Bovine images, they say, were associated with obscenity.

It is said that the gods of the old religion become the devils of the new. The Patriarchs despise not only the Great Cow, but Her Bull as well.

*Could it be, my husband, that they revile You because You service me . . . because you are the occasion of my passion, because with you I may lose myself inside that energy, that grand, animal thrash-*

*ing, and become as fecund, as willful and wild, as awesome as Earth Herself? They will not soar with me, as you do; they want to own me, to ride me—so that they may control me, so that they may control themselves, so that they may control sex, so that they may control flesh, so that they may control Life.*

Illusion . . . folly . . . sin . . . to refuse the gift. It is to refuse our kinship with the others and with Process; it is to refuse Nature and Earth itself, our links with them, our connection with Life, and therefore, with God. It is an affront to Her and to Her creation.

Physical, animal, sentient sexing does, in fact, remind us that as human animals we are indeed transitory creatures. But it reveals to us too that we are connected to the Infinite. For when we are placed so close to the rest of our living kind, we are afforded a sharper view of our place in the range of existence.

Our carnality serves Nature in the creation of new beings; but it also serves when generation is not at all the issue, not desirable, nor even possible, as when we pleasure ourselves or lovers of our own sex, or when we are past conceiving. In the very seeking of pleasure there is a yes-ness—to myself, to another, to bonding, to aliveness. In unity with the creatures in the fields, the squirrels, and the deer, and all who thrust and thrash and call out and share in the dance of life, we are lovely: in our making being, in our making goodness, in our making love.

The "Act" itself? Not ridiculous: no, just uncivilized—decivilized, remanded to roots, to the source, to the Mother, re-bound, re-ligamented, religious.

Done for the joy of it, in good spirit, sexing is a merging with divinity and a meditation on Life. Representing all the fecundities of Earth and animality, it is the ultimate metaphor for vitality, for Spirit; and it symbolizes the continuity and authority of Nature.

Sexing is Life acting in us and through us. It is Life worshiping Itself, and its pleasure is the gift of the Mother for doing her work.

let there be

quiet

## Attending

To hone our spiritual lucidity we must ardently attend.*

Indifference robs us of intensity. It makes us bland. It reduces our sense of participation in life and thus our belief that life has meaning or value.

As much as we are able, we must keep ourselves fully awake, alert to what transpires around us and to how we experience it. We must endeavor not to become just flat receptacles, sleepily receiving the colors of events and reflecting them back to life in watery consistency. Of the moments in our lives, we ought to be asking ourselves: What shall I notice here and, equally important, what must I slough off? How may I best use this moment to heighten my vitality and enlarge my soul, to tie me closer to the core of Being, and to deepen my conviction that life matters? Since I am right now defining my self, in what direction shall I press it?

---

*To attend: " . . . to accompany or wait upon as an attendant or servant . . . to take care of . . . to take charge of . . . to listen to; heed . . . to wait for, expect . . . to pay attention . . . to remain ready to serve . . . from the Latin *attendere* to heed: *ad-* to + *tendere* to stretch" (*AHD*).

## *Attending to Spirit*

What is it to attend to spirit (to heed, to wait upon), to stretch toward (S)spirit?

Most essentially, to attend to my soul is to wait upon, to serve deity in me, to enlarge in myself that portion of my existence that is Life-loving, that is beautiful, that seeks and connects with the rest of What Is.

To attend to my soul is to develop in myself spiritual literacy— a sharper ability to identify the questions of spirit, to recognize the component in each act or event that touches my being-in-the-world-in-relation-to-all-other-being—and to understand the consequences to my being of the choices I make.

To attend to my spirit is to try to live art-fully, with concern for design, beauty, harmony, balance, perspective; to create out of my life, as much as possible, a work of my choosing, one that I believe to be grace-full; to arrange, as much as possible, in the events of my days a vision to which I may assent, so that I may say at the close, "It was good."

To tend to spirit includes bringing myself internally into a finer state of integration and externally into a closer harmony with the Soul of Life. It is to keep the Soul of Life in the forefront of my awareness when choosing how to act in the world, so that my acting serves not only myself, but the others as well and the Harmony of which we are a part and upon which we depend.

To tend to spirit is to *choose* to pay attention, to stretch. It is to know that I am doing so, to do it purposefully, to know why I am doing so, and increasingly to know how.

We come to spirit in many dispositions of mood and purpose: we come in confusion, to ask questions and to be directed; we come in pain, to place our experience in wider perspective and thus to receive some modicum of peace; we come in joy, to celebrate; we come in need, to garner our strength and be empowered; we come seeking Vision; we come most especially to make contact with All-ness, to give ourselves over to that frame of mind that sees and judges, so much as possible, through the eyes of the Mother, through that largest of perspectives and that deepest of feelings.

We come to the Allness; we come to the self.

Each time we come—seeking Connection—each time we touch the Soul of Life and are touched in return, we enlarge the ability to be spirited, to seek, and to listen for its voice. Each time, we grow more confident that the Voice is real and the words are right, and we are convinced again to return. Each time, the umbilicus that holds us tight to the Source is drawn closer and made stronger.

## *Stillness*

The primary entrée into spiritual lucidity is intense, personal *engagement* with the most immediate and commanding events of experience—birth, sex, relationship, aging, death, and all the rest. Such engagements, interactions, when we confront them authentically, when they are intimate, emotional, self-conscious, and reflective, lead us directly to what have been called the ultimate questions, and so they propel us into engagement with Being itself.

Other strategies also lead us in: meditation, ritual, rational contemplation, study, ordeal, discussion, experiences, art, perhaps even revelation.

Ultimately, we must be alone—with our existence and our reflections upon it. It is in aloneness, in absolute psychic privacy, that we form our most authentic responses to life and thereby direct our spiritual process.

We must not shun aloneness, but treat it as a gift. To be alone is to be without only human company. Otherwise, if we but invite it, our presence is filled with Being.

In solitude we may be infinitely more in contact with Allness, with the Earth, and with Her children. There is a silence and a stillness which diminish only the *static* of awareness; if we learn to use the silence, it opens us to a range of hearing we never before imagined. In such stillness resides Enchantment.

To bring ourselves lucidly to aloneness, to the stillness, is to place ourselves in the presence of That Which Is.

## Praise

Praise the Mother, honor the Earth
Bend the knee (but do not kneel) before Her,
   She Who feeds and sustains us with
   Her fruit and beauty.

# Notes

1. *Webster's First New Intergalactic Wickedary of the English Language,* conjured by Mary Daly in cahoots with Jane Caputi (Boston: Beacon Press, 1987) pp. 75–76.

2. Ibid., p. xiii.

3. Mary Daly, *Pure Lust: Elemental Feminist Philosophy* (Boston: Beacon Press, 1984), pp. 7–8.

4. From *The Feminist Book of Light and Shadows*, ed. Helen Beardwomon (California: Luna Press, 1976). Reprinted by permission of the author. A later expanded version of the ritual appears as "Self Blessing" in Zsuzsanna Budapest, *The Holy Book of Women's Mysteries* (Oakland, Calif.: Wingbow Press, 1989), p. 107. (Distributed by Bookpeople, 7900 Edgewater Drive, Oakland, CA, 94621.)

5. Nelle Morton, "Journal Jottings" in *The Journey is Home* (Boston: Beacon Press, 1977), p. 218.

6. From Carol Ochs, *Behind the Sex of God: Toward a New Consciousness Transcending Matriarchy and Patriarchy* (Boston: Beacon Press, 1977), pp. 86-87. Copyright © 1977 by Carol Ochs. Reprinted by permission of Beacon Press.

7. Excerpts from the *Spiral Dance* by Starhawk. Copyright © 1979 by Miriam Simos. Reprinted by permission of HarperCollins Publishers, Inc.

8. *Oxford Dictionary of the Christian Church*, 2nd edition; ed. F. L. Cross and E. A. Livingstone (New York: Oxford University Press, 1974).

9. Apuleius, *The Golden Ass*, translated by W. Addlington, Book XL; Campbell's endnote. The citation he refers to is in *The Masks of God: Primitive Mythology* (New York: Viking Press, 1959), p. 56.

10. From *Masks of God: Occidental Mythology*, pp. 42–43, by Joseph Campbell. Copyright © 1964 by Joseph Campbell. Used by permission of Viking Penguin, a division of Penguin Books USA Inc.

11. John A. Hardon, S.J., *Modern Catholic Dictionary* (New York: Doubleday, 1980), p. 337.

12. Merlin Stone, *When God Was a Woman* (San Diego, Calif.: Harvest/HBJ, 1978), pp. 154–55.

13. Diane Wolkstein and Samuel Noah Kramer, *Inanna: Queen of Heaven and Earth: Her Stories and Hymns from Sumer* (New York: Harper and Row, 1983), pp. 36–37. Reprinted by permission of Diane Wolkstein.

14. Merlin Stone, p. 19.

15. Starhawk, pp. 93–94.

16. *Oxford Dictionary of the Christian Church*, p. 579.

17. Barbara G. Walker, *Woman's Encyclopedia of Myths and Secrets* (New York: Harper and Row, 1983) p. 125.

18. *Modern Catholic Dictionary*, p. 233.

# The Religion of the Fathers: How and Why It Went Awry

## *Bar Mitzvah: A Story*

After several years away, I had returned to the Bronx in New York City to visit my family. There was to be a celebration; the last of the boys of my generation had reached thirteen, and he was to make his Bar Mitzvah. The clan was assembling at the synagogue for the event, greeting and congratulating one another—*Mazel tov, mazel tov*—and I was caught up in the pleasure of seeing yesterday's faces and smiles. Held and hugged by aunts, great-aunts and cousins, amiable women with ample bodies and flesh as soft as marshmallow, I was carried back to the euphoria of belonging. A pleasant nostalgia conjured up warm images of vast family dinners, of candles flickering on the sideboard, of Baba, my grandmother, teaching me how to make *pirogen* in the mellow light of her kitchen, while in the living room my grandfather labored with the boys, stumbling over their Hebrew.

It felt good to be in the midst of this at first, yet quite soon, almost spitefully, a blip of some other feeling, hard to identify, was emerging along the farther edges of my awareness. Annoyance? Anger? Ambivalence? Confusion. Why have I been so sour about these people? Why have I been so reluctant to return home? What could I have . . .

For a moment, I had almost forgotten. I had left this place years before on a dead run, as if escaping from jail. There were reasons. . . .

Glancing around, I caught sight of my husband, standing alone at the far corner of the lobby—the *goy*, the outsider. He looked liked an outsider. My mother used to say (with a disappointed sigh) that he had the map of England for a face—straight nose, green eyes, blondish hair. Unfortunately, she had said, he was a nice boy. (Another sigh.) Now, as a favor to me (to my mother? to my grandmother? to . . .?), acquiescing to the family, as I was, he stood by himself, at a distance, unacknowledged, so that Baba would not learn that I, her favorite, once the most pious of all her grandchildren, had committed the ultimate betrayal and married "out." It would kill her, they all agreed.

It was one more secret we all would have to keep from Baba, who had always been to the family the embodiment of Jewish law and culture, even more so than my grandfather, the Rabbi. I remembered then the countless secrets that had emerged from countless almost unkeepable rules. I remembered how the rules had pervaded our lives with constant watchful self-denial, with family espionage concerning who might be growing careless, with endless daily irritations that had long before lost any bit of sense or meaning or even tradition, beyond that of keeping the rules. And because there were so many rules, there were so many secrets, big and small, "don't tells": Don't tell Baba about the ice cream Mama bought me on Saturday (It is forbidden to touch money on Sabbath); about the milk Mom snuck into her coffee cup after dinner (It is forbidden to take dairy after meat); about brother's tattoo (It is forbidden to mark the skin); about catching Daddy eating a hamburger at the candy store across the street (Not kosher).

"Don't tells" more serious than the others cut deeper: "Don't tell Rabbi," Baba had warned me, "how troubled you are that God had allowed Hitler to murder so many of us, his Chosen" (or that I didn't like being "Chosen," because it was so dangerous).

Don't tell anyone what Mama told me when she was past sixty and a new widow, that she had been raped when she was sixteen, and only Baba had known, and she had taken Mama to the doctor, and he had sewn her up and put everything back together again, so Daddy never knew. (No one could ever know—it would be a shame—Jewish women go pure to their husbands.) But Baba was dead now, and Daddy was dead now, and . . .

And don't tell the family you are serious about this *goy*. One doesn't marry a *goy*, an outsider. It's a rule. God said so. It is written . . . somewhere.

I had almost forgotten all the hiding.

As a young child, I had not felt the rules, not yet having had a chance to bang against them. When I was very young, I could walk to the lake with my dog. We could sit quietly at the water's edge, look up at the sky and the clouds, feel the sun all warming and light, and be happy that God was so nice. I could go to the temple on Saturday morning and sit upstairs in the women's balcony with my grandmother, stand when she stood, sit when she sat, look happily into her affectionate eyes, and be glad that God was so nice. I had told her once on the way home that I would be a rabbi when I grew up. She laughed good-naturedly, tenderly amused. "You can marry a rabbi," she corrected, "and that would be a great honor."

I had almost forgotten that as I grew older, the rules and the doubts pressed harder. And I pressed harder.

Everyone agreed, I used to be such a nice girl. Suddenly there I was, asking questions. And serious about marrying a *goy*? It was the final straw.

In fact, it turned out to be the final straw. My mother threatened to "jump" out of our fourth-story apartment window. Relatives I had barely known came around "to talk," heart to heart, until they found me obstinate. In the end, my mother did not jump, and relatives turned polite. Some were never polite again, but most had come to the wedding—for my mother's sake, because she had "suffered enough." Never mind. I had had enough, enough of rules without reason, of people without bend, of Gods without voice or shape or sense, of lies and hiding, of insiders and outsiders. Physically and mentally, I left.

Now I was back—for a visit, an outsider myself finally, forgetting for the moment, seduced by the warm feel of it all, the bodies, the laughter, the smell of wood and brass, the outlines of candelabra and lions on the giant doors to the sanctuary, the presence of . . . ? It would last only a moment though, the seduction, ended by yet another reminder of why I had left.

On this day, the day of the Bar Mitzvah, the reminder took the form of one of my great-uncles, Baba's younger brother and occasional past visitor to our kitchen. I looked up to see him approaching, politely smiling. I moved toward him. "Uncle," I said, family-glowing, "how good to see you," and I extended my hand in greeting as my brother, standing beside me, had done. Error. I had indeed forgotten. The smile shot from his face, and he jerked his hand back. "Mustn't," he instructed in Yiddish. Of course. I knew that. Women do not touch men, certainly not in Temple. It is forbidden, defiling. Women do not touch the Torah, the holy objects, the prayer shawls. We sit upstairs in the balcony, safely removed, in our own place, watching the activities on the floor, where the men direct the service. Women have a special role to perform in Judaism, we had always been told, different from men's. Not less, the more modern rabbis would tell us, different. They tell us, the men. Not less. You could see that on my uncle's contorted face as he pulled away.

It is a common enough story. Women all over the world have recounted similar histories. Places, times, and people may vary; one religion replaces another, but the substance of the tale abides. Women tell of early abduction by a mind-set and an institution not our own and not of our making; of self-killing experiences at the hands of the priests and their brethren; of slow doubt and confused realization; of halting, uncertain resistance turning ultimately to rebellion; of a shocked sense of betrayal, followed by anger, and finally—disgusted, scarring repudiation. We fled, and there was reason enough to do so. Traditional religion, a mind-kill for humanity, has been a holocaust for women.

## What Went Wrong?

The religions of the Fathers are severely afflicted. They may have been rooted in healthy soil, born of the needs and desires that normally underlie the spiritual venture. They still contain in varying measure that pure strain of positive religion that serves the monumental aims of the interior life: reflective introspection, interconnectedness with being, reconciliation with existence, meaningfulness. However, because of their centuries-old control by a certain kind of masculine consciousness and by patriarchal political structures, today's institutions of the "great religions" are permeated by and tainted with perverse and corruptive strains: obsession with power, aversion to nature, and misogyny. These strains in turn have lead to characteristics that place patriarchal religion at odds not only with the essential goals of spiritual pursuit, but with its own stated ethos as well. Those characteristics are (1) a contempt for physical existence and (2) an insistence upon only one truth that can be legitimated by only one authority. The first, contempt for physical existence, creates a dolorous and ultimately deadening life orientation. The second, an absolutist control of truth, opposes individual self-determination and thus human becoming.

Religion does not by its nature need to be a distortion of human experience, but for many of us, that is exactly what it has become. While some *individuals* may elude the distortions that have penetrated most of the contemporary religions, the *institutions* have not. In patriarchy, clearly identifiable themes and practices have sent them awry: (1) The first, and most all encompassing, is *masculism*, which is the adoration of a perverse masculinity represented in the person of Mars, the ancient god of war. A masculist orientation contains the worship of power, an acceptance of violence, an obsession with death, and an inclination toward the morbid and negative aspects of life. (2) The twin to masculism, perhaps its alter ego, is the absolute erasure of the female in its symbol system and the substitution of a one-sex metaphor for a two-sex reality. The abuse and exploitation of women in the world follow from and reinforce this theme. (3) Perhaps most fundamental is the element that undergirds the entire system: a rigid dualism pervading both its metaphysic and its social system. (4) Finally, and as a result of the others, is a definition of meaningfulness that renders life meaningless.

To maintain these essentially counter-rational themes and to implement their consequences in society, patriarchal religious institutions have resorted to an array of antisocial conduct—enforced subordination of reason and good sense to ideology, the oppression of women, and the tolerance, even encouragement, of violence.

In patriarchal religion these themes are closely related, each component giving rise to and supporting the other.

## Masculism: the Core of Patriarchal Consciousness

> The orthodox discourse, on the other hand, is the discourse of a god on power and its dispensation; it is the source and origin of a vision that takes total charge of the organization and management of the universe and everything in it, including pleasure. The orthodox discourse is power, the exercise of power, and the delegation of power, all in one.
> —Fatna A. Sabbah, *Woman in the Muslim Unconscious*[1]

What has most distorted the spiritual process in patriarchal religion, to the degree that it is present, is *masculism*. Its essence is the glorification of the traits of masculinity as defined by the ancients in the person of Mars, the god of war. It includes (1) the elevation of the male as the standard of human worth and (2) the perception of all life from the point of view of masculine experience. Its corner-stones in Judaism, Christianity, and Islam are the militant quest for power and an aversion to femaleness and nature (which in patriar-chy have been treated nearly as cognates).[2]

Masculism is the ethos of patriarchy, its underlying world-view and guiding principle. At its simplest level, it is the living out of the martial ideals—a lust for power and control over others and self; absorption by the abstract and unfelt, by duties, principles, and behaviors legitimated essentially by rationalistic argument; the mys-tification of battle in all its aspects; a passion for order, the sol-dier's order; a belief in hierarchy, in the rights of the strong over the weak, in God over men, in men over nature and women, in winners over losers.

On a more profound level, masculism is an orgasm of rigidity. Because it collapses without absolute order, it diminishes anything relaxed, spontaneous, or wild. It fears sex and sensuality because passion contravenes the worship of control. Because in patriarchy femaleness is associated with both sex and disorder, masculism must neutralize it; it must silence "the feminine" and immobilize wom-en.

Popular representations of the "world's great religions" tend to rhapsodize on their "rich diversity" and then on their commonali-ties. Feminists have come to see those commonalities even more clearly than we are bidden, for we realize that the alleged diversity of "the religions of man" is illusory. Driven by the same fuel, pur-suing similar agendas, each has become but a different version, venue changed, of masculism.

Over dinner one afternoon in Boston in 1974, Mary Daly asked me why I thought her recently published book, *Beyond God the Father*,[3] had such a powerful impact upon me. After all, she point-ed out, we had come from such different places: she from Catholic orthodoxy, I from Judaism. I answered that what she had described in Catholicism and what I had experienced in Judaism *felt* the same. Indeed, she replied, they are the same. As Daly elaborated the idea later, at their core the world's great religions are only "One Great Religion," and that one religion is patriarchy:

> Western society is still possessed overtly and subliminally by chris-
> tian symbolism, and this State of Possession has extended its influ-
> ence over most of the planet. Its ultimate symbol of processions is

the all-male trinity itself. Of obvious significance here is the fact that this is an image of the procession of a divine son from a divine father (no mother or daughter involved). In this symbol the first person, the father, is the origin who thinks forth the second person, the son, the word, who is the perfect image of himself, who is "co-eternal" and "consubstantial," that is, identical in essence. So total is their union that their "mutual love" is expressed by the procession (known as "spiration") of a third person called the "Holy Spirit," whose proper name is "Love."* This naming of the "three Divine Persons" is the paradigmatic model for the pseudogeneric term *person*, excluding all female mythic presence, denying female reality in the cosmos. . . .

This mythic paradigm of the trinity is the product of christian culture, but it is expressive of *all* patriarchal patterning of society. Indeed, it is the most refined, explicit and loaded expression of such patterning. . . .

*Patriarchy is itself the prevailing religion of the entire planet*, and its essential message is necrophilia. All of the so-called religions legitimating patriarchy are mere sects subsumed under its vast umbrella/canopy. They are essentially similar despite the variations. All— from buddhism and hinduism to islam, judaism, christianity, to secular derivatives such as freudianism, jungianism, marxism, and maoism—are infra-structures of the edifice of patriarchy. All are erected as parts of the male's shelter against anomie. And the symbolic message of all the sects of the religion which is patriarchy is this: Women are the dreaded anomie.† Consequently, women are the objects of male terror, the projected personifications of "The Enemy," the real objects under attack in all the wars of patriarchy.

—*Gyn/Ecology*[4]

Grounded in the character of Mars, riddled as they have been by masculist thinking, one would expect these institutions, then, to reflect a military bent. One would expect them to feature a male god, one and only one, utterly powerful and self-sufficient, apex of a hierarchy enormous enough to encircle all reality—"heaven and earth," executor of a system of perfect order, rigidly defined principles, and unbreakable rules. One would expect an army of subordinate enforcers, supreme commanders, and petty officers; written codes supported by reams of analytical addenda; and a fixed system of rewards and punishments, mostly punishments. One would

---

*Thomas Aquinas, *Summa theologiae*, I q. 37. (Daly's note.)
†Conversation with Jane Caputi, Boston, May 1977. (Daly's note.)

expect the emphasis to be on obedience over feeling, duty over joy, abstraction over experience, death over birth or even life. One would expect a constant harping on struggle and conflicts—between God and the Devil, good and evil, God and the angels, God and humanity, the faithful and the infidels, spirit and flesh, will and desire, soul and body, pride and submission, this part of the self and another. One would expect a history of battles and murder, of military campaigns, of in-groups and out-groups, of bad guys and good guys and better guys. One would expect a reality or "truth" subordinated to the exigencies of the system, a logic as flexible as its rules are not, techniques of deceit and manipulation so consummately wrought as to fool all but the most wary. In fact, far too often, one finds precisely what one would expect.

In the interactions of the various powerful religions, even the protocol is decidedly military. Convinced that it alone has the perfect alliance with the One True God, each proudly proclaims its superiority in understanding the dictates of monotheism (as if there were no contradiction at all in the existence of so many "one true" gods and "one true" religions, as if there were no question at all of the superiority of monotheism over other theologies). Magnanimously granting to opposing priests the outward forms of deference, like gentleman generals of medieval armies, they secretly repair to their tents to assess relative strength: How does the enemy stand in terms of the great principles of patriarchy—order, system, abstraction? How tightly are the opposition's arguments packed, where are the loopholes, and how do you get to them? How many adherents does each have, how many are falling away, and who is getting them?

All is carefully analyzed—degree of piety, commitment, devotion. It is a matter of sizing up the competition, for the stakes are high, not only validation and the sheer ecstasy of winning, but booty— money, power, and foot soldiers.

As on a battlefield, one finds oneself relentlessly trained upon the lessons of death, upon the vileness of human behavior—"pray for me, a sinner," chants a child of seven—upon the necessity for obedience to the commanders to find safety, upon the risks of failure and the glory of sacrifice, upon guilt and reparation.

There is talk of love, kindness, and tolerance; joy and beauty are granted mention, but it is only thinly convincing because these are portrayed without passion, without urgency, and only on condition. Such values, it would seem, survive more typically in the faithful than in the institutions, and then perhaps despite, rather than because of their fidelity. It is not a proper model of decency, because the priorities and actions of the institutions are more concerned for the body politic, for proving right and writing proofs, for "certitude," than for human beings and their needs. There appears to be more love for fetuses than for people dying on the battlefield or dying of hunger and neglect in the streets; it seems to be more important to furnish the temples than to house the poor.

While given lip service by the powers that be, the gentler virtues are not given center stage; they are background, pale in color, slight in substance, and they seem so far away, so ephemeral. Those within the fold who hold them in the foreground and for whom the colors of life are primary must move with caution. For them the power elite holds barely disguised disdain. As a politically off-center minority, they never seem to come to power.

It has been argued by many modern followers of the various patriarchal religions that this dark picture depicts a spiritual landscape that is completely unfamiliar to them. Theirs, they say, is a religion of joy, celebration, and harmony. So many interpretations are possible, they argue; one ought not to blame the images themselves, but the uses to which they have been put. In other words, the argument goes, the symbols have been abused.

They are quite correct, for the symbols have been abused. It is certainly true that the best of ideas can be contaminated by misuse, but in this case, the mis-use and the contamination are exactly the point. The original symbols might have been developed in more positive ways, but in fact they were sent spinning in a different direction. A particular group of people with a particular way of looking at the world sent them spinning where they did, approved what emerged, and were in turn reinforced by it.

That particular way of looking at the world *is* the problem, because it perpetuates itself through the religions it created, and, in a continuing spiral, it perpetuates its perpetuation.

A blanket of pessimism, of dolor, hangs over the practice of religion in patriarchy. The effect of the embrace of suffering is ubiquitous. For so many, too many, laughter and gaiety are suspect. Idle hands are the devil's workshop, beauty is a snare, and pleasure is the ultimate enemy. Grim austerity is taken for a mark of piety; self-denial, obsessive discipline, and self-reproach receive applause. Offer it up, offer it up.

One of the most sacred stories in all three Western father-god religions, told over and over, is the tale of the great prophet Abraham, so pious, so obedient to his Master, he would sacrifice without question what he held most dear, he would murder his only son, the beloved, miraculously conceived child of his later years. Regarding Abraham, the tale may be understood perhaps as a story of loyalty and of trust. So far as the Master may be judged, however, in other words, so far as the value set that must promote such obedience, there are undeniable intimations of a strain of cruelty and of demanding, tyrannical power.

How striking that the entire myth is not called into question, that it is said to demonstrate the virtue of Abraham and the mercy of the Father rather than the terrible vulnerability of anyone subject to the whims of such a mean-spirited sovereign.

It is striking, but not surprising, for this jealous, angry, unfathomably capricious god-who-punishes-and-tests materializes time and again among his servants, who are turned to salt, condemned to be drowned, cast to the crowd to be raped, skinned alive, beaten, beset with disease, burned, buried, and crucified. And when he does materialize, it is not loathing and fear that are expressed by his subjects, but praise and exultation. Misery, after all, is the surest route to heaven.

Bloody battles are common in patriarchal sacred history. A holy day of great significance in Islam (central to Shiites, less so to Sunnis, but important as well) is the tenth day of Muharram, which commemorates the murder of Husayn, grandson of Muhammad, by the Caliph Yazid in a terrible battle in Karbala, Iraq, in 680. It is a story of tragedy and sacrifice, of love, death, loss, cruelty, duty, revenge, pain, and suffering reenacted every year in passion plays staged by actors and members of the community.

> On the tenth of Muharram emotions reach a crescendo in the staging of the Karbala tragedy. Actors representing both sides in this sacred drama—the forces of Yazid and the Alid family of Husayn—recreate the religious Passion of Islamic, particularly Shi-ite, history. . . . Toward the end of the Passion, the central theme has become clear: *suffering and martyrdom are exalted virtues, the way to salvation* [italics mine]. Through the ultimate vicarious suffering and martyrdom of Husayn, sinners are released from the flames of hell.[5]

What is questionable is not that by this ritual the community is given an opportunity to express and resolve some very painful themes of human life; it is not that sacrifice and duty cannot be exalted or are not virtuous. Rather it is the centrality of those themes to the definition of virtue or the character of piety. What is questionable is the idea that martyrdom is desirable, "the way to salvation," or the idea that by one's experience of suffering other evils may be neutralized.

In fact, the story of the Crucifixion in Christianity portrays the identical theme: through suffering we are made clean; sacrifice and martyrdom are exalted virtues, the way to salvation. By the death of one sacred to the Father, the rest of us are delivered. What is more, the Passion story occupies the same place in this religion, absolute center, and has the same effect—imbalance, an emphasis on dolor.

Christianity contains many of the same myths that appear in other traditions, especially the paradigm of death-descent-rebirth. The Jesus story is the classic tale of the perfect demigod, born of an extraordinary human parent, following his fate as decreed by the gods. We see his wanderings, his trials, his descent into darkness, and the final victorious ascent into the place of the gods. Like so many other characters touched by deity, he is to be remembered and emulated by the wise. Around him in the story are all the ingredients of mythic drama: mystical seasons mirroring natural ones—seasons of youth and maturity, of birth, death, and rebirth, of joy and sorrow and joy again, circling, ever repeated, ever told. Evil and virtuous personalities jostle for success, winning and losing, portraying moral contests. There are mystery and magic, unfathomable events, awesome, good happenings and terrible ones. Here is wonderfully rich raw material, containing potentially so many lessons, so many possible visions. But what becomes of this story?

We must wonder why this god, this shining young man, came to be depicted without a family of his making, without a sexual partner, or children, or grandchildren, or any of the complications of daily human life. Surely a story meant to provide a blueprint for human living ought to treat matters so large in human affairs. Of all the events recounted in this life of more than thirty years, why do we not see him working as a carpenter, worrying about income, deciding how to treat his customers? We are left to wonder why the dying takes so much precedence over the living. The dying god, the sacrifice, is but one available symbol. So is his birth—a truly delightful tale, but in the history of institutional Christianity, the Christmas story has been treated mainly as an enchanting aside. It is not the image hung over every door and every bed, hung about the neck, fastened to the waist. If one image must predominate, why the *cross* and not the *cradle*, why the death and not the life? Why is it not the *road* He traveled, the *"fish"* He caught, the *wine* He provided? The *dove*, the *heart*, the *staff*, all are symbols associated with the god. Each is replete with meanings and meditations and could serve as primary sign, as primary focus. The fish appeared first, but the crucifix won.

The image of the crucifixion recounts a story about the willing sacrifice of a demigod for the good of the people. A tale meant to connote, perhaps, absolute love, ultimate generosity, it holds the potential for many positive and constructive lessons, but a separate force directs elsewhere, and the tone that prevails is lamentation. The primary message seized upon and sent forward by the patriarchs is the glory of sacrifice of the self—for the good of the sacrifice, as reparation and payment for our flaws. For the majority of the faithful, the message is death, guilt, and blame: He died for *your* sins!

Everywhere, the faithful go in mourning black, to remember the death, to honor the death, to commemorate the death, to pay for the sins, to remember the sins, always the sins. . . . Images of agony, tales of horrors that were and horrors to come predominate over the message of hope and comfort.

From one religion to another, the names of the martyrs may change, and their sufferings occur in a different locale, but the themes are constant—death, pain, punishment, and denial. The morals of these stories and their warnings are perfectly obvious. Greater even than the cost of survival exacted by an unconscious and unyielding natural order is the terrible price tag for salvation by the father-god. We must pay the price, and gladly. Because we are flawed. We are tolerated on condition.

The tone, the slant of the symbols is significant, for it has gigantic consequences. Surely, the image of a brutally murdered man (or worse yet, man-god), hanging bleeding and humiliated, the scapegoat for an essentially corrupt humanity, as the *preeminent* symbol of a world-view creates the bleakest orientation to existence. It certainly generates a very different perception of life than would the image that preceded it for thousands of years, that of a vital woman and her consort, full of natural power, and generally at ease with themselves and their creations. The picture of a universe of gods, reflecting a similar universe of mortal beings, human and other than human, good and not so good, living out their seasons in harmony with their own natures, leads to a very different set of values than a heaven governed by a Being fashioned to appear antagonistic to nature, at odds with His creations, and removed from the cycle of life and the exigencies of physical existence.

## Destruction of the Goddess and the Nullification of the Female

Earliest patriarchal religions were not so thoroughly distorted as the current ones; in fact, they were not wholly different from their predecessors. There is ample documentation[6] that infant patriarchies fed liberally upon pagan religions, preserving and adapting a great portion of the old stories, ceremonies, metaphors, and beliefs before supplanting and suppressing them. Indeed, the lexicon of spirit is surprisingly consistent from earliest history to the present. We see holy families in culture after culture. Time and again, with small variations in name and appearance, the same cosmic personalities play upon the scene, the father or mother gods, their obedient or rebellious offspring, their foils and their followers. There are stories of extraordinary human beings conceived of gods, of holy ones dead and ultimately reborn, of priesthoods established by the gods themselves, and of magical beings who influence natural forces and human events. The drama of the changing seasons and its cycle marked by mystical rites reappear in every tradition. Conflict between the forces of good and those of evil erupt into cosmic war. Wrongdoers are punished by earthly cataclysms while the steadfast are wondrously rewarded. The old images blend into the new as modern religions recapitulate archaic ones: the pagan festivals of spring equinox, celebrating renewal after winter, appear again in another festival of rebirth, Easter, named for Oestre, the Great Goddess, Mother and Source of all life. Christmas reenacts the celebration of winter solstice, sacred to the old religions as the turning point in the year when the days begin to grow longer once again, signifying that in the midst of deepest darkness, light (warmth, life, spring, hope) is born. Today as before, ceremonies of communion join gods with people and people with each other, as all share in the breaking of bread and the taking in of the body of their deities and ancestors.

Paganism and the current patriarchal religions share a common ancestry. They have similar goals and overlapping beliefs. But crucial elements separate them, and their differences are very instructive. As the new monotheistic, father-god theologies were born, they consciously set about to distinguish themselves from earlier traditions, emphasizing their dissimilarities, especially in their sexual codes and in their rejection of the goddesses and their consorts, whom they branded idols, "false" gods. (Monotheism always settled on a father-god.)

The old religions did not just die. They were smashed by the new, their altars destroyed, their priests and followers slain or enslaved, their communities decimated, their values and beliefs maligned. The obliteration of the ancient earth religions and the defamation of their images were no accident of history. There were objectives.

One purpose of savagely vilifying earlier gods has to do, of course, with power. Consolidation of authority relies on the elimination of rivals. Former religions must be reviled if their priests and institutions are to be thoroughly disempowered; if one is to claim to speak exclusively for god, all other speech must be invalidated. Nonexclusive religions do exist, those that do not claim sole possession of cosmic truth and that can therefore tolerate the presence of other gods and religions. However, such inclusivity is impossible for patriarchy because its very essence is the glorification of power, dominance, and therefore absolute hegemony. Among the emerging patriarchal religions there could be no place for coexistence: "I am the Lord thy God. . . . Thou shalt have no other gods before me" (Exodus 20:1–3).

More importantly, the followers of the Father would never feel safe, in the world or in their minds, as long as the Goddess reigned anywhere. His power (and theirs) could not be shared; Hers would have to be annihilated. But even more was required: Her memory had to be defamed, obliterated as sacred. In the masculist mind-set, She represents the ultimate profanity and the consummate danger— the ascendancy of women and the female principle. For the patriarchs, the Goddess is associated with physical life, with sex and the generation of physical life and, therefore, with death.

Much is revealed in how the gods of the old religion were transmuted into the new: Baal (literally *husband*), Lord of the ancients, was demoted from Consort of the Great Goddess to Beelzebub, essence of evil. As Satan, he is depicted with the horns and tail of the Bull, symbol of masculine sexual potency. His cloven hooves and hairy physicality recall the salacious goat-god, Pan; he is said to possess an irresistible sexuality—powerful, filthy—that is so seductive, even the most virtuous women stand in peril without the constant attentiveness of their male protectors.

Baal's essential crime, of course, was liaison with the Great Goddess, the ultimate corruption in patriarchy, a female deity/female principle. Not only was She a female out of Her place, but like Her consort, She too was guilty of unbridled physicality—fleshliness—which was the source and the consequence of Her sin. It is noteworthy that in Her transmutation She has little power. No great god of evil does She become—no Satan or Devil. Rather She is devolved into a mere helper, subordinate in her evil as she will be in life. The Great Goddess becomes the witch, ugly, malignant, but diminutive in comparison with her lord of the underworld. Her various representations too are small and lowly: spiders, pigs, cats, snakes. Only the great Serpent of Regeneration, a most positive manifestation of the Great Mother as life principle, retains its power, but this time it is recast as evil, the monster of the Garden of Eden, the ultimate bearer of calamity. But in this telling, the snake is portrayed as male.

Ishtar and Baal, it was said, were disgusting. They committed the sin of nature, of carnality. Moreover, She was disobedient, usurping the proper authority of man, and He, Her respectful consort, tolerated, even encouraged Her and in so doing tempted the pride of woman. Both, therefore, are not only contemptible, but damned. They and their followers deserved their destruction.

The destruction, in religion and in the heart, of the Goddess and what She represented was not an easy task, because Her existence in both places is natural and suitable. The effort it demanded then and continues to require even now has blighted the history of patriarchal religion with terrible atrocities, against women and against human nature.

## The Oppression of Women

It is not possible to deify the masculinity of Mars and then grant parity to women. To do so would be to allow equal value to the very traits originally devolved upon women by the patriarchs so that they could be free of them—all the uncontrollable, unpredictable idiosyncrasies of concrete living and dying that cannot be subsumed under fixed rules and principles, that cannot be adjudicated by neat categories and hierarchies, that create insecurity and dread because they suggest irreparable imperfection, the capriciousness of nature, and the likelihood of mortality.

There is no alternative. Womanhood, if it must exist at all, must be held in control and in contempt. Woman must be contained: she must serve men, manhood, and manhood's god; she must play counterpoint—female smallness (inferiority, etc.) enhances male bigness; and she must be limited to the nonsacred realms of existence (earth and nature).

Masculism is the celebration of the masculine. Patriarchy is its political expression. It should come as no surprise, therefore, that its misogyny should be codified and sanctified by its religions.

In each society, institutional religion fulfills a variety of purposes. One of its functions is to legitimize cultural structures in an ultimate way. Institutionalized religion serves as the quintessential expression of a society's values, ethos, and beliefs about life.

Societal agendas and religious morality generally interlace, often becoming indistinguishable. Social custom would be deemed little more than collective habit were it not given special validity by the institutions claiming cosmic truth; nor could priests enforce their will without popular convention functioning as an enabler. The relationship between patriarchal societies and their institutional religions is symbiotic: the "good people" of the community serve the temple by modeling propriety and by vigilant watchfulness of others—signaled by their approval or their rebuff. In return, they receive enhanced legitimacy and status. For the priests and the social elite, it is a most effective alliance: the goals and needs of each become integrated. Holy writ becomes legal statute, and the social expediencies of the powerful gain the force of God's will. When the two realms support one another in this way, the possibility of rebellion is reduced.

This alliance, of course, has generally been a foil to liberty of thought and action. For women, systematically excluded from positions of power in either religion or social government, systematically debased by both, the enormity of the effect is beyond measure. Any abuse can be justified:

The story is told of an Egyptian girl made ready for her future husband. She must be prevented absolutely from any opportunity for infidelity, in body or in thought. She must be rendered totally "innocent," totally submissive. One very effective solution—brutal clitoridectomy: A child of six and her four-year-old sister are torn from their beds in the middle of the night. Confused and terrified they are carried by strangers' hands to the icy tiles of the bathroom, where, amid cheers of exultation, they are restrained and, writhing in pain, they are mutilated.

I screamed with pain despite the tight hand held over my mouth, for the pain was not just a pain, it was like a searing flame that went through my whole body. . . .

I did not know what they had cut off from my body. . . . I just wept . . . . Now we know where lies our tragedy. We were born of a special sex, the female sex. We are destined in advance to taste of misery, and to have a part of our body torn away by cold, unfeeling, cruel hands.

—Nawal El Saadawi, former Director of Public Health in Egypt[7]

This is clearly an act of control and hatred, a practice created by and for the community of men. Such a truth, in its nakedness, would be intolerable to look upon, even to those whom it serves. A transgression of such magnitude must be masked. To render it excusable, to clothe it, it must be given entirely different meaning, transmuted, as it were, into to some other reality. Here "religion" may serve: "*This is done according to the will of God.*" Sexual mutilation perpetrated by a group of ordinary men would be an abomination, but stipulated by the word of God, a power greater than men's and over which they have no control (and for which, therefore, they have no responsibility), the entire procedure may be safely set back in society, thoroughly justified, and (because God is good) cleansed of evil.

The act of sexual mutilation, horrible as it is, is not alone of its kind. Little would be gained in describing again in detail the countless violations of women, physical and otherwise, that are sanctioned by religion. What is crucial is to understand the strategy behind the institutionalization of these practices and the impact: To detoxify the actual intent of the act, to neutralize the guilt of the aggressors, both in their own consciences and in appearance, and to forestall resistance by the victims, brutal acts are transformed into divine decrees; from mere societal conveniences each is recast into a rite of the institution that defines what is right.

If it suits the masters to have their women altered, mutilated, rendered docile, it can be done. What is more, it will be done without apparent culpability and with a minimum of overt force on the part of the perpetrators; "custom" and piety will supply the force. To be full members of society, acceptable in the sight of God and man, women must "willingly" participate in their own violation, giving it further validation; after all, it is done by their own hand! And they offer up not only their own bodies and minds, but those of their sisters and daughters. And so the barbarities are made to appear wholesome, virtuous, even in the face of contrary reason, even in the face of contrary experience that would be otherwise obvious.

For such ends, patriarchal religion provides the ideal vehicle. The contempt for *"experience"* relative to *"logic"* enables its followers to manipulate ideas for their own ends. The obsession with submission (to the will of god, to the priests, to the temple) allows the dictates of the self to be nullified. The penchant for masochism provides justification for any misery incurred. Suffering, after all, cleanses the soul.

Practices or ideas that are serviceable but morally or existentially problematic can be rehabilitated by reference to sacred principles. Miraculously, the origins of questionable activities can be transported back into time to when He directed that the Holy Books be made. In The Book they can be located, highlighted, chanted, and invoked: Thou shalt, you must, God wishes it: to have your feet bound, to have your organs torn, to have your body burned, to have your sexuality appropriated, to have your freedom extinguished, to have your hair shorn, to have your head (face, body, being) covered, to have your creativity exploited, to be formed into sacrificial mothers and obedient wives, to . . .

It is written: God wishes for this to be done. It is not for you to question. It is in the Holy Book. It is not for you to understand. If there is suffering and pain, it is holy decree, not human decree. *Good* women, godly, pious women, accept without question, without understanding, without hesitation or doubt or resistance, for it is written. Such a woman is pleasing in the eyes of God and in her husband's as well. It is written. No man who loves God would have any other kind of woman; any other kind of woman must die alone, shunned and unwanted, an abomination in the eyes of God, men, and the human community. It is written.

Will woman not comply?

To ensure that any existing loopholes in the logic will not be discovered, discussion is prohibited:

> There is no doubt that to write about women in Arab society, especially if the author is herself a woman, is to tread on difficult and sensitive areas. It is like picking your way through territory heavy with visible and hidden mines. Almost every step might touch an electrified wire, a sanctified and sacred spot which is meant to be untouchable, a value that is not to be questioned because it is a part of the religious and moral structures that rear themselves up like

heavy iron bars whenever questions related to women are raised and hands stretched out to set her free.

—Nawal El Saadawi[8]

Disobedience may be punished:

And this is so much in accordance with the natural order, that the head of the household was called paterfamilias; and this name has been so generally accepted, that even those whose rule is unrighteous are glad to apply it to themselves. But those who are true fathers of their households desire and endeavour that all the members of their household, equally with their own children, should worship and win God, and should come to that heavenly home in which the duty of ruling men is no longer necessary, because the duty of caring for their everlasting happiness had also ceased; but, until they reach that home, masters ought to feel their position of authority a greater burden than servants their service. And if any member of the family interrupts the domestic peace by disobedience, he is corrected either by word or blow, or some kind of just and legitimate punishment, such as society permits, that he may himself be the better for it, and be readjusted to the family harmony from which he had dislocated himself.

— Augustine, *The City of God* [9]

Now, as earlier, it is still a justification frequently propounded for granting males dominion over the lives of women: on Earth, men alone represent God and know His will. For the good of all, and most particularly for those less favored than men—women and children—males must discern, promulgate, and when necessary enforce Holy intentions.

Ultimately, for the stubborn, a final excommunication may be meted out:

In December of 1979, Ms. Farrokhrou Parsa, the first woman to serve in the Iranian cabinet, was executed after a trial by hooded judges— a trial at which no defense attorney was permitted, no appeal possible, and the defendant had been officially declared guilty before the proceedings began. She was charged with "expansion of prostitution, corruption on earth, and warring against God." Aware of the hopelessness of her case, she delivered a reasoned, courageous defense of her career decisions, among them a directive to free female schoolchildren from having to be veiled and the establishment of a commission for revising textbooks to present a nonsexist image of women. A few hours after sentence was pronounced she was wrapped in a dark sack and machine-gunned.

Ms. Parsa, whose mother had been exiled for *her* stance on women's rights (especially her opposition to the veil), had been educated as a medical doctor but chose to serve as a teacher and, later, as principal of a girls' high school. In 1964 she was one of the first six women elected to Parliament. In 1968 she was appointed Minister of Education. At the time of her death she had been retired for four years.

She was not a heroic figure but a hard-working, disciplined woman who struggled to achieve her position in government. She was a practical, level-headed feminist. The significance of her position for the Iranian women's movement rested not so much in her considerable personal achievements but in that *she was one of hundreds of thousands*. Those who executed her also understood this and staged the event as a symbolic attempt to reduce her—and through her the type of woman she represented—to an insignificant, lifeless shape in a dark sack. In the year following her death, many women marched against the tyranny of the mullahs. Many were beaten, stabbed, imprisoned. Some of the very young were tried and executed without ever identifying themselves as other than "fighters, daughters of Iran." No further identification was necessary. It was a type of woman the regime meant to destroy.
—Mahnaz Afkhami[10]

## Internal Logic of Patriarchy—Terror and Denial: Dualism and the Flight from Life

It has become almost banal to remark the presence of martial violence in the burning of women and the burning of libraries, in the sacking of cities, in inquisitions and holy wars, murders of entire "heretical" communities by the faithful, and the death of the faithful at the hands of the heretics (faithful too, albeit to another god). We see Mars in the spectacle of priests blessing weapons, praying for victory, assuring everyone that God had picked the right side (or the side was right because God had picked it, or both). Time and again when circumstances have coalesced to produce the potential for suffering and damage, when they might have done otherwise, the powers of the patriarchal religions have failed to position themselves stoutly on that side most aligned with life. Instead, like virtuous warriors, they have capitulated to death.

Patriarchy (and masculism, which is its heart) romances death. That much is obvious. In its wars, its violation of nature and women, its quest for increasingly effective violence and its growing desensitization to pain, its religion that pursues death after life as a solution to life, patriarchy reflects a profound necrophilia, the embrace of death.[11]

But in masculism the romance of death is not an end in itself. Rather, the place of necrophilia in patriarchy is determined by a paradox: masculists are seduced by death because they fear it so. The key to the martial embrace of death is the denial that is locked within.

*I had been summoned to his office, the chairman of the Department of Philosophy and Religion in a small university that had once been a religious college. He was, in fact, a minister of that religion. In facial features a handsome man, rather young, yet he seemed to me older, unrelievedly stark, rigid. He moved with little grace, as if not at home in his body. His smile needed warmth. In front of him on his desk lay a yellow pad, covered with scribblings— apparently about me. He held it between us as he spoke, deliberately, in measured tones: "Sheila, there have been some complaints about you. . . ."*

*Two ladies from a church in a little town south of the college had called to report that they had heard me use "dirty words" during a public lecture. The Dean of Nursing had called; one of her "girls" had told her that in class I had referred to the nursing students (or was it their uniforms?) as virgins (or virginal, she couldn't remember which). It was rumored I had assigned Lady Chatterley's Lover in the introductory philosophy course. Was it true? I began to explain: I had been exploring the attitudes of Western culture towards the body and sex. I had raised the question of. . . .*

*Suddenly, interrupting, "Did you say 'fuck' in class?" he blurted, blushing, losing composure. I answered yes. I began to explain again. Again he cut me off. "You can't. . . . You may not. . . ." There were protestations from me, mumbled utterances of academic freedom. (I was very young.) A few days later, I received the proverbial pink slip. Following, there were meetings with the Dean and the Provost, subtle accusations of "misconduct," lectures on the nature and needs of society and academe, reports in the press, controversy, student delegations. Time passed. The pink slip prevailed. I lost.*

It was a telling incident. As I recall it now, it is clear to me as it was not then that no other outcome was possible. In the Provost's unwitting words, I was guilty of "massive cultural conflict." In underestimating patriarchy's hysterical ambivalence toward sex and in overestimating the power of rationality in its resolution, I had forced patriarchy's consciousness (expressed through its religion) into psychic proximity with the reality of human sexuality. In that very traditional, very patriarchal community, such an action could not be tolerated.

In its sexual mores reside the quintessential principles of patriarchy. Notwithstanding all their obsessive attention to matters of the body, particularly the genitals, masculists revile sex as the ultimate symbol of all they fear and resist. So deep is their hatred, so complete the prohibition, that even speech, the mentioning of sex, is prohibited, and language has become unavailable.

Even now it is difficult to articulate precisely the heart of the subject. How can one communicate with precision about a set of events for which there are no accurate words? I am speaking of what takes place experientially, externally, intersubjectively, and phenomenologically when one sexes. I am referring to a whole range of events and perceptions involved when one . . . (does it?). It is not that we need a better definition of intercourse and company. Quite the other way around: we know what we mean; there simply are no words for it, at least not ones that work.

One may have sex, have sex with, copulate with, make love to, lie with, sleep with, take someone to bed (none of these terms even near accurate representations), but one cannot simply _____ (insert appropriate verb). In the slang, one can fuck (screw, bang, jump, etc.); yet for nonsexist people the slang does not work. Were it even less illicit, less associated with the sleazy, the current slang lexicon would still be inadequate to capture the range of activities and experiences involved. Essentially masculist, the terms are single-mindedly genital and almost exclusively heterosexual. What is more, they are violent and contemptuous, sharply reflective of the society and the mind-set that give rise to them.

How odd that this ubiquitous animal activity claims in our language no acceptable verb that expresses precisely what one does when one does it! *To sex?* To sex someone or sex oneself or be sexed. *Sexing, the act of.* In the absence of anything better, this term will have to do.

It seems, at first, peculiar that we should be in such a quandary to find a word for an event that is so common in human experience. Generally, language reflects society's reality. Phenomena that are experienced often or that have powerful effect on life are typically assigned many terms or words, each reflecting some nuance of difference or definition. In this way a language is said to be "rich" in that area. In English, for example, numerous terms refer to various forms of precipitation—*rain, snow, sleet, fog, storm,* and so on. There are *bushes, shrubs, trees, flowers, weeds, thickets, scrubs, grass,* which allow us to name with minute accuracy different varieties of plant life. Surely, sexing is as common as plant life, certainly as powerful, and yet in this regard our language is not merely "unrich," it is poverty-stricken.

Given this insufficiency, do we have other options? If in our need to communicate the intricacies or intimacies of sexing, we abandon the barrenness of "polite" language, we appear to be left with only one alternative—what is referred to (incorrectly) as "cursing," that is, the slang that has been outlawed by propriety as "foul" or "dirty" language. In other words, we are taught that when one mucks about with sex or sexuality in our culture, one lowers oneself to the dirt. It is perhaps equally instructive to observe the converse: should one wish to deal in dirt verbally, i.e., curse, one has little choice in our language but to refer to sexing or to parts of the body. The foulest of words or epithets refer to body parts and functions in place of something of the sort popular in some other cultures, "May the shadow of a goat fall upon your mother's grave." Even more ironic, the only two truly serious cursing words, *hell* and *damn,* are considered by most to be mild expletives, totally eclipsed by what in any sane universe might be a rather pleasant wish, "get sexed."

This talk about sexual language might be little more than wryly funny or mildly informative were it not for the fact that, generally speaking, sex talk is a map of sex thought, and in Western culture the destinies of sexuality, women, and nature have become entwined. There are profound reasons why the idea of sexing is omitted from polite language.

In patriarchy, sex thought is decidedly schizophrenic: sexing exists, and it does not exist. *For the record* it is absent, what one might call a nonevent, something that happens, which yet does not happen. Too disturbing, too out of sync with the patriarchal construction of life, too dissociating even to utter, sexuality is "unspeakable," not formally acknowledged, and so in "official" public awareness it is erased, in a sense deactualized. It is reactualized only in different, even quarantined, psychic locations: either in the medico-technical retreat, where it may be isolated, scrubbed of *af-*

fect, and rendered harmless, or in the nether regions of some slea-zy, subordinate reality, where slang and id and sin reside.

Two opposed realities, then, function concurrently to manage our relationship to sex: In the foreground—formally supported, main-tained by nice people behaving nicely, consistent with the princi-ples of the patriarchs as expressed in their religions, hailed as vir-tuous—stands the antiseptic realm of nonsensuality, non-sex. In this place one is pure, clean, and virginal. Here one is modest, covered, and in control, unbothered by the chaos of need or the dark confu-sions of physical fantasy or shared secrets.

In the background looms another reality, sinister, troublesome, shameful. Here is struggle and pain, for here is pleasure, passion, an intensely felt reality. In this place we experience carnality in its widest sense. We eat, digest, gurgle, and belch. We sex and lust. We imagine and fantasize and act out.

Patriarchy presents us with two seemingly incompatible yet simul-taneously operative realms of consciousness, two layers of exist-ence both psychological and social, each with its own correspond-ing truths, rules, values, expectations, and mores. We are required to balance precariously between them, learning early the intricacies of the dance—my body lives and acts; now I may speak of it, now I may not. At home, alone with my friends, we sometimes say this or that; in school, publicly, never. These words I hear, these acts I see in films at the theater, others on television, but some are re-served only for pay (private?) television. This I share with my fam-ily, this with my friends, this with my teacher. We are presented very early with the public and private realms and the system of judging what goes where, but soon we learn that the division is even deeper than public and private. It is legitimate and illegitimate. Although we may share certain publicly unmentionable items with Mother, at home alone, we may share only a portion of them and only in certain terms. Other awarenesses we share not at all. We do not speak of the pleasure of touching ourselves or the curiosity we feel for other bodies. We guard carefully dreams and fantasies that seem bizarre, because no one else appears to have them.

Later, although not much later, we discover the place for the ille-gitimate. We are young when we encounter our first "dirty joke," when we discover the girlie magazine, when we hide ourselves away with the rest of the gang to play "Doctor." Experience teaches us when to go underground (or, more accurately, into background) with a certain portion of our reality. As we mature, each of us is initiated into the mysteries, trained to know precisely how to negotiate the terrain, how to bridge the chasm, how far and when the dominant upper reality may be penetrated by the lower.

*Upper* and *lower* serve us as fair names for the fractured experiential realms, corresponding as they do to the two realms of being posited by patriarchy: respectively, the one where God, goodness and spirit reign, the other where animals and unenlightened humans thrash about in ignorant slavery to the material. *Upper* and *lower* serve us as well in connoting higher and base, civilized and animalic, righteous and sinful, good and bad, powerful and subordinated. By resolving into pairs of contrasting concepts, they lead us directly into dualism, a thought strategy that supports and explains patriarchy's treatment of sexuality.

Appearing in many cultures, ancient and new, in the Orient and in the Occident, dualism is a mode of thinking that structures reality around two opposing realms of existence, relevant phenomena then being categorizable into the appropriate realm, as one of a pair of opposites.

Reflective of the primal dualities that are perceived in nature—night and day, dark and light, male and female—dualism is more than merely an expression of that experience. Frequently it becomes a statement of the most profound existential puzzles of life and a schema for resolving them.

What matter in life could be more fundamental, more primordial than the twin mysteries of life and death, what awareness more compelling than female and male, than fecundation and generation? What proportion of the way we live is ordered by the realities of night and day, of the moon and the sun, which are their symbols, and of the separate meanings that become attached to them? These are dualities.

Gradation, the continuities between the poles, may be noticed—night to dawn to day to dusk—but does not gradation form the background in our experience rather than the foreground? At least primarily, is it not the difference, the opposition, that taunts the mind and captures the soul, which demands resolution?

Nonetheless, although it requires a subtler, more complex turn of mind than the immediate recognition of duality, the background—the context of connection or gradation in which the pairs reside—should not be omitted from an analysis of the philosophy of dualism. For one thing, background and foreground themselves form a duality of their own, one more basic and defining than the others.

Continuity or gradation, the relational element, suggests change and process: heat blending by degrees into cold, liquid shifting progressively through viscosity into solidity, motion slowing to rest and returning gradually to speed again. Change—growth, movement, the endless cycles of evolution and devolution, occurrence and recurrence, equally as apparent in nature as polarity—process, can be opposed to stasis, to the absolute and unchanging separateness of the subordinate polarities. In one sense then, change and stasis, gradation and opposition, compose the ultimate oppositions.

In a different sense, however, in another gestalt, taken together, change and stasis can provide the resolution for the entire split. Relationship (process that houses difference), connection, may be perceived as the more powerful, prevailing reality.

> The fundamental duality of existence was observed in the opposition of male and female, of the active and the passive (reflected in grammar), of heaven and earth, of the sun and the moon. Such duality could not be left unresolved. Otherwise the cosmos would break in two, and that was unthinkable if there actually was a cosmos. To emerge from this dilemma one can deny the reality of one or the other of the conflicting beings, find some third thing which will be the source of them both, or see their connection as phases of a single process which is more real than either.
> — George Boas[12]

The ancients, matriarchal and nature-oriented, assigned preeminence to Process, to the cycle of being and becoming, and to the integration of the dualities within it. Patriarchy, much younger, chose a different option. There had to be a victor and a vanquished, a hierarchy of better and worse, higher and low. Ultimately, stasis would prevail.

One of our earliest examples of dualism in Western tradition is the work of the Greek, Pythagoras, who more than 2,500 years ago, proposed his schema for the structuring of reality that included among its principles the well-known table of opposites.

Close in time to ancient matriarchal perspective, but yet already showing clear signs of the emerging masculist mind-set, this table is more than simply an objective analysis of the structure of reality. Obviously it has attached to it a schema of values, preferences, and prejudices; the left side of the chart is valued over the right.

At first glance the categories may seem puzzling. We might have a feeling for why the concepts *straight, right,* or *light* might be

| Table of Opposites[13] | |
|---|---|
| limited | unlimited |
| odd | even |
| one | many |
| right | left |
| male | female |
| rest | motion |
| straight | crooked |
| light | darkness |
| good | evil |
| square | oblong |

grouped with *good*. Knowing who created this scheme and the society out of which this emerged, we might see why *male* might reside with them. Perhaps even *square* may be intuitively obvious as their preference. Why, however, are *limitation, oddness, oneness, rest* preferred?

The notion of certainty or control, proposed earlier in this chapter as an essential of masculist consciousness, provides the solution, the organizing principle. *Limitation* implies order. It is countable, definable, ultimately predictable. It has sharp, discernable edges; it is ascertainable, thus controllable; limitlessness is elusive. *Oddness* cannot break comfortably into equal parts, as *evenness* does, and so it too implies a resistance to alteration, hence to elusiveness. *Oneness* is absolute limitation, connoting as it does allness, totality, universality, thus completeness, inclusiveness. *Rest*, of course, is the absence of change. Stasis is comfortable, reassuring; obviously, then, process must be avoided. *Motion*, of course, is a cognate of change.

Change itself is the demon, the converse of control. Conceptually, change is the foil to perfection. If a thing is perfect and changes, must it not have moved from perfection? Is not change itself, then, imperfect, undesirable? Is this imperfection of change-ability not reflected in the "worst" aspects of concrete existence (for masculist consciousness), in the process of nonbeing, moving through to life, to nonbeing again—death?

Perfection, in this mind-set, all that is seen as desirable and good, associates with changelessness, a kind of stop-action control: it connotes definability, predictability, and certainty. Clear echoes of fear are heard in such an orientation, fear that goes well beyond insecurity, fear for all things that cannot be secured, kept under surveillance, and made to submit, to conform to expectation. Somehow one senses in this the notion that if anything moves, in any way at all, it is dangerous.

*Evenness* has the tendency to break easily into parts (as *oddness* does not) and is perceived therefore as less stable. *Many* has not the completeness of *One*, and with *crooked*, *oblong*, and the other "imperfections," it resides together with the absence of light, the frightening *darkness* (where unseen, uncontrolled things happen), and with the evil even darker than *evil—woman*.

By this period in the "evolution" of cultures, as masculine supremacy had taken hold, femaleness had come to be seen as an imperfection in itself, women being, in Aristotle's words, "misbegotten males," conceived in error during unpropitious weather conditions (too much humidity). Earlier, before women had come to be denigrated, femaleness had been associated with motion and process taken in the very positive sense, with fecundation, growth, life, and Earth. The left side of the body, associated with femaleness, had special value and signified feminine divinity. Maleness, although in a sense less divine because less associated with the giving of life, was nonetheless honored for its particular vitality. Maleness was different from, in opposition to, femaleness, certainly not superior, but not inferior either. Femaleness and maleness themselves were a metaphor for all the essential dualities of life, for duality itself. Reflecting the truths of the lived existence of women and men, the two were perceived as a constant, integrated unity representing the interdependent processes of life: The fields needed the heavens to give forth the grain; the stag served the deer, who in turn gave forth new life; land and water together were the source of fertility and nourishment.

It took patriarchy's special fear to invest a balanced duality with the unbalancing element of hierarchy and to affix the notions of good to one side and evil to the other.

In time, with different philosophies created by different men, the table has grown (historically and conceptually). Dualism has crystallized into something even greater than a conceptual schema; it has metamorphosed into a modus for ordering all reality, political and social, as well as psychological and ontological. As additional concepts have been assigned to one side or the other, the chasm between the two sides has widened and taken on new consequences. Most significantly, the decision to place "God" on the side of *oneness*, *light*, and *good* has compelled or permitted (it is hard to say which) the placement of the "Devil" and all his retinue and evils on the other side, further differentiating the character of the two realms and setting each into a particular valuation, one side now clearly adjudged better, the other more completely relegated to the distaff. Gone is any attempt at the original complementarity. The now familiar hierarchy of one over the other, dominance and subordination, good and evil, is solidly in place, the Pythagorean table finally elaborated into the pervasive modern mind-set expressed so clearly in patriarchal religion. One rendering of that mind-set may be presented as follows:

| | |
|---|---|
| one | many |
| God | the Devil |
| perfection | imperfection |
| eternal | transitory |
| spirit | body |
| Heaven | Earth or Hell |
| life | death |
| salvation | damnation |
| mind | passion |
| rationality | emotion |
| ethereal | carnal |
| right | wrong |
| virtue | sin |
| good | bad |
| light | dark |
| male | female |
| straight | crooked |

In this newly elaborated patriarchal schema and in the religions that both create and reflect it, the formula is vividly clear:

> *Eternal life, godhood, goodness, and salvation together form one reality, and this reality stands in strict opposition to a second reality that includes physical existence, sense, sensuality, emotion, feeling, sex, and women.*

As we consider this formula, we are faced with certain provocative questions. Most simply and fundamentally, what agenda (besides a rationalization of power) underlies this particular configuration? Given the realities of masculine sexuality, its ever-ready ubiquity, why align sex and sexuality with women? Why then affix that combination, women and sexuality, to evil, earthly life and death, and oppose all to God, spirit, and perfection?

*The key to understanding this mind-set is the equation of women, bodies, and death. In patriarchy, dualism becomes a strategy for avoiding death.*

How can death be denied? It is visible everywhere. Creatures finish, their bodies decline and finally putrefy right before our eyes, displaying to us in painfully vivid terms the meaning of mortality. Could there be a way out? Assuredly so, we are told by the patriarchs; there is a defense.

If we are not to die, we must somehow separate from these dying things, our bodies, and yet not, as we might usually expect, separate from life. We must instead posit a different part of ourselves to be ourselves, one that is conveniently detachable, but which does not die and which, therefore, may connect us with all that is eternal and eternally pleasant, good, and unending. That detachable essence could be fashioned "spirit," not-body, that is, the opposite of body and badness, hence good.

"Creatures" die, but for human beings, formed by and from the stuff of gods, just a little lower than the angels (and to the degree that they resemble the angels), there is the possibility of life without end. For humans, provided they dwell apart from nature, the being within, the real being, the one that counts, does not have to die. One is safe so long as one is not-body, but is instead "spirit," "in this world, but not of it."

Man that is born of woman is of few days, and full of trouble. He comes forth like a flower and withers. (Job 14:1–2)

[I]f you live according to the flesh you will die, but if by the spirit you put to death the deeds of the body, you will live. (Romans 8:13)

One need not die, one need only keep to the un-dying realm. One need only eschew the mortal, the physical—Nature and all that she is—sensing, feeling, experiencing, and its signs—pleasure, sensuality, sexuality. One need only reject life to have it forever.

Body must be denied. Now, it is not simply the having of a body that must be forsworn; that would be impossible. Having a body could be rationalized away, justified, so to speak: "It is a trial, a test; we never wanted one in the first place, but God said we must because we were bad. It will not be long before we are shed of it," and so on. No, it is not the having of a body that requires denial; it is the affirmation of it, the choosing of it; it is the delight in body and in physicality, the taking of pleasure there, that marks one as a citizen of the realm of mortality and as the Devil's own. Affirmation of body and materiality, willful appreciation of sense and sensation, their election, is the sin that damns.[14]

What could be more clearly an election of materiality than willful, happy sensuality? As the one physical need or drive that can be controlled or denied, as the most intense and demanding of the pleasures of the body, sexing—sensual, experiential, noninstrumental, for-its-own-sake—sexing must be forsworn. If for a male sexing is to be forsworn, then woman too must be renounced, not just because she is one with whom he may likely share sex, but because woman *is* sex; for him she is the essence of carnality. In patriarchy, woman is body, primarily, essentially, and by design. In the various "holy texts," she is never designed as an equal, a full partner in spirit or mind. Her unique service lies elsewhere. As pure biology, as animal, it is women's essential purpose to reproduce their mates' animal aspect.

> It was necessary for woman to be made, as the Scripture says, as a helper to man; not, indeed, as a helpmate in other Works, as some say, since man can be more efficiently helped by another man in other works: but as a helper in the work of generation. . . . Among perfect animals, the active power of generation belongs to the male sex, and the passive power to the female. . . . But man is further ordered to a still nobler work of life, and that is intellectual operation. Therefore there was greater reason for the distinction of these two powers in man; so that the female should be produced separately from the male, and yet that they should be carnally united for generation. . . .
>
>     . . . [W]oman is defective and misbegotten, for the active power in the male seed tends to the production of a perfect likeness according to the masculine sex; while the production of woman comes from defect in the active power, or from some material indisposition, or even from some external influence, such as that of a south wind, which is moist, as the Philosopher observes. On the other hand, as regards universal human nature, woman is not misbegotten, but is included in nature's intention as directed to the work of generation.
>     — Thomas Aquinas[15]

For the male the definition of Woman as carnality, as flesh rather than spirit, is likely a primal perception and a happy device. To be sure, in his eyes, Woman displays herself as animalic, grounded, as she appears to be, in physical process. Monthly, in synchrony with the moon, she bleeds from her most secret, hidden recess. She opens her legs and with a great animal groan she squeezes out living creatures. Into her body she receives him, the man, and when in this act, he is himself most physical—sharply sensing, processing stuff, participating in animal conception.

Nonetheless, she might yet be understood as only partly carnal, and like himself, spirit as well. But that would not do. Where then could man dump the aspects of his being that estrange him from perfect, infinite life? What would he do with, and who could keep for him, sensation, passion, and sense? On whom could he blame his mortality? Was it not she, after all, who supplied him with this putrefying vessel of flesh? He that is born of woman, of the flesh, is transient, full of trouble, and destined to die. Only he that is *born again*, a second time, *not in the body*, but in the spirit (un-body) is immortal. If woman were equally spirit with man, would he not then be equally body with her? It cannot be. To ensure immortality, woman's carnality must not only be acknowledged, but insisted upon, detested and, finally, punished.

In the myth of Eve and Adam,[16] man, alone and pure, lives in perfect harmony with creation, needing nothing, provided with everything, certain of the protection of God (fate and power) and the eternality of life. Woman appears, like him but secondary (created not by fiat for herself alone, as was Adam, but for Adam as a "help meet"), and inferior (undisciplined, disobedient). She succumbs to the appeal of the flesh, to appetite, and leads Adam to his downfall. So obviously carnal, Eve, the woman, is therefore obviously the author of all catastrophe.

The story is a neatly packaged rationale for the total subordination not only of women to men, but of femaleness (understood as body–nature) to maleness (understood as spirit–god). In one stroke, women are separated forever not only from their physical freedom, but from any claim to sanctity.

Even giving birth, once a magical, wondrous power and source of prestige for women, is declared a punishment and demoted to an abomination. Physical life is disdained. Instead, the honor of creating human life, once ascribed to the Great Mother, who opened her legs and with a groan gave forth the cosmic egg, is settled upon the male god and his first male child, Adam. The first birth is now accomplished more neatly, cleanly, first by male Jahweh's fiat, and then again without blood or pain by Adam, who consequently becomes the first human giver of life. Ever after, women are held responsible for the production and maintenance of the *bodies* of their offspring (and by generalization all others), but men have charge of their spirits.

Though rarely understood, the most pivotal element of the story is the enmity that is placed between the woman's "seed" and the snake, one of the oldest and most venerated symbols of matriarchal deity and women's priesthood.[17] The symbolic significance of the snake's debasement and its separation from Eve and her children, is clear: They represent the absolute suppression of the old, matriarchal religion and the permanent exclusion of women from priestly activity. The father-god, his manly purity, and the males in its image may now be supremely triumphant.

A story often told and repeated in various forms, in various cultures, the myth is a way for the community of men to tell again and again to each generation of men that they are in danger, that the threat is mortal, and that escape can be secured only by the suppression of appetite and of its ultimate symbol—Woman. Furthermore, the myth articulates in symbol the horrible consequences of a carnality unchecked, let loose in the world.

We are now ready for a final amendment of the dualistic table. To the side of God and perfection, we must add the rigors of an antibody, antinature ethic, and its opposite we must assign to the realm of death.

| God | the Devil |
|---|---|
| power | anti-power |
| | (powerlessness) |
| | or |
| | (Evil, Earthly power—the |
| | refusal to submit to Jahweh) |
| one | many |
| perfection | imperfection |
| order | chaos |
| eternal | transitory |
| spirit | body |

| | |
|---|---|
| Paradise | Nature (i.e., the world) |
| Heaven | Earth and Hell |
| immortal life | death |
| salvation | damnation |
| mind | emotion and feeling |
| rationality | passion and appetite |
| control | licentiousness |
| ethereality | carnality |
| virtue | sin |
| good | evil |
| light | dark |
| men | women |
| male | female |
| asceticism | sensuality |
| instrumental sex (reproduction) | experiential sex (sexing) |
| pain, mortification | pleasure |
| abstinence | indulgence |
| pure | impure |
| clean | dirty |
| right | wrong |
| straight | crooked |

The list now reveals nearly all the first principles of patriarchal consciousness. Everything associated with physical life is swept away, banned to the sphere of death. Gone to perdition is Nature, animal bodies, and the earth they live upon. Banned from the sphere of perfection is anything that suggests process, change, or movement. Passion, freedom, sensuality, and all living experience join sin, dirt, and damnation on the side of the Devil, on the side of chaos, by the side of the woman. Earth and Hell together oppose God's realm.

For men, reality has been purified. Like the inside of a monastery, all is order, austere and pristine. Decay and disease are no longer the threats they were; there is nothing important to rot. No passion to tempt, no needs to satisfy, no self to indulge—only Spirit–God and spirit life in a one-sex, unsexed Spirit place.

But a strange inversion has taken place. The signs and symbols of life (Earth, women, birth, sensation) have now become signs and symbols of death: life itself is death, and death alone brings life.

## Dilemma of Meaning

It is an odd sense of life that survives in the patriarchal schema. Life as we understand it, as we experience it—earthbound, natural, sensed, and sensing—now becomes a form of death, and the life that is allowable, the one upon which God smiles—eternal life—is oddly vacuous and decidedly unappealing except for its longevity. A trade has been made: everything that could possibly be thought of as vitality has been swapped for a nondescript always-ness.

But a devastating mistake has been made. This was not the bargain the patriarchs were seeking, for, in fact, it is not simple survival by itself that drives their system; it is the quest for meaning. It is not avoidance merely of ending, of finishing. Instead, what propels the patriarchal system is escape from dissolution, from nonexistence (which is subtly different from end, from death), and from the sense of pointlessness that may be carried with it.

What is probably most essentially fearful about death for anyone is the fact of nonbeing. It is not the dying but the not-being that is so dissociating to our emotions and our consciousness. It threatens our sense of purpose and of the significance of existence itself. What is the point of a life that merely begins, carries on, and ends? This is the ultimate puzzle we all must face, and its solution is the goal of metaphysical systems.

The system the patriarchs have devised, however, has led them directly away from their goal—meaningfulness—and straight to the nightmare they were struggling so hard to elude. Abstract life, survival of any sort so long as it is not subject to death, cannot really be so precious that it would be worth surrendering what substance or joy that lived existence may offer. In fact, it is utterly pointless.

Patriarchal religion seeks meaningfulness through the vanquishing of death rather than through the embrace of life, and because in reality death cannot be vanquished but must be dealt with, masculist consciousness has committed itself to a course bound to go awry.

To address their self-imposed crisis of meaning, the patriarchs have turned once again to an old ally, power. If meaning is not to be found in simple, mortal being, then it has to be sought elsewhere, in a different kind of being, Total Being, Always Being, Being that is beyond limit, beyond smallness, powerlessness, and finitude. Martial men can have meaning in their own lives, and power over death can be achieved—through identification with this Being which is greater than death. Moreover, if the strategy is to succeed, the identification with Being-bigger-than must be very close, as close almost as identity. Mortal martial man must become one with Great Being, and Great Being must exist.

And so patriarchy's God is born.

Here is God, the metaphor for Allness, broken off from the universe, catapulted into the Far Away, placed into angry opposition to His own children, the children of the earth, fulminating against the very nature that Life and He have given them.

Here is the Progenitor—creator, procreator, and maintainer—rendered as male, the he-Mother of us all, alone and unaided in conception and procreation, the one-sex metaphor for a two-sex reality, a wrong sex symbol for a nature that it is meant to exemplify.

So now the Father gives birth, the Mother is made offspring, the Son becomes the One, and the Family Holy is turned upside down. The deception is so extraordinary, it takes one's breath away.

There is a craziness in all this that is profoundly disturbing. It is not that we cannot assimilate the counter-realities of fantasy. Rather we cannot but perceive the distorted intentionality beneath: the creation of a universe in which woman and women's power are erased so that her cognate, Earth, and its cognate, natural life, may also be erased, because it contains death. Finally, to complete the craziness and make the distortion absolute, at its worst, patriarchal religion reifies its metaphors: there really is such a God, such a Father, such a Devil, such a heaven and hell. No longer are we dealing with abstractions that we may at least interpret and make our own, but with actual entities that must be reckoned with in the concrete world.

No longer a symbol of All That Is, God is now a person, not spirit/vital center, but spirit/movie ghost. He sits enthroned in the heavens and manipulates the realities He was meant to represent. Into concretization with this deity goes the entire lexicon of spirit: grace, redemption, salvation, reconciliation, faith, and sin. When God the metaphor becomes God the thing, all the aspects of spirit become externalized, and as such they are lost to the spirit and the spirited. As metaphors they are profound experiences, problems to be solved, forces of life to be dealt with, questions to be pondered, goals to be achieved, deep places in the mind or heart. As "things," outside of us, they are not unlike all the other things that populate the world, externalities: separate, unattached to our core, hostile, friendly, or neutral.

With God as thing, it is far more difficult to stand face-to-face with Truth, responsible for one's own decisions and decipherings, for the meaning we create, for the quality of the path we choose. Instead, in patriarchy one is dependent on this God–Person–Father for truth, morality, and choice. One has but to bend the will and the knee. In place of insight, there is dogma; in place of community, there is church; in place of quest, there is surrender; in place of wisdom, abnegation. With God as thing, the essential responsibility is obedience, all other ethical responsibilities are subsumed beneath it.

Is this what tending the spirit is meant to be?

## Conclusion

So long as a religion remains pervaded with masculism, so long as it insists upon the exclusive authority of men who continue to cling stubbornly to that ideology, and to the degree that it reviles the female principle, which might salvage it, it will be distorted and noxious. Reality, after all, is not simply an expression of the human male experience, and Mars is probably the least desirable of the deities to invoke for sustenance and meaning.

It is a question whether patriarchal religion is redeemable. Some argue that its flight from life and from the female has made it an unsalvageable crookedness and guaranteed its own eventual self-destruction. They reason that patriarchy's denial of the "fleshly" side of the dualistic dichotomy and its consequent suppression of women's participation in the institutions of religion ensures a progressive intensification of its original warp. Furthermore, the distortion contained within the single-gendered reality is so deep that it poisons everything it touches, so deep that were it excised, the religion would no longer be Judaism or Christianity or Islam or what-have-you, but some other completely different thing. Perhaps that is so. Perhaps then the world's great religions would be what they have the potential to be and what religion is supposed to be.

Certainly, unless the masculine–masculist death grip held over these institutions is loosened, we shall never find out. Indeed, it is ironic that in separating themselves from women and silencing women's voices, the patriarchs have denied themselves the very perspectives that might restore their balance and save their Vision.

## Notes

Portions of this chapter were published earlier in "A Feminist Analysis of the New Right," *Women's Studies International Forum* 6, no. 4 (1983), pp. 345–51, reprinted with kind permission from Pergamon Press Ltd., Headington Hill Hall, Oxford OX3 OBW, UK.; and from "Bodies and Souls/ Sex, Sin, and the Senses in Patriarchy: A Study in Applied Dualism," reprinted with permission from *Hypatia: A Journal of Feminist Philosophy* 2, no. 1 (Winter 1987).

1.  Fatna A. Sabbah, *Woman in the Muslim Unconscious*, tr. Mary Jo Lakeland (New York: Pergamon Press, 1984), p. 18.

2.  Discussions of the patriarchal association of women and nature are numerous, both within and without the women's movement. See, for example: Thomas Aquinas, "Whether Woman Should Have Been Made in the First Production of Things," *Summa Theologica*, Part 1, Q. 92 (The Production of Woman), Art. 1 in *Basic Writings of St. Thomas Aquinas*, ed. Anton C. Pegis (New York: Random House, 1945); J. J. Bachofen, *Myth, Religion, and Mother Right*, tr. Ralph Manheim (London: Routledge and Kegan Paul, 1967); Diana H. Coole, *Women in Political Theory: From Ancient Misogyny to Contemporary Feminism* (Boulder, Colo.: Lynne Rienner Publishers, 1988); Susan Griffin, *Woman and Nature: The Roaring Inside Her* (New York: Harper & Row, 1978) and *Pornography and Silence: Culture's Revenge against Nature* (New York: Harper & Row, 1981); and Helen M. Luke, *Woman, Earth and Spirit: The Feminine in Symbol and Myth* (New York: Crossroad, 1981).

3.  Mary Daly, *Beyond God the Father* (Boston: Beacon Press, 1973).

4.  Daly, *Gyn/Ecology* (Boston: Beacon Press, 1978), pp. 37–39. Copyright ©1978, 1992 by Mary Daly. Reprinted by permission of Beacon Press.

5.  Richard C. Martin, *Islam* (Englewood Cliffs, N.J.: Prentice-Hall, 1982), p. 13.

6.  See among them: Joseph Campbell, *The Masks of God* series (New York: Viking Press)—*Primitive Mythology* (1959), *Oriental Mythology* (1962), *Occidental Mythology* (1964), and *Creative Mythology* (1970); Campbell, *Myths to Live By* (New York: Viking Press, 1972); *The Mythic Image* (Princeton, N.J.: Princeton University Press, 1974); James A. Frazer, *The Golden Bough* (New York: Macmillan, 1922); Robert Graves, The *White Goddess* (New York: Vintage Books, 1958); Robert Graves and Raphael Patai, *Hebrew Myths* (New York: Doubleday, 1964); and more recently the feminist works of Merlin Stone, *When God Was a Woman* (New York: Dial Press, 1976) and *Ancient Mirrors of Womanhood: Our Goddess and Heroine Heritage*, vols. 1 and 2 (New York, New Sibylline Books, 1979); Barbara G. Walker, *The Woman's Encyclopedia of Myths and Secrets* (San Francisco: Harper and Row, 1983); and Riane Eisler, *The Chalice and the Blade* (New York: Harper and Row, 1987).

7.   Nawal El Saadawi, *The Hidden Face of Eve: Women in the Arab World*, tr. Dr. Sharif Hetata (Boston: Beacon Press, 1982), p. 8.

8.   Ibid., p. 3.

9.   Augustine, *The City of God*, Volume I, Book XIX.

10.   Mahnaz Afkhami, "IRAN: A Future in the Past—The 'Prerevolutionary' Women's Movement," in *Sisterhood Is Global: The International Women's Movement Anthology*, edited by Robin Morgan (New York: Anchor Books, 1984), p. 330. Copyright ©1984 by Robin Morgan. By permission of Edite Kroll Literary Agency.

11.   In *Beyond God the Father* and even more pointedly in *Gyn/Ecology*, Mary Daly articulates the notion that patriarchy is essentially necrophilic.

12.   George Boas, "Preface" to Bachofen, p. xv.

13.   Quoted in Wilhelm Windelband, *A History of Philosophy*, vol. 1 (New York: Harper Torchbooks, 1958), pp. 66–67.

14.   Christianity's unrelenting hostility to pleasure, especially sexual pleasure, has been documented repeatedly. An excellent resource on the subject is Uta Ranke-Heinemann's *Eunuchs for the Kingdom of Heaven: Women, Sexuality and the Catholic Church* (New York: Penguin Books, 1990).

15.   Aquinas, "Whether Woman Should Have Been Made."

16.   An interesting discussion of the Adam and Eve episode is found in Merlin Stone, *When God Was a Woman*, especially Chapter 10.

17.   See "serpent" in Walker, *The Woman's Encyclopedia* and in Campbell, *The Masks of God: Occidental Mythology*, Chapter 1.

# Bibliography and Related Readings

Adler, Margot. *Drawing Down the Moon: Witches, Druids, Goddess-Worshippers, and Other Pagans in America Today.* Revised and expanded edition. Boston: Beacon Press, 1987.

Adler, Mortimer J. *How to Think About God: A Guide For the Twentieth Century Pagan* (*One who Does not worship the God of Christians, Jews, or Muslims; irreligious persons).* New York: Bantam, 1982.

Allen, Paula Gunn. *Grandmothers of the Light: A Medicine Woman's Source Book.* Boston: Beacon Press, 1991.

Aquinas, Thomas. "Whether Woman Should Have Been Made in the First Production of Things." *Summa Theologica*, Part 1, Q. 92 (The Production of Woman), Art. 1 in *Basic Writings of St. Thomas Aquinas.* Edited by Anton C. Pegis. New York: Random House, 1945.

Austen, Hallie Iglehart. *Heart of the Goddess: Art, Myth, and Meditations of the World's Sacred Feminine.* Oakland, Calif.: Wingbow Press, 1990.

Bachofen, J. J. *Myth, Religion, and Mother Right.* Translated by Ralph Manheim. London: Routledge and Kegan Paul, 1967.

Belenky, Mary Field. *Women's Ways of Knowing: The Development of Self, Voice and Mind.* New York: Basic Books, 1986.

Berger, Pamela. *The Goddess Obscured: Transformation of the Grain Protectress from Goddess to Saint.* Boston: Beacon Press, 1986.

Bianchi, Eugene C., and Rosemary Radford Reuther. *From Machismo to Mutuality: Essays on Sexism and Woman-Man Liberation.* New York: Paulist Press, 1976.

Bloom, Harold. *The Book of J.* New Haven, Conn.: Yale University Press, 1990.

Bolen, Jean Shinoda. *Goddesses in Everywoman: A New Psychology of Women.* New York: Harper Collins, 1985.

Budapest, Zsuzsanna. *The Feminist Book of Lights and Shadows.* Edited by Helen Beardwoman. California: Luna Press, 1976.

———. *Grandmother Moon.* San Francisco: Harper San Francisco, 1991.

———. *The Grandmother of Time: A Woman's Book of Celebrations, Spells, & Sacred Objects for Every Month of the Year.* San Francisco: Harper and Row, 1989.

———. *The Holy Book of Women's Mysteries.* Oakland, Calif.: Wingbow Press, 1989.

Bynum, Caroline Walker. *Gender and Religion: On the Complexity of Symbols.* Boston: Beacon Press, 1986.

Campbell, Joseph. *The Masks of God: Occidental Mythology.* New York: Penguin, 1976.

Christ, Carol P. *Diving Deep and Surfacing: Women Writers on Spiritual Quest.* Boston: Beacon Press, 1986.

———. *Laughter of Aphrodite: Reflections on a Journey to the Goddess.* San Francisco: Harper and Row, 1987.

Christ, Carol P., and Judith Plaskow, editors. *Womanspirit Rising: A Feminist Reader in Religion.* 2nd edition. San Francisco: Harper and Row, 1992.

Daly, Mary. *Beyond God the Father: Toward a Philosophy of Women's Liberation.* Boston, Beacon Press, 1973.

———. *The Church and the Second Sex.* New York: Harper and Row, 1975.

———. *Gyn/Ecology, the Metaethics of Radical Feminism.* Boston: Beacon Press, 1978.

———. *Outercourse: The Be-Dazzling Voyage. Containing Recol-lections from* My Logbook of a Radical Feminist Philosopher *(Being an Account of My Time/Space Travels and Ideas—Then, Again, Now, and How)*. San Francisco: Harper San Francisco, 1992.

———. *Pure Lust: Elemental Feminist Philosophy*. Boston: Beacon Press, 1984.

Dexter, Miriam Robbins. *Whence the Goddesses: A Source Book.* Athene Series in Women's Studies. New York: Teachers College Press, 1990.

Evans, Shawn, editor. *The Goddess Remembered*. Freedom, Calif.: Crossing Press, 1990.

Gage, Matilda Joslyn. *Woman, Church, and State: A Historical Ac-count of the Status of Woman Through the Christian Ages, With Reminiscences of the Matriarchate*. Watertown, Mass.: Perse-phone Press, 1980.

Giles, Mary E. *Feminist Mystic and Other Essays on Women and Spirituality*. New York: Crossroads, 1982.

Gimbutas, Marija. *The Civilizations of the Goddess*. San Francisco: Harper San Francisco, 1991.

———. *The Language of the Goddess*. San Francisco: Harper San Francisco, 1989.

———. *Goddesses and Gods of Old Europe, 7000 to 3500 B.C.: Myths, Legends, and Cult Images*. Berkeley: University of Cali-fornia Press, 1982.

Goldenberg, Naomi. *Changing of the Gods*. Boston: Beacon Press, 1979.

———. *Returning Words to Flesh. Feminism, Psychoanalysis, and the Resurrection of the Body*. Boston: Beacon Press, 1990.

Gottner-Abendroth, Heide. *The Dancing Goddess: Principles of a Matriarchal Aesthetic*. Boston: Beacon Press, 1991.

Graves, Robert. *The White Goddess*. New York: Vintage Books, 1958.

Graves, Robert, and Raphael Patai. *Hebrew Myths*. New York: Dou-bleday, 1964.

Gray, Elizabeth D., editor. *Sacred Dimensions of Women's Experience*. Wellesley, Mass.: Roundtable Press, 1988.

Gray, Elizabeth Dodson. *Green Paradise Lost*. Wellesley, Mass.: Roundtable Press, 1979, 1981.

―――. *Patriarchy as a Conceptual Trap*. Wellesley, Mass.: Roundtable Press, 1982.

Hampson, Daphne. *Theology and Feminism*. Cambridge, Mass.: Basil Blackwell, 1990.

Harding, Sandra, and Merrill Hintikka. *Discovering Reality: Feminist Perspectives on Epistemology, Metaphysics, Methodology, and Philosophy of Science*. Hingham, Mass.: Kluwer Academic, 1983.

Hardon, John A., S.J. *Modern Catholic Dictionary*. Garden City, N.Y.: Doubleday, 1980.

Highwater, Jamake. *The Primal Mind: Vision and Reality in Indian America*. New York: New American Library, 1982.

―――. *Myth and Sexuality*. New York: Meridian, 1991.

Hurcombe, Linda, editor. *Sex and God: Some Varieties of Women's Religious Experience*. New York: Routledge and Kegan Paul, 1987.

Hoyt, Charles Alva. *Witchcraft*. Edited by Beatrice Moore. Carbondale, Ill.: Southern Illinois University Press, 1981.

Iglehart, Hallie. *Womanspirit: A Guide to Woman's Wisdom*. San Francisco: Harper and Row, 1983.

James, William. *The Varieties of Religious Experience: A Study in Human Nature*. New York: Collier Books, 1961.

Janeway, Elizabeth. *Man's World, Woman's Place: A Study in Social Mythology*. New York: William Morrow, 1971.

Johnson, Buffie. *Lady of the Beasts: Ancient Images of the Goddess and Her Sacred Animals*. San Francisco: Harper and Row, 1988.

Johnson, Sonia. *Going Out of Our Minds: The Metaphysics of Liberation*. Freedom, Calif.: Crossing Press, 1987.

Jong, Erica. *Witches*. New York: Abrams, 1981.

Keller, Catherine. *From a Broken Webb: Separation, Sexism, and Self.* Boston: Beacon Press, 1986.

Kolbenschlag, Madonna. *Kiss Sleeping Beauty Goodbye: Breaking the Spell of Feminine Myths and Models.* 2nd edition. San Francisco: Harper and Row, 1988.

Kramer, Heinrich, and James Sprenger. *The Malleus Maleficarum (The Hammer of Evil),* 1928. Translated by Montague Summers. Reprint. New York: Dover Publications, 1971.

Kuo, Mo-Jo. *Selected Poems from the Goddesses.* Translated by John Lester and A. C. Barnes. 2nd edition. Peking: Foreign Language Press, 1978.

Larner, Christina. *Enemies of God: The Witchhunt in Scotland.* Baltimore, Md.: Johns Hopkins University Press, 1981.

Larue, Gerald. *Sex and the Bible.* Buffalo, N.Y.: Prometheus Books, 1983.

Laura, Judith. *She Lives! the Return of Our Great Mother.* Freedom, Calif.: Crossing Press, 1989.

Lerner, Gerda. *The Creation of Patriarchy.* New York: Oxford University Press, 1986.

Logan, Vincent Kruse. "A Pagan's Progress." *Religious Humanism* 22, no. 1 (Winter 1988): 43–46.

Luke, Helen M. *Woman, Earth and Spirit: The Feminine in Symbol and Myth.* New York: Crossroad, 1981.

Mariechild, Diane. *Mother Wit: A Guide to Healing & Psychic Development.* New revised edition. Freedom, Calif.: Crossing Press, 1989.

————. *The Inner Dance: A Guide to Psychological and Spiritual Unfolding.* Freedom, Calif.: Crossing Press, 1987.

Martin, Richard C. *Islam: A Cultural Perspective.* Prentice-Hall Series in World Religions. Englewood Cliffs, N.J.: Prentice-Hall, 1982.

Mascetti, Manuela Dunn. *The Song of Eve: An Illustrated Journey into the Myths, Symbols, and Rituals of the Goddess.* New York: Fireside Books, 1990.

Matthews, Caitlin. *The Celtic Tradition*. Longmead, Shaftesbury, Dorset, U.K.: Element Books, 1989.

Merivale, Patricia. *Pan the Goat-God: His Myth in Modern Times*. Studies in Comparative Literature, no. 30. Cambridge, Mass.: Harvard University Press, 1969.

Midgley, Mary. *Animals and Why They Matter*. Athens: University of Georgia Press, 1983.

Mollenkott, Virginia Ramey, editor. *Women of Faith in Dialogue*. New York: Crossroad, 1987.

Monaghan, Patricia. *The Book of Goddesses and Heroines*. New York: Dutton, 1981.

Morris, Thomas V., editor. *The Concept of God*. Oxford: Oxford University Press, 1987.

Morton, Nelle. *The Journey is Home*. Boston: Beacon Press, 1986.

Noble, Vicki. *Motherpeace: A Way to the Goddess Through Myth, Art, and Tarot*. San Francisco: Harper and Row, 1982.

Ochs, Carol. *An Ascent to Joy: Transforming Deadness of Spirit*. New York: Meyer Stone Books, 1989.

―――. *Behind the Sex of God: Toward a New Consciousness Transcending Matriarchy and Patriarchy*. Boston: Beacon Press, 1977.

―――. *When I'm Alone*. Minneapolis: Carolrhoda Books, 1992.

―――. *Women and Spirituality*. Totowa, N.J.: Rowman and Allanheld, 1983.

Oda, Mayum. *Goddesses*. Berkeley, Calif.: Lancaster-Miller, 1981.

Olsen, Carl, editor. *The Book of the Goddess: Past and Present*. New York: Crossroad, 1983.

Orenstein, Gloria Feman. *The Reflowering of the Goddess*. Athene Series in Women's Studies. New York: Teachers College Press, 1990.

Pagels, Elaine. *Adam, Eve and the Serpent*. New York: Random, 1988.

Patai, Raphael. *The Hebrew Goddess*. 3rd enlarged edition. Detroit, Mich.: Wayne State University Press, 1990.

Person, Ethel Spector. "Sexuality as the Mainstay of Identity: Psychoanalytic Perspectives." *Signs* 5 (1980): 605–606.

Pesek-Marous, Georgia. *The Bull: A Religious and Secular History of Phallus Worship and Male Homosexuality.* Rolling Hills, Calif.: Tau Press, 1984.

Pomeroy, Sarah B. *Goddesses, Whores, Wives, and Slaves: Women in Antiquity.* New York: Schocken Books, 1975.

Prell, Riv-Ellen. "The Vision of Woman in Classical Reform Judaism" *Journal of the American Academy of Religion* 50 (December 1982): 575–589.

Preston, James J., editor. *Mother Worship: Theme and Variations.* Chapel Hill: University of North Carolina Press, 1982.

Ranke-Heinemann, Uta. *Eunuchs for the Kingdom of Heaven: Women, Sexuality, and the Catholic Church.* New York: Penguin, 1990.

*Roget's International Thesaurus.* New York: Thomas Y. Crowell, 1946.

Ruether, Rosemary, and Eleanor McLaughlin, editors. *Women of Spirit: Female Leadership in the Jewish and Christian Traditions.* New York: Simon and Schuster, 1979.

Ruether, Rosemary Radford, editor. *Gaia & God: An Ecofeminist Theology of Earth Healing.* San Francisco: Harper San Francisco, 1992.

———. *New Woman–New Earth: Sexist Ideologies and Human Liberation.* San Francisco: Harper and Row, 1982.

———. *Religion and Sexism: Images of Woman in the Jewish and Christian Traditions.* New York: Simon and Schuster, 1974.

———. *Sexism and God-Talk: Toward a Feminist Theology.* Boston: Beacon Press, 1983.

———. *Womanguides: Readings Toward a Feminist Theology.* Boston: Beacon Press, 1985.

———. *Women-Church: Theology and Practice.* San Francisco: Harper and Row, 1988.

Ruether, Rosemary Radford, and Rosemary Skinner Keller, editors. *Women and Religion in America.* San Francisco: Harper and Row, 1982.

Russell, Letty M. *Household of Freedom: Authority in Feminist Theology.* Philadelphia: Westminster Press, 1987.

Ruth, Sheila. "Bodies and Souls/Sex, Sin and the Senses in Patriarchy: A Study in Applied Dualism." *Hypatia* 2 (1987): 149–163.

———. "A Feminist Analysis of the New Right." *Women's Studies International Forum* 6 (1983): 345–351.

El Saadawi, Nawal. *The Hidden Face of Eve: Women in the Arab World.* Zed Press, 1980 (original). Beacon Press edition: Boston: Beacon Press, 1982.

Sabbah, Fatna. *Woman in the Muslim Unconscious.* Translated by Mary Jo Lakeland. New York: Pergamon Press, 1984.

Sarton, May. *Journal of a Solitude.* New York: Norton, 1973.

Seymour, Miranda. *The Goddess.* 1st American edition. New York: Coward, McCann and Geoghegan, 1979.

Sjoo, Monica, and Barbara Mor. *The Great Cosmic Mother: Rediscovering the Religion of the Earth.* San Francisco: Harper and Row, 1987.

Smithson, Isaiah. "Great Mothers, Son Lovers and Patriarchy." *Journal of American Culture* 4, no. 2 (Summer 1981).

Snitow, Ann, Christine Stansell, and Sharon Thompson. *The Powers of Desire: The Politics of Sexuality.* New York: Monthly Review Press, 1983.

Spretnak, Charlene. *States of Grace: The Recovery of Meaning in the Postmodern Age.* San Francisco: Harper San Francisco, 1991.

Sproul, Barbara C. *Primal Myths: Creating the World.* San Francisco: Harper and Row, 1979.

Stanton, Elizabeth Cady. *The Woman's Bible* 1895–98. Reprint. New York: Arno Press, 1972.

Starhawk. *Dreaming the Dark: Magic, Sex, and Politics.* Boston: Beacon Press, 1982.

———. *The Spiral Dance: A Rebirth of the Ancient Religion of the Great Goddess.* San Francisco: Harper and Row, 1979.

Stein, Diane. *Casting the Circle: A Women's Book of Ritual.* Freedom, Calif.: Crossing Press, 1990.

Steinberg, Milton. *Basic Judaism.* 1947. Reprint. New York: Harcourt, Brace, & Jovanovich.

Stone, Merlin. *Ancient Mirrors of Womanhood: A Treasury of Goddess and Heroine Lore From Around the World.* Vols. 1 & 2. Boston: Beacon Press, 1990.

————. *When God Was a Woman.* New York: Harvest/HBJ, 1978.

Storrie, Kathleen. *Feminist Theology.* (Sound recording.) Seattle, Wash.: Evangelical Women's Caucus, 1982. (Cassette) Recorded at the Fifth Plenary Conference of Evangelical Women's Caucus, "Women and the Promise of Restoration" in Seattle, Wash., July 1982.

Teubal, Savina J. *Hagar the Egyptian: The Lost Tradition of the Matriarchs.* San Francisco: Harper and Row, 1990.

Treacy, Gerald C., Rev., S.J. *On Christian Marriage by Pope Pius XI with Discussion Club Outline.* Glen Rock, N.J.: Paulist Press, 1941.

Valiente, Doreen. *An ABC of Witchcraft: Past and Present.* 1973. Reprint. Custer, Wash.: Phoenix Publishing, 1984.

————. *Witchcraft for Tomorrow.* Custer, Wash.: Phoenix Publishing, 1983.

Vance, Carol S., editor. *Pleasure and Danger: Exploring Female Sexuality.* Boston: Routledge and Kegan Paul, 1984.

Van Dyke, Annette. *The Search for a Woman-Centered Spirituality.* New York: New York University Press, 1992.

Walker, Barbara G. *The Crone: Woman of Age, Wisdom and Power.* San Francisco: Harper and Row, 1985.

————. *The I Ching of the Goddess.* San Francisco: Harper and Row, 1986.

————. *The Skeptical Feminist: Discovering Virgin, Mother and Crone.* San Francisco: Harper and Row, 1985.

————. *Woman's Dictionary of Symbols and Sacred Objects.* San Francisco: Harper and Row, 1988.

————. *Woman's Encyclopedia of Myths and Secrets.* San Francisco: Harper and Row, 1983.

————. *Women's Rituals*. San Francisco: Harper and Row, 1990.

Washbourn, Penelope. *Becoming Woman: The Quest for Spiritual Wholeness in Female Experience*. New York: Harper and Row, 1979.

————, editor. *Seasons of Woman: Song, Poetry, Ritual, Prayer, Myth, Story*. San Francisco: Harper and Row., 1982.

Weinstein Marion. *Positive Magic: Occult Self Help*. Custer, Wash.: Phoenix Publishing, 1981.

Windelband, Wilhelm. *A History of Philosophy*, Vol. 1. New York: Harper Torchbooks, 1958.

Wolfson, H. A. *The Philosophy of the Church Fathers*, Vol. 1. Cambridge, Mass.: Harvard University Press, 1956.

Wolkstein, Diane, and Samuel Noah Kramer. *Inanna: Queen of Heaven and Earth: Her Stories and Hymns from Sumer*. New York: Harper and Row, 1983.

"Women—Sex and Sexuality," *Signs* (Special Issues) 5, no. 4 and 6, no. 1.

Young, Serinity, editor. *Sacred Writings By and About Women: A Universal Anthology*. New York: Crossroad, 1992.

Young-Bruel, Elisabeth. "The Education of Women as Philosophers." *Signs* 12 (Winter 1987): 207–221.

# Index

215

# About the Author

Sheila Ruth was born in New York City in 1940 and took her B.A. (Political Science, 1962) at Hunter College in the Bronx and her M.A. (1965) and Ph.D. (Philosophy, 1969) at the State University of New York at Buffalo.

Dr. Ruth is professor of philosophy at Edwardsville and teaches in the Women's Studies program, which she founded in 1973 and directed until 1985. Her textbook *Issues in Feminism: An Introduction to Women's Studies* (Mayfield, 1990) is in wide use, and she is a frequent speaker at universities and other institutions. She is a member of the St. Louis Religious Society of Friends (Quakers).